D1576902

DISCARDED

THE BURMA AIR
CAMPAIGN

By the same author

Red Sky in the Morning: The Battle of the Barents Sea, 1942
The Ohio *and Malta: The Legendary Tanker that Refused to Die*

THE BURMA AIR CAMPAIGN

December 1941–August 1945

MICHAEL PEARSON

Pen & Sword
AVIATION

First published in Great Britain in 2006 by
Pen & Sword Military
an imprint of
Pen & Sword Books Ltd
47 Church Street
Barnsley
South Yorkshire
S70 2AS

ISBN 1-84415-398-3

A CIP catalogue record for this book is available from the British Library.

Typeset in 10/12pt Sabon by
Concept, Huddersfield, West Yorkshire

Printed and bound in England by
Biddles Ltd

For a complete list of Pen & Sword titles please contact
PEN & SWORD BOOKS LIMITED
47 Church Street, Barnsley, South Yorkshire, S70 2AS, England
E-mail: enquiries@pen-and-sword.co.uk
Website: www.pen-and-sword.co.uk

For Corporal Leslie Pearson RAFVR
Headquarters 226 Group
My father.

Contents

Acknowledgements

To the following individuals and organizations I would like to offer my grateful thanks for their invaluable cooperation during the preparation of this book:

Wireless Operator Ken Armstrong, RAF.
Flight Sergeant Les Brazier, 167 Wing, 224 Group RAF.
Flight Sergeant Alex (Paddy) Calvert, 607 Squadron RAF.
The Embassy of Japan, London.
F.A. Galea, 355 Squadron RAF.
Flight Lieutenant Wilfred Goold DFC, 607 Squadron RAF.
Imperial War Museum Photographic Archive, London.
The Library of Congress, Washington DC.
Mr J.W. Loosemore, 67 Squadron RAF.
The National Archive, Kew.
National Archives and Records Administration, Modern Military
   Branch, Maryland USA.
Steven Ramsey for his excellent work on the maps.
Royal Air Force Museum, London.
607 (County of Durham) Squadron Association, Northumberland.
Harold Staines, 34 Squadron and the RAF Regiment, and his
   daughter Diana.
Ronald White, 152 Squadron armourer fitter.
Basil Wood, 159 Squadron RAF.

Michael Pearson

Abbreviations Used in Text

AATO	Army-Air Transport Organisation.
ABDACOM	American, British, Dutch and Australian Command.
ACM	Air Chief Marshal.
ACSEA	Air Command South East Asia.
AHQ	Air Headquarters.
AOA	Air Officer Administration.
AOC	Air Officer Commanding.
AOC-IN-C	Air Officer Commanding-in-Chief.
ATC	Air Transport Command, USAAF.
AVG	American Volunteer Group.
CAF	Nationalist Chinese Air Force.
CCTF	Combat Cargo Task Force.
CMU	Command Maintenance Unit.
COL	Chain Overseas Low (radar).
DZ	Drop Zone.
EAC	Eastern Air Command.
FAA	Fleet Air Arm.
FAMO	Forward Airfield Maintenance Organisation.
GCI	Ground Controlled Interception (radar).
GHQ	General Headquarters.
GOC	General Officer Commanding.
GR	General Reconnaissance.
IAF	Indian Air Force.
IOGROPS	Indian Ocean General Reconnaissance Operations.
JAAF	Japanese Army Air Force.
JNAF	Japanese Navy Air Force.
MT	Motor Transport.
MU	Maintenance Unit.
NCAC	Northern Combat Area Command.
POW	Prisoner of War.

PR (U)	Photographic Reconnaissance Unit.
PSP	Pierced Steel Planking.
RAAF	Royal Australian Air Force.
RAF	Royal Air Force.
RAMO	Rear Airfield Maintenance Organisation.
RCAF	Royal Canadian Air Force.
RDF	Radio Direction Finding (later known as radar).
RNZAF	Royal New Zealand Air Force.
RP	Rocket Projectile.
RSU	Repair and Salvage Unit.
SEAC	South East Asia Command.
3 TAF	3rd Tactical Air Force.
TCC	Troop Carrier Command.
USAAF	United States Army Air Force.
VCP	Visual Control Post.
VHF	Very High Frequency.

Japanese Terms Used in Text

Chutai   Squadron.
Hikodan   Air Brigade.
Hikodan Shireibu   Air Brigade Headquarters.
Hikosentai   Flying Regiment.
Hikoshidan   Air Division.
Hikoshidan Shireibu   Air Division Headquarters.
Kokugun Shireibu   Air Army Headquarters.

Burma – Principal Geographical Features

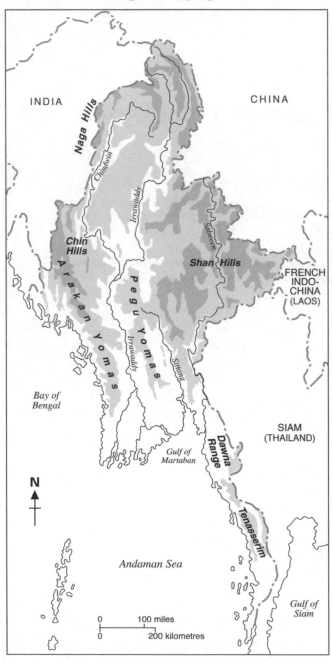

The Japanese Plan

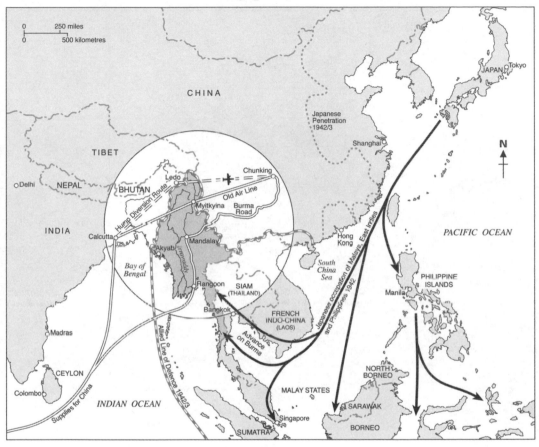

The Japanese Imperial High Command believed that by conquering Burma they would cut off the last supply route to China and protect their vast conquests in the south-west Pacific. The possibility also existed for further gains westward into India.

They also believed that mountains and jungles would set the Allies an impossible task should they attempt to reconquer Burma from bases in India to the north.

Airfields in Burma/Siam – December 1941–April 1942

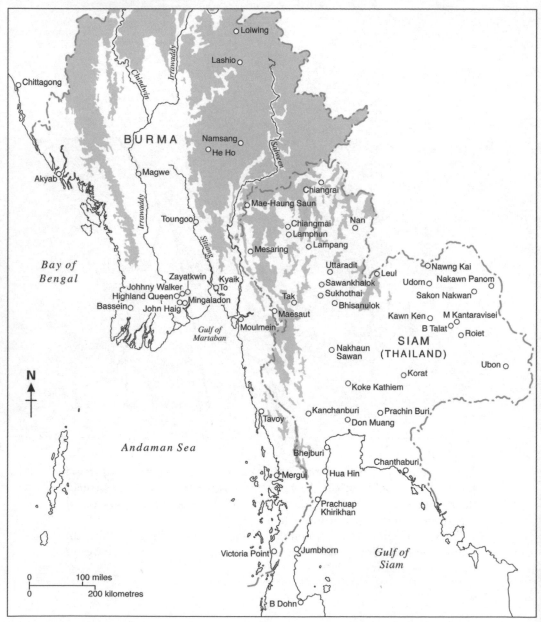

The Japanese Invasion of Burma

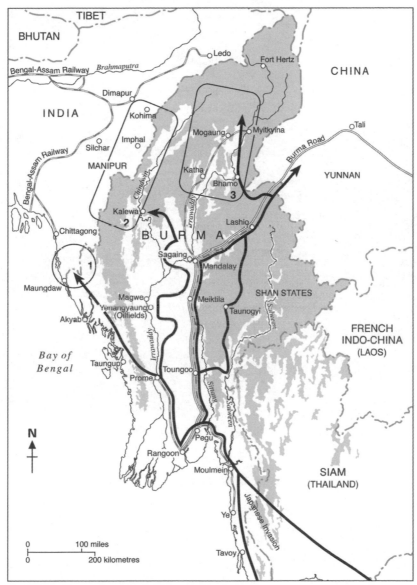

Key. The three fronts along which battle lines stabilized:
1. The Arakan.
2. The Central Front around Imphal.
3. Northern Combat Area Command.

Operation Thursday – the Second Chindit Expedition

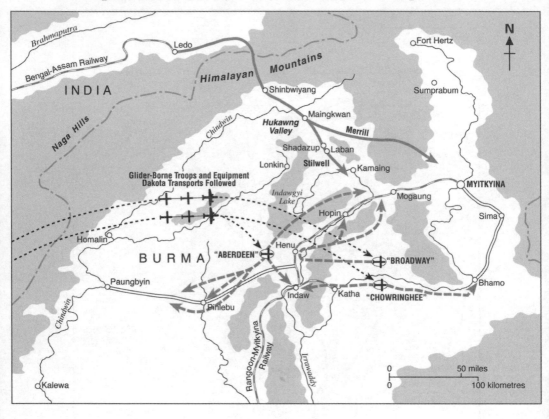

Imphal and Kohima

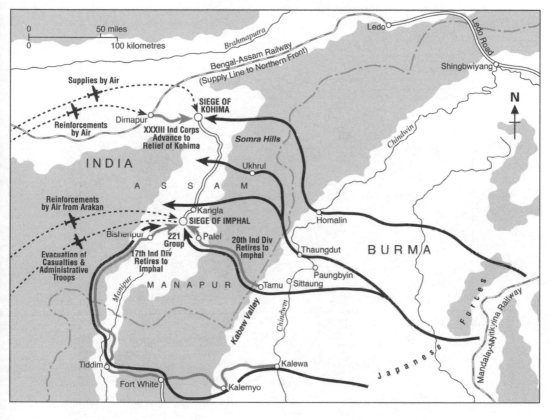

The Reconquest of Burma

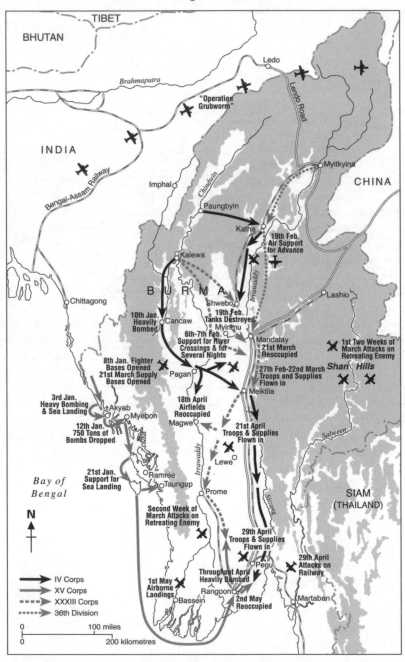

Introduction

The campaign for Burma during the Second World War has been called the 'Forgotten War' and the soldiers of the Fourteenth Army the 'Forgotten Army'. It has also been said, with some justification, that nobody considered the air forces involved in the campaign long enough to forget about them. This is particularly unfortunate since air power in all its facets truly came of age in the China/Burma/India theatre during 1941–1945. The Japanese capture of Rangoon in March 1942 denied large-scale seaborne support to Allied ground forces in Burma, consequently, without compensating supply from the air, the Fourteenth Army could not have achieved the complete victory that it ultimately did. Air Chief Marshal Sir Keith Park, Air Commander in Chief, South East Asia Command from February 1945, probably encapsulated the essential interlocking of the two arms when he said that on the Western Front 'the Armies of Liberation are advancing under the protecting wings of the Air Forces. But here in Burma our Armies are advancing *on* the wings of the Allied Air Forces.'

The battle to first win and then hold the air superiority necessary to enable the massive air supply operation to take place would be a difficult and dangerous one. The Japanese Army Air Force would prove to be a tough and courageous opponent, despite ridiculous pre-war assertions which sought to maintain that the Japanese would make bad pilots because they wore thick spectacles, or because, one leading newspaper reported in all seriousness, the tradition for Japanese mothers to carry newborn babies in papoose baskets on their backs upset their children's sense of balance in later life! Such nonsense would be rapidly disproved in combat. In terms of equipment the Japanese also had the edge to begin with. While the famous Mitsubishi A6M Zero Fighter, principally operated by the Japanese Naval Air Force (JNAF), rarely put in an appearance over Burma and India, the Japanese Army Air Force (JAAF) in that theatre had in its armoury the equally formidable Nakajima Ki-43 Peregrine Falcon (Allied code name Oscar), and others.

1

What impressed Allied air forces was the speed and manoeuvrability of the Japanese fighters in comparison with their own equipment, however these advantages were often gained at the cost of reduced or in some cases non-existent armour protection for the pilot, which in turn led inexorably to a high mortality rate among Japan's experienced airmen. The reasoning behind this short-term approach might well lie rooted in the Imperial Japanese High Command's belief that the 'effete' Western democracies were simply not willing or able to fight a protracted war and would rapidly sue for peace; ironically the same mistake made by that other totalitarian military state of the time, and Japan's principal ally, Nazi Germany.

Both the topography and climate of Burma would prove to be significant factors as the ground and air campaigns fought for control of the country. At more than 240,000 square miles Burma (now Myanmar) covers a vast area, and was in 1941 populated by some 17 million people. The natural grain of the country runs north to south, fixed by four major rivers with intervening mountain ranges (see map on p. 00). The source of the Irrawaddy River lies in the Himalayas far to the north near Fort Hertz, the river flowing southward down the spine of the country across a dry central plain to the Rangoon delta. The Chindwin also rises in the north to flow into the Irrawaddy at Pakkoku, south of Mandalay. The Sittang River starts its journey to the east of the Irrawaddy just south of Meiktila in central Burma and runs south to the Gulf of Martaban. The last of the country's great rivers, the Salween, is also the farthest east. With its source in China the Salween and its tributaries flow through deep gorges that cross the 3,000-foot-high tableland that constitutes eastern Burma, to debouch from the Tenasserim Peninsula into the Gulf of Martaban at Moulmein. All four rivers have numerous tributaries, most of which formed a serious obstacle to movement.

The eastern border of Burma runs along mountain ranges that stretch from China in the north, south and south-eastward to the border with Indo-China (Laos), and further south and south-westward along the border with Siam (Thailand). Mountains also comprise a major feature of the country's western border with India, and comprise the Naga Hills and Himalayas to the north, the Chin Hills in the centre and the Arakan Yoma farther south. The Naga Hills rise to some 12,000 feet, the Chin Hills peak at between 8,000 and 10,000 feet, while the Arakan Yoma is somewhat lower at around 3,000 feet, and separates Burma proper from its western coastal region, the Arakan. Between the Irrawaddy and Sittang rivers rise the hills of the Pegu Yoma. The mountain ranges are sheathed with dense jungle to a height of some 6,000 feet, while the lower hills of the Arakan and Pegu Yomas are completely covered.

From mid October to March the Burmese climate is temperate and pleasant, but in April both temperature and humidity rise dramatically, heralding the arrival of the monsoon in mid May and lasting until around mid September. Monsoon affected all of Burma and Assam (eastern India), with the exception of the dry Burmese plain around Mandalay and Meiktila. Rivers, valleys and flat areas would flood, while disease associated with unclean water was rife. British and Allied forces reported 250,000 cases of malaria and dysentery in the year 1943/44 alone.

For the airmen thick cumulonimbus thunderclouds made flying extremely hazardous. On one memorable occasion observers watched a Dakota transport aircraft fly into thunderclouds only to emerge some minutes later travelling in the opposite direction *upside down!* In the turbulence of the cloud formation the pilot lost all control of the aircraft.

The indigenous Burmese, the Burmans, were located mainly in central Burma and were highly resentful of British rule, their hostility fuelled by the many thousands of Indian and Chinese brought into Burma by the British. With their naturally industrious outlook these immigrant workers proceeded to corner sections of the Burmese economy for themselves. The Burmans shared their country with a number of minority tribes, the Karens, Shans, Kachins and Chins, who for the most part inhabited, and in several instances gave their names to, the mountain regions of the borders. The Burmans acquired an unpleasant reputation for their persecution of these tribes.

Burma having over a long period of time developed a reliance on cheap sea communications with India across the Bay of Bengal, little attention had been paid to overland routes, in part due to the extremely difficult nature of the area to be traversed. Although strategically important to the defence of India no railways connected the two countries and only one road, 185 miles of little better than cart track stretching from Imphal to Kalewa. Almost all other communications followed the geography of the country in running north to south, including the country's main railway artery which stretched from Rangoon to Mandalay. Railway lines also ran from Mandalay to Lashio, Rangoon to Prome and from Pegu across the Sittang to Martaban.

The internal road system was primitive in the extreme, often amounting to little more than dirt tracks. The main all-weather routes were from Rangoon to Mandalay, from Meiktila through the Shan State, from Toungoo through the Karen Hills to Loilem, from Rangoon to Prome and then on to Mandalay, although this last was not always passable in heavy rain.

3

The vital Burma Road supply route to a Chinese army that had been fighting the Japanese invader since 1937 began in Mandalay and wound its way (literally) to Lashio. From there the road led to Wantung on the Chinese border, traversed the only bridge across the Salween and ended at Chunking. Lend-Lease supplies landed at Rangoon were sent by road or rail to Mandalay and on to China, in the process ensuring that Burma would be high on any Imperial Japanese list of potential targets.

For this vast mountainous country one of the most innovative campaigns in military history would be fought, a campaign in which air power would have a truly indispensable part to play.

Of the Allied forces engaged it is important to note that of the British and Commonwealth troops by far the majority, 340,000, were Indian, although predominantly under British leadership. There were also 100,000 British and 90,000 Africans, in addition to which 65,000 Chinese and 10,000 Americans also made their vital contributions to ultimate victory.

Chapter One

A Wing and a Prayer

I

On 16 June 1921 the British cabinet opted to establish Singapore as a bastion from which to strike back at any threat to Britain's empire in the Far East. Air power being in its infancy Singapore was initially built up as a naval base, the strategy being to hold the island 'fortress' against all comers for the thirty to forty days necessary for a reinforcing fleet to arrive from Britain to defeat the invader. With Germany comprehensively defeated in 1918, and riven with political dissent in the years that followed, this strategy did not envisage Britain having to fight for her life against an aggressor in Europe while simultaneously being required to despatch a fleet to relieve Singapore. By the mid 1930s, however, with the rise of expansionist military regimes in Japan, Germany and Italy, a swing away from naval to air power to defend Singapore had been proposed and was under consideration.

Japan gained a toehold in China at the end of the First World War, and off and on from that time attempted to extend its authority. As an expanding industrialized nation Japan had urgent need of raw materials, and in September 1931 occupied the Chinese state of Manchuria, a territory traditionally the subject of hot dispute between Japan, China and Russia. With an eye to further military operations in China, Japan improved the underdeveloped Manchurian infrastructure and Japanese corporations set about developing the area's coal, iron ore and timber reserves for the exclusive benefit of the Japanese economy, now increasingly turning to a war footing. Hoping to forestall any prospect of a Sino-Soviet agreement to the detriment of Japan, the Japanese ultra-nationalist Kwantung Army occupying Manchuria, and at times seemingly impervious to control from Tokyo, engineered open war with China in July 1937. With even the Chinese Communists ultimately accepting that Nationalist Generalissimo Chiang Kai-shek was the man to unite the nation in resistance,[1] China fought back and a bloody war of attrition developed.

With the outbreak of the European war with Germany in September 1939, and the defeat of France in June 1940, Britain could no longer rely on the large, modern fleet of its ally to contain the aggressive Italians and keep open essential links with the Middle East and Suez. The Royal Navy would have that task to do as well as keep open Britain's crucial transatlantic supply lifeline, and as a consequence would be quite unable to provide a relief force of any substance for Singapore. The die, therefore, was cast – air power would have to step into the breach in the Far East in an attempt to deter Japanese expansionism. In the meantime, until the RAF could be reinforced, ground forces would be built up as far as possible.

In Japan a schism between the Army, which favoured further advances in China, and the Navy, which favoured expansion to the south, became more pronounced. In Manchuria during 1938–9 two disastrous engagements with Russian troops, at Changfukeng and Nomonhan – Japan suffering 50,000 casualties in the latter engagement alone – combined with the German/Soviet Non-Aggression Pact, which in the event of open war with Russia would release more Russian units for the Manchuria front, served to convince the Army to maintain the status quo in China for the time being, while falling in with the Navy's 'Southward Advance' strategy. The strategy gained credibility in the eyes of the Army when the fall of France left its colonies in Indo-China (now Vietnam, Laos and Cambodia) cut off from any hope of assistance from the mother country and therefore open to Japanese incursion from Manchuria. The strategic importance of Indo-China to Japan lay in its proximity (i.e. within bomber range) to Burma and the Burma Road, a tortuously narrow, twisting, highway leading northwards from the port of Rangoon through Mandalay to Kunming in China. Along this road the Western democracies, chiefly the United States, poured supplies for the use of the Chinese Army in its war with Japan. As the colonial power responsible, the Burma Road proved to be a source of much friction for Britain, which, being sorely pressed in its war with Germany, closed the Burmese section of the road in July 1940 in the hope of pacifying Japan, but reopened it three months later following pressure from the United States.

Japan was an industrialized nation without indigenous oil supplies of its own and for more than ten years coveted the islands of the Dutch East Indies (now Indonesia), supplier of the great majority of its oil imports. German occupation of the Netherlands added this coveted prize to that of the Burma Road, bringing both within Japan's grasp. On 16 July 1940 the Army in Japan seized its opportunity and effectively removed the government, replacing it with one in which General Hideki Tojo, until recently commander of the notorious Kwantung Army in Manchuria, occupied the key appointment as Minister of War. Two months later, 22 September, the same day that Japanese Foreign Minister Yosuke Matsuoka signed the Tripartite Pact with Germany and Italy in Berlin, Japanese forces invaded French Indo-China, later withdrawing but paving the way for Tokyo to put intense pressure on the puppet regime in Vichy to have Saigon close the Haiphong–Yunnan railway supply route to Chiang Kai-shek's forces and allow Japanese military bases in Indo-China. Despite all demands being met by the French administration, in July 1941 Tokyo ordered the occupation of Saigon anyway. Japanese forces having already seized control of most of China's coastline in 1938, the Burma Road became the principal supply route to China. Should Japanese forces press forward into Siam (now Thailand), the safety of Singapore, the Malay Peninsula and Burma itself would hang by an exceedingly precarious thread.

Japanese annexation of French Indo-China prompted a swift response from the governments of the United States, Britain and the Dutch East Indies, which froze Japanese assets in those countries, imposed a ban on oil exports, and effectively brought the simmering cauldron that was the Pacific and South East Asia to the boil. Without oil Japan's war in China would grind to a halt and any plans for future expansion would be significantly curtailed. The Imperial High Command had taken the precaution of building up a six-months oil reserve and now faced the problem of obtaining a resumption of supplies before the reserve ran out, but without enduring the loss of face involved in backing down to the Western democracies, a course of action which would in any event be intolerable to the military hard liners in the government. Future supplies must be brought firmly under Japanese control and the most inviting possibilities therefore appeared to be the Indies themselves, the Philippines and Malaya/Burma, the principal port and capital of which, Rangoon, was also the terminus for the Burma Road. The Imperial High Command duly opted to try for all three simultaneously, in stark contrast to Allied planning which confidently assumed that Japan would *not* challenge the combined might of Britain, the United States and the Netherlands all at the same time and that therefore whichever of these three Far Eastern Allies was not attacked would come to the aid of those that were.[2]

Even prior to its Chinese adventure Japan was considered the most likely aggressor in the Far East and if the principal method of defence for Singapore was to switch from sea to air power a substantial force of fighters, bombers and torpedo bombers with which to interdict Japanese convoys transporting troops and equipment to South East Asia, would need to be based in Malaya and Singapore. Britain's Chiefs of Staff agreed that a total of 582 aircraft would be the ideal for the defence of all her Far East interests, the majority being allocated to Singapore/Malaya, but given the inevitable restrictions, financial and otherwise, a mixed force of twenty-two squadrons comprising 336 aircraft should suffice. Events overtook the plans, however, and the war in Europe proved to be almost as much of a drain on aircraft as on ships, with all the most modern aircraft types and the bulk of the numbers being retained for home defence. As an indication of the gap between intent and reality, in November 1940, with the air war over Britain raging and war with Japan just over a year away, the number of front-line aircraft available in Malaya amounted to eighty-eight:

- Bombers – two squadrons of Blenheim Mk Is (twenty-four aircraft).
- Reconnaissance – two RAAF squadrons of Hudsons (twenty-four aircraft).
- Torpedo bombers – two squadrons of Vickers Vildebeest biplanes (old – the first prototype flew in April 1928 – and slow), twenty-four aircraft.
- General purpose – one RAAF squadron of CAC Wirraways, originally designed as a two-seat trainer, twelve aircraft.
- Flying boats – one squadron of Singapores, four aircraft.[3]

Fighters are conspicuous only by their absence. Also, given the necessity to inflict a crippling blow against an approaching Japanese invasion force while it remained at sea, a replacement for the obsolete Vildebeest torpedo bombers required urgent attention. The answer to this latter problem at least appeared to be the monoplane twin-engine Bristol Beaufort, which entered production in Britain during the late 1930s and in Australia early in 1940. The first ninety of these Australian Beauforts were earmarked for Malaya but with much of the raw material and certain complete sections of the aircraft still having to come from either Britain or the United States, there were considerable delays, and Vildebeests remained in front-line service long past their sell-by date.

The command structure in the Far East also posed problems, all the services, army, navy and air force, having their own headquarters and lines of communication stretching back to their respective ministries in London, each jealously guarding its own area of responsibility. As early as 1936 General Dobbie, the then GOC Singapore, recognized the need for a unified command centre to enable the three services to work together to develop a single mutually supportive strategy. Regrettably he attempted to take control unilaterally and trod on air force corns in the process, a certain amount of inter-service strife being the inevitable result. The idea, however, was sound and in October 1940 Prime Minister Winston Churchill approved a proposal for a unified Far East Command to be established under Air Chief Marshal Sir Robert Brooke-Popham. The new C-in-C, although somewhat prone to underestimate Japanese capabilities (in which he was not alone), determined to make his new command operate effectively but found himself hamstrung by the way in which it had been established. For one thing he was allotted a staff of only seven. Representations to Whitehall resulted in an increase to fifteen in August 1941 but not all the new posts were filled by the time the Japanese war broke out in December. Even more damaging to the new Headquarters was the operational compromise under which it was forced to operate. RAF and Army commanders were allowed to retain direct links with their respective ministries in London, a counter-productive compromise that inevitably made the breaking down of single-service loyalties and chains of command even more difficult than it should have been. Additionally Brooke-Popham was given no authority whatsoever over naval operations, for which C-in-C China continued to liaise directly with the Admiralty. Without being allotted the overall authority that he required from London, time would be needed for the Air Chief Marshal to be seen by the other service chiefs as the impartial commander that he needed to be. The problem was that time, along with everything else in the Far East, was in very short supply.

On 11 November 1940, one week prior to Air Chief Marshal Brooke-Popham commencing his appointment, a fateful event occurred that was destined to cast a long shadow over British plans and preparations in the Far East. On that day the eighteen-year-old, 9,370 tons deadweight British flag steamer *Automedon*, en route from the UK to Singapore, was shelled and subsequently captured by the German auxiliary cruiser *Atlantis*. Aboard were British war cabinet minutes to be delivered by hand to C-in-C Far East. The minutes outlined British policy towards Japan and included a Chiefs of Staff assessment which came to the conclusion that Singapore, Hong Kong, French Indo-China, Malaya and the Netherlands East Indies were all indefensible. One month after their capture, the documents and the priceless information contained in them were forwarded to the Japanese. The fact that the highly confidential information contained in the cabinet minutes had been compromised was known to the British Government by the end of 1940, but Brooke-Popham was never informed.

From the time of the Dobbie incident relations between the RAF and Army in the Far East had been at best cool, but in April 1941 Air Vice-Marshal C.M. Pulford was appointed Air Officer Commanding RAF Far East and the following month Lieutenant General A.E. Percival took

9

over as GOC Singapore. The two new commanders made a conscious effort to improve matters between the services and set about establishing a pattern of good cooperation, assisted no doubt by having their living quarters as well as their respective headquarters in close proximity; but despite the good intentions problems persisted. The European war proved to be not just an insatiable black hole through which equipment poured, it also sucked in the most talented field and staff officers. Good, efficient staff officers are as important as good combat officers and all too many staff members in the various Far East command headquarters were either inexperienced or not of the highest quality. Air Vice-Marshal Pulford was not in the best of health on his arrival in Singapore and having to shoulder more of the burden than was necessary in order to make up for staff deficiencies did not help.

Finding himself saddled with a less than perfect remit did not prevent Air Chief Marshal Brooke-Popham from bringing the parlous state of the air defences available for the Malay Peninsula to the attention of the Chiefs of Staff in London on several occasions. Following yet another chivvying telegram to London on 23 July 1941,[4] emphasizing the need for more aircraft to attack shipping, the Chiefs of Staff responded by pointing out the many production difficulties faced and further pointing out that the Middle East urgently required aircraft replacement and reinforcement. Worse still for the Far East Germany had invaded Russia on 22 June 1941 and Churchill had promised all the material support that Britain could give. Brooke-Popham was consequently faced with the fact that he would be unlikely to receive substantial reinforcement before the end of 1941. This then was the problem with which all three services in that far-flung theatre of war would have to wrestle for the next three to four years – they languished at the bottom of the list of priorities for men, equipment, spares, everything. A similarly bitter pill to swallow must have been the realization that given the massive requirements that industrialized warfare on this scale imposed upon limited resources, it is difficult to see how things could realistically be different.

By early 1941 the problem of the non-existent fighter establishment in Singapore had been addressed, but even here it was on a strictly hand-me-down basis. From February of that year numbers of modern monoplane Brewster Buffalo aircraft began arriving in crates from the Unites States, permission having been given by the Air Ministry for the initial formation of two squadrons. The Buffalo was an American aircraft designed as a carrier-borne fighter, entering service with the US Navy in 1938 and subsequently ordered first by Belgium and then by the British Purchasing Commission as a land fighter. Britain's intention was to use the 170 aircraft allocated (which finally included the Belgian order, that country having fallen before being able to take delivery) as a stop-gap while Hurricane and Spitfire production was hurried along. The first examples to arrive in Britain were given to the American-manned No. 71 Squadron (the first Eagle squadron), but feedback was extremely disappointing, the aircraft being deemed well below European requirements for a front-line fighter. With the exception of a few aircraft operated in Egypt and Crete, the balance of the order was transferred to the Far East, where, it was thought, they would be more than a match for anything the Japanese had to offer.

Drawing pilots with substantial flying experience from existing squadrons, the first two fighter squadrons, Nos 67 and 243, were established in Singapore and reached operational standard by the middle of April. On 30 May 1941 the Air Ministry sanctioned a further two Buffalo squadrons, No. 453 RAAF and No. 488 RNZAF, and here difficulties began to surface. Having utilized all the experienced pilots locally available new drafts were brought in from Australia and New Zealand, for the most part promising pilots but straight from Flying Training Schools, a number of the New Zealanders having flown nothing more demanding than a Hawker Hart biplane trainer and were consequently completely unused to retractable undercarriages, variable pitch propellers, or flaps. While happy to authorize the new squadrons the Air Ministry was not prepared to authorize an Operational Training Unit, advising Brooke-Popham that neither personnel nor aircraft were available. Attempting to proceed without a unit of any kind would gravely hamper the operational effectiveness of the crews and a training section was cobbled together from local resources and based at Kluang. The unit performed well but with time fast running out and the new pilots inevitably taking longer to bring up to full operational effectiveness than their more experienced colleagues, the onset of the Japanese war the following December found the two Commonwealth squadrons still not operationally effective. Most sorely missed was a good leavening of combat-seasoned pilots from other theatres to pass on the practical methods of aiming and manoeuvring that can only be developed in the heat of battle, the tricks of the trade that make the difference between hitting the target or having him get away to fight another day.

As training proceeded the Australian Government requested Brooke-Popham to do what he could to ensure that the RAAF Wirraway squadron (No. 21) be re-equipped with modern aircraft and as a result they too converted to Buffaloes. No. 67 Squadron relocated to Burma in October while the remaining four Buffalo squadrons, totalling sixty-seven aircraft, remained for the defence of Singapore and Malaya. This was undoubtedly better than no fighters at all but the raising of five squadrons at short notice created its own share of problems. The number of aircraft remaining as replacements with which to keep the

11

five squadrons fully equipped was limited, spares scarce, cannibalization already in progress, and the fear expressed that without a regular flow of supplies the fighter force would rapidly dwindle away to nothing in the face of inevitable mechanical problems and battle casualties. The Chiefs of Staff had set an acceptable level of aircraft availability at 336, with a level of reserves calculated at 50 per cent for flying boats and 100 per cent for all other aircraft types, or 327 aircraft, making a grand total of 663.[5] As the situation in the Far East deteriorated and November drew uneasily into December, aircraft actually available for the defence of the Far East were:

Malaya
- Blenheim Mk I bombers – 31
- Blenheim Mk IV bombers – 16
- Brewster Buffalo fighters – 60
- Hudson reconnaissance aircraft – 24
- Vickers Vildebeest torpedo bombers – 24
- Catalina flying boats – 3
- Maintenance units – 2

Reserve aircraft
- Blenheim Mk I and Mk IV – 15
- Brewster Buffalo – 52 (21 of which were out of commission due to teething problems with the valve gear on their engines).
- Hudson – 7
- Vildebeest – 12
- Catalina – 2

Burma
- Blenheim Mk I – 4
- Brewster Buffalo – 16

Reserve aircraft
- Blenheim – none
- Brewster Buffalo – 16 (of the total of 32 Buffaloes in Burma 24 were out of commission due to the same valve gear problem).[6]

Also available were two Catalina flying boats based in Ceylon, amounting to 180 front-line aircraft plus 104 reserves, a total of 284. Compared to the expressed aims of the Chiefs of Staff this amounted to a glaring deficit of 379 aircraft, which, when discounting the hopelessly obsolete Vildebeests, ballooned to 403.

In anticipation of hostile actions on the part of Japan, the Commander-in-Chief had awaiting his go-ahead an agreed plan known as Operation Matador, in which British ground forces supported by four squadrons of bombers and two squadrons of fighters would advance into southern Siam to capture Singora, the port facilities and attendant aerodromes of which formed the key to any invasion of Malaya and Singapore. Inevitably circumstances surrounding the implementation of the decision were complex. At 1400 hours 6 December Brooke-Popham received notification that air reconnaissance had observed two large Japanese convoys, complete with warship escorts, off the southern tip of Indo-China steaming westwards. Further west a third smaller Japanese force was seen steering north-westwards. In consultation with his fellow commanders Brooke-Popham concluded that the two large convoys would in all likelihood follow the smaller force and make for Koh Tron on the west coast of Indo-China, probably with the intention of landing sufficient forces to march on Siam. Concurrent with these events talks with Japanese Ambassador Kurusu in Washington were known to be still in progress, and only one week previously, 29 December, the Chiefs of Staff in London reaffirmed a policy of avoiding war with Japan, confirming that on no account should a Japanese force at sea be attacked unless Japan had first carried out a hostile act against British, US or Dutch territories. Already fighting one war for survival in Europe, Britain could not afford another in the Far East unless assured of military assistance from the United States, and President Roosevelt was not empowered to declare war on Japan without the support of Congress, which he would not get unless Japan attacked US troops or civilians first. Based on the information at his disposal Brooke-Popham decided not to order 'Matador', but brought all forces to the highest degree of readiness.[7]

On 7 December 1941 the Japanese attacked Pearl Harbor. Also on that fateful day Brooke-Popham was informed that Japanese ships had been seen in the vicinity of Singora, and at 0200 hrs Singapore time on 8 December he received the news that Japanese troops were ashore at Kota Bharu on the north-east coast of Malaya. It was now too late for 'Matador' in any event.

II

From its beginnings in 1911–12, military aviation in Japan developed along the lines of two separate air forces, the Japanese Army Air Force and the Japanese Navy Air Force, each, as the names imply, a wholly integrated arm of the Army and Navy respectively and each completely independent of the other.

13

To observers in the West in the late 1930s the JAAF appeared inferior to the JNAF, their calculations perhaps based in part on an over-optimistic reading of the results of the sizeable air battles fought by the JAAF against the Russian Air Force during the clashes at Nomonhan on the Manchuria/Mongolia border in May–August 1939. Fighter pilots the world over are, like fishermen, prone to exaggeration, and independent confirmation of claims is often impossible. For example, at Nomonhan the Russian Air Force claimed over 650 Japanese aircraft destroyed, the actual number being closer to 162. For their part the Japanese claimed to have shot down 1,162 aircraft and destroyed an additional 98 on the ground. Actual Soviet losses were closer to 207.[8] With the Japanese a more likely aggressor than Russia it would not be impossible for Western observers to hail Russian claims while decrying those of the JAAF as fanciful. With the coming of the Far East war proper the JAAF was to prove every bit the equal of its sister service and an extremely tough proposition for any of the Allied air forces to have to take on. It was true for a time, however, that the JNAF did have the better fighter in the Mitsubishi A6M2 Zero, which entered service in 1940. The JAAF would have to wait until late 1942 to have the Nakajima Ki-43 Oscar in significant numbers.[9] From an air war perspective the true significance of the China flare-ups was the acquisition by pilots of the JAAF and the JNAF of priceless combat experience, in the process handing them a crucial advantage over their opponents when full-scale war came.

Organization of the JAAF in December 1941 centred on the Air Division, the *Hikoshidan*, a flexible organization made up of a varying number of Flying Regiments, or *Hikosentai*, dependent upon the type of operation to be undertaken. Each regiment would normally be divided into three squadrons, or *chutai*, the aircraft establishment of a regiment varying according to the location of the regiment and the type of aircraft operated, along the lines of the following:

- Fighter regiment, 42 or 49 aircraft
- Light bomber regiment, 27 or 42 aircraft
- Medium bomber regiment, 27 or 37 aircraft
- Reconnaissance regiment, 27 aircraft, or 18 if two *chutai*.

Each fighter or bomber regiment would include in its complement one repair and maintenance company (also known as a *chutai*) divided among the three airborne *chutai*.

With the Japanese decision to go to war irrevocable, operating to a closely coordinated timetable, three fleets set sail – an attack formation

14

with which to destroy the US fleet at Pearl Harbor, and invasion fleets bound for the Philippines and the Malay Peninsula respectively. Initially allocated by the JAAF to the Malaya/Burma area was the 3rd *Hikoshidan*, comprising 14 *chutai* of fighters, 12 of bombers, 15 of light bombers and 5 of reconnaissance aircraft, plus tactical reconnaissance and ancillary support aircraft.[10] An additional 117 fighters, three *Hikosentai* and one *chutai* (the latter operating nine of the initial production version of the Ki-43) were also moved within supporting range of the intended landing areas.

In April 1937, following what might well have been a physical and mental breakdown, 44-year-old chain-smoking Colonel Claire Lee Chennault of the US Army Air Force went into retirement at his substantive rank of captain. Chennault, however, had no intention of merely fading away. During his time in uniform the former USAAF Colonel, no mean pilot himself, made the acquaintance of Colonel Mao Pang-chu of the Nationalist Chinese Air Force and with retirement impending negotiated a three month assignment with a view to improving the performance of the Chinese air arm against the formidable Japanese airmen to whom they were opposed. On 31 April 1937, the day following his 'retirement', Chennault set off for China.

The journey by rail and sea was tortuously slow and included a stopover in Kobe where Chennault is said to have been impressed by what incendiary bombs could do to Japanese houses, built, as was the custom, largely of wood. Having arrived in China, on 3 June 1937 Chennault found himself ushered into the presence of the secretary-general of the China Aeronautical Commission, Her Excellency Madame Chiang Kai-shek, the wife of the Generalissimo, younger than her husband, and by all accounts beautiful, charming and with a razor-sharp mind. Chennault got on well with the Chiangs and developed a love of China; consequently his initial three-month assignment stretched into years, during which time he was effectively made Chief of Staff of the CAF and Chief Flying Instructor.

As with many of the Chinese warlords Chiang Kai-shek employed foreign pilots, notably Russians, but with the 1930s drawing to a close and the situation in Europe worsening almost daily, the Generalissimo feared that if war broke out these would be recalled to Russia. Chiang initially suggested hiring American pilots for the CAF and from this grew the notion of a 'semi-detached' mercenary air force manned by American pilots and ground crew, recruited from the US armed forces with the blessing of the Government. By January 1941 the idea had crystallized into what was to become the American Volunteer Group

(AVG) or Flying Tigers as they are more popularly known. Utilizing loans from American banks China purchased 100 Curtiss P-40 (Tomahawk) fighters, to be serviced and maintained by American ground crew and flown by American pilots. Claire Lee Chennault would command the force under the overall direction of Chiang Kai-shek. Pilots would be tempted out east in search of adventure – they would almost certainly see action – and for an attractive pay package amounting to $600 per month, two or three times the rate for a pilot enlisted in the US Army or Navy. Undoubtedly a good deal, especially if the talked of bonus of $500 for every Japanese aircraft destroyed materialized, but by the standard of the times not exceptional – mercenary pilots in the Spanish Civil War were able to obtain $1,500 per month with a $1,000 bonus for each aircraft shot down, and civilian pilots ferrying bombers to Britain commanded $1,500 per month plus a bonus of $2,500 for ten successful deliveries.[11] Ground crew for the AVG would sign on for $300 per month, also significantly higher than regular army pay.

The morning of 8 July 1941 in San Francisco was, in the tradition of the Bay, misty with a definite nip in the air, as the Dutch liner *Jagersfontein* slipped her moorings and steamed out under the Golden Gate Bridge. Course was set across the Pacific for a voyage that would conclude with her arrival in Singapore on 11 August, the liner including in her passenger manifest the first contingent of the one hundred pilots and getting on for two hundred ground crew that would ultimately form the American Volunteer Group.

The original destination for the AVG had been Kunming in southern China; however with the Japanese advance into French Indo-China this area was now regularly bombed and, to make matters worse, in August flooded with monsoon rains. As an alternative the British authorities in Burma were persuaded to allow the AVG to use Kyedaw airfield, close to Toungoo in the south of the country, until the Americans were able to move on into China. Kyedaw was also subject to monsoon but had an all weather (asphalt) airstrip and was not, as yet, under Japanese attack. Whether or not as some form of quid pro quo Air Chief Marshal Brooke-Popham, desperate for reinforcements, was able to persuade Chiang Kai-shek to permanently base one squadron (of the three into which the AVG would be divided) in Burma. Chennault was apparently not a party to the agreement, which nevertheless made perfect military sense for the Generalissimo, acutely aware as he was of the necessity to keep open the Burma Road as his principal source of military supplies.

At 0300 on 8 December 1941 Singapore suffered its first attack by Japanese bombers, the initial wave traversing the island in a formation of nine at an estimated height of around 12,000 to 14,000 feet. No bombs were dropped by these aircraft, evidently tasked with drawing searchlight and anti-aircraft attention away from a closely following group using a much lower approach, 4,000 to 5,000 feet attacking various targets as they came, but paying particular attention to aerodromes. Thirty minutes warning of the arrival of hostile aircraft had been obtained; however, inexplicably the headquarters of the Air Raid Protection organization was not manned. As a consequence air-raid sirens sounded only minutes before the attack commenced, blackout was not in force in civilian areas and delighted Japanese aircrew were handed a brightly lit target – the first pebble dislodged in what was to become a landslide of disaster for the colony.

At first light that same morning aircraft based in and around Kota Bharu, comprising 9 Hudsons of No. 1 Squadron RAAF, plus 2 locally available Buffaloes of No. 243 Squadron RAF and 7 Vildebeests of No. 36 Squadron RAF, attacked the Japanese landings and subsequently reported a number of landing craft and a transport containing tanks sunk in the river. Two Hudsons were shot down and a third badly damaged, as was one Buffalo. The Japanese ships retired northward, but their infantry were ashore and some infiltration into British defensive positions was reported.

III

Force Z, comprising the battleship HMS *Prince of Wales* and the battlecruiser HMS *Repulse*, under the command of Admiral Sir Tom Phillips, arrived in Singapore on 2 December 1941, five days prior to the outbreak of the Japanese war. At less than two years old and with a main armament of ten 14-inch guns *Prince of Wales* was one of Britain's newest and finest battleships, and had already experienced an eventful war. In May 1941, off the coast of Iceland, she accompanied the battlecruiser *Hood*, the then pride of the Royal Navy, in an attempt to prevent the German battleship *Bismarck* and her consort the heavy cruiser *Prinz Eugen* from breaking out through the Denmark Strait into the shipping lanes of the North Atlantic. In the ensuing engagement *Hood* was sunk but *Prince of Wales*, although damaged, managed to hit *Bismarck* and cause an oil leak which significantly contributed to the destruction of the 'unsinkable' German leviathan days later by ships of the Home Fleet. Fully repaired, in August 1941 *Prince of Wales* carried Prime Minister Winston Churchill to Placentia Bay, Newfoundland, for a person-to-person meeting with President Franklin D. Roosevelt.

Like all Britain's battlecruisers the sleek graceful lines of *Repulse* made her beautiful to look at – even Japanese aircrew were later to comment on the fact – but she was twenty-five years old.[12] As a battlecruiser she had the main armament (six 15-inch guns) of a battleship, but armour plating was sacrificed to increase speed. In the years since her construction some improvement had been made to her armour, but the main belt around her hull was still only 9 in thick, as against 14–15 in for *Prince of Wales*. An armament refit to upgrade anti-aircraft protection had been scheduled for the end of 1941, but instead she found herself on her way to Singapore.

The exact composition of Force Z is still open to interpretation, although the original intention appears to have been to balance the capital ships with inclusion of the new aircraft carrier *Indomitable*. The issue became academic on 3 November when the carrier grounded in the West Indies and was unable to proceed, thereby removing any prospect of an accompanying air umbrella for Force Z as it set course for an area where compensating land-based air cover was known to be significantly understrength. The decision to despatch to the Far East two extremely valuable naval assets and their crews without adequate air support appears to show a significant underestimation of both the seriousness of Japanese intentions and their potential for war, and should certainly have been rescinded when *Indomitable* was forced to stay behind.

The resolve of the Prime Minister, with the reluctant backing of First Sea Lord Admiral Sir Dudley Pound, to reinforce Britain's naval presence in the Far East seems to have been based upon an imprecise notion to deter the Japanese from opening hostilities – despite the fact that Force Z as finally constituted would make little if any difference to the naval balance of power in the East – and with no clear idea of what the operational strategy for the ships would be if war with Japan broke out anyway. General Sir Hastings Ismay, Winston Churchill's personal staff officer and representative on the Chiefs of Staff Committee, was later to comment that up to 8 December, the day after Pearl Harbor, no decision had been reached as to what to do with the ships.[13] It was thought that they might disappear into the ocean wastes to exercise a vague menace like 'rogue elephants', an option that appears to take little note of the fact that *Prince of Wales* was not designed as a raider and with consequently high fuel consumption did not have the range for the task, or they might head south to join the United States fleet, which necessarily planned to operate in the Pacific, not the Indian Ocean.

In 1941 the Royal Navy, already facing substantial problems in the Atlantic, the Arctic and the Mediterranean, sorely needed every ship it could lay its hands on and could ill afford a risky venture in 'gunboat diplomacy' to the Far East.

Prince of Wales departed Scapa Flow on 23 October for South Africa and thence on to Singapore in company with *Repulse*, Admiral Phillips arriving in Singapore by air two days after his command. Air Chief Marshal Brooke-Popham later reported that due to the Admiral's commitments – he was taking over as C-in-C Eastern Fleet from Sir Geoffrey Layton – the two men had no opportunity for a full consultation before war broke out. Nevertheless, when war did come, Admiral Phillips opted to take action with his ships in the form of an attack on the Japanese landings at Singora. To this end he requested of AOC Singapore, Air Vice-Marshal Pulford, three things:

1. Reconnaissance 100 miles to the north of his force from daylight on Tuesday, 9 December.
2. Reconnaissance to Singora and beyond, 10 miles from the coast starting at first light on 10 December.
3. Fighter protection off Singora at daylight on 10 December.

Following some toing and froing of messages between Air HQ and Naval HQ Singapore Pulford's response amounted to:

1. Affirmative.
2. Possible, but reconnaissance to Singora would have to be undertaken by Blenheim Mk IVs operating from Kuantan and it was uncertain whether this airfield was out of action or not. (NB. Two reconnaissance sorties from Kuantan were in fact flown by the Blenheims although one aircraft had wireless problems.)
3. Not possible as the northern airfields from which fighters would have to operate were either untenable or too badly bomb damaged. The short range of the Brewster Buffalo meant that flying from airfields farther afield would leave a very short time over the Singora area.[14]

Force Z, comprising the two capital ships accompanied by four destroyers, left Singapore on the afternoon of 8 December and Pulford's reply was signalled to Admiral Phillips that evening. At 1345 the following day the ships were sighted by Japanese submarine *I-65*, and again at 1700 by an aircraft operating from the cruiser *Kinu*. Having lost the element of surprise Admiral Phillips called off the operation but did not order the ships to turn for Singapore until 2015, after dark. In order not to betray his new course to Japanese sources he also maintained strict radio silence and did not inform Singapore of his change of plans. At 1835 on the 9th HMS *Tenedos*, a Force Z destroyer low on fuel, had already turned back for Singapore.

Approaching midnight Admiral Phillips received two signals from Admiral Palliser, Chief of Staff Eastern Fleet, in Singapore. The first warned of a substantial force of Japanese bombers in the area capable of mounting an attack within five hours of Force Z being sighted. The second signal reported Japanese landings at Kuantan on the Malay Peninsula. If successful these landings would cut off all British troops in northern Malaya, therefore Admiral Phillips set course for Kuantan, still maintaining radio silence. The reported landings at Kuantan were in fact false, but it may be doubted whether the diversion adversely affected subsequent events as, following numerous submarine and aircraft sightings, Japanese commanders assembled substantial air and sea forces ready to bring Force Z to battle at the earliest opportunity the following day.

At 0952 on the 10th, *Tenedos*, on her way back to Singapore, was attacked by a solitary Japanese aircraft, the destroyer signalling the incident to Singapore. Shortly thereafter she spotted more Japanese aircraft and at 1030 was attacked by another nine, emerging unscathed. The destroyer reported the sightings and the subsequent attack, her signals being picked up by Force Z.

Some way to the north, shortly before the attack on *Tenedos*, a twin-engine Mitsubishi G3M2 Nell Naval attack bomber spotted Force Z proceeding toward Kuantan, signalled its find and remained in contact with the ships. Admiral Phillips issued orders in readiness for air attack, increased speed to maximum 25 knots and altered course for Singapore. Crucially, despite his force having been located he maintained radio silence, did not report his position and did not request air cover.

The first that Singapore knew of events at sea was a message just after noon from *Repulse* stating that she was being bombed some 60 miles east-south-east of Kuantan.[15] A fighter squadron was immediately despatched but arrived just in time to see *Prince of Wales* slip beneath the waves, *Repulse* having already been sunk. The two ships had been overwhelmed by a force of sixty Nell bombers, plus twenty-six twin-engine Mitsubishi G4M1 Betty torpedo bombers operating from bases in southern Indo-China. Coming just three days after Pearl Harbor the attack confirmed the demise of the big-gun battleship and the arrival of air power in naval warfare. In defiance of colleagues in both the Navy and the Air Force, Admiral Phillips maintained an unshakable belief that the big-gun battleship, with its multifarious anti-aircraft armament, would have nothing to fear from air attack. He had been proved wrong in the cruellest manner and did not survive the encounter.

IV

Japanese ground forces made rapid progress down the Malay Peninsula and despite not being specifically trained for jungle warfare adapted to it far more quickly than their British and Commonwealth opponents, who remained dependent on mechanized units and supply columns and were therefore operationally restricted by the need for good roads. By contrast the Japanese, on foot or mounted on nothing more sophisticated than bicycles, used jungle tracks to outflank their adversaries and force them to retreat or risk being surrounded. It was a tactic that Japanese commanders were to use repeatedly and with great success in the coming campaigns in South East Asia.

From 8 December onwards requests for reinforcement of both ground and air forces issued from Singapore with increasing urgency and as the emergency became ever more pressing troops, aircraft and personnel were diverted from other commands, notably the Middle East. By 25 December Air HQ Far East had either been promised or had received the following:

- Six Hudson Mk IIs arrived from Australia to reinforce Nos 1 and 8 (reconnaissance) Squadrons, RAAF.
- Fifty-two Hudson Mk IIIs to be flown out from the UK commencing 20 December to re-equip No. 62 (bomber) Squadron, and Nos 1 and 8 Squadrons, RAAF.
- Twelve Blenheim Mk IVs to reinforce No. 34 (bomber) Squadron. Of these, seven had arrived from the Middle East by 20 December, the remainder were en route.
- Fifty-one crated Hawker Hurricane fighters en route by sea from the UK to the Middle East were diverted to Singapore and expected to arrive on or about 8 January. Aboard ship with the aircraft were twenty-four pilots, the expectation being that these aircraft would be based at Kallang and Johore in defence of Singapore. It was anticipated that little or nothing would be left of the outclassed Brewster Buffaloes by the time the Hurricanes arrived.
- Four Catalina flying boats en route with two spare crews. One to be based in Ceylon, the remainder to reinforce No. 205 Squadron at Seletar.[16]

Prior to the outbreak of the Japanese war a decision had been taken in London for General Sir Henry Pownall to replace Air Chief Marshal Brooke-Popham as Commander-in-Chief Far East, the changeover ultimately taking effect on 27 December. If Brooke-Popham's remit had been unsatisfactory then General Pownall's was even more so, his instructions being to deal with matters of major military policy and strategy, but not to assume operational control. Events moved with such speed, however, that the appointment proved short lived. In mid December, at a conference held in Washington to hammer out a coordinated response to Japanese aggression, the Far Eastern Allies, America, Britain, the Netherlands and Australia, formed a new joint command, designated ABDACOM, the principal area of responsibility being operations in all theatres of the Far East with the exception of the Pacific. General Sir Archibald Wavell took over as C-in-C Far East, setting up his headquarters in Java. General Pownall became Wavell's

Chief of Staff and Air Marshal Sir Richard Peirse assumed command of all Allied air forces. Another important appointment, but one with a complicated pedigree, was that of Air Vice-Marshal P.C. Maltby. Originally designated Pownall's Chief of Staff, with the formation of ABDACOM and the new command structure, the Air Vice-Marshal received instructions to carry out a thorough review of the air defences of Singapore. Maltby found that Pulford's already fragile health, plus the strain of having to conduct operations with minimal staff to assist him, were taking their toll. Pulford nevertheless handled the squadrons satisfactorily and as a consequence, despite being Pulford's senior, Maltby proposed taking the post of Deputy AOC himself in order to remove some of the administrative burden from Pulford's shoulders. With General Pownall's agreement the Air Vice-Marshal duly took up the appointment on 12 January. Although Pulford's deputy, Maltby generously advised the AOC that being senior officer he, Maltby, would take responsibility for all that might happen thereafter.

The formation of ABDACOM was an essential step towards the coordination of Allied military operations, but before the new command could get into its stride events moved on with alarming rapidity.

In northern Malaya British and Commonwealth forces had insufficient strength in both ground troops and aircraft to repel the furious attacks to which they were subjected. As a consequence the area, including vital air bases which Japanese forces then put to their own use, quickly fell to the invader. On 23 December all Allied fighter units were withdrawn to Singapore, only Kuala Lumpur and Port Swettenham being retained as forward landing grounds; and by 25 December approximately half the Malay Peninsula was in Japanese hands.

Piling on the pressure the Japanese Imperial High Command despatched substantial seaborne reinforcements toward the furthest advanced of their land forces at Endau on the Malay Peninsula. Two Hudson reconnaissance aircraft located the convoy, comprising two large troop transports and a substantial naval escort, as it approached landfall early on the morning of 26 December, however finding their W/T transmissions jammed the aircraft were unable to pass on the information until their return to base. Upon receipt of the news at Air HQ Singapore the decision was taken for an immediate air assault. The Vickers Vildebeests of Nos 36 and 100 Squadrons made up the only relatively intact formations remaining to the RAF, the slow vulnerable aircraft having been used mainly at night. Now, however, these outdated biplanes were to make a daylight attack on enemy ships in a dive-bombing role, the waters around Endau deemed too shallow for the torpedoes with which the crews had chiefly trained.

At approximately 1505 the first attack, 12 Vildebeests plus 9 Hudsons, escorted by 15 Buffaloes and 9 Hurricanes, went in at the Vildebeest's maximum 90 knots (approximately 100 mph). A number of enemy ships were hit but five Vildebeests were shot down. At 1730 a second attack, nine Vildebeests and three naval Fairey Albacore biplanes transferred to 36 Squadron, plus Hudsons and fighter support, made further strikes on the Japanese shipping. A further 5 Vildebeests were shot down as were 2 Albacores and 2 Hudsons. The transports, a cruiser and two destroyers, were later believed to have been damaged but at a cost of 12 Vildebeests – two being written off in addition to those shot down – 2 Albacores, 38 aircrew including Squadron Leaders R.F.C. Markham and I.T.B. Rowland, the commanders of 36 and 100 Squadrons. Also among the casualties were two Hudsons, a Hurricane and many damaged aircraft.[17] Compounding the tragedy, by the time the attacks materialized it was already too late, the Japanese troops and their equipment were already ashore.

V

By 29 January Japanese troops in force were approaching the Straits of Johore separating Singapore Island from the Malay Peninsula. With the exception of the fighters, what remained of the air establishment at Singapore had already been ordered to depart for Java or Sumatra while attempts were made to arrange for stores, spares and equipment accumulated over many years to follow them. With no air transports available everything leaving Singapore had to go by ship from docks that were increasingly under air attack, congested and devoid of civilian labour.

The following day, 30 January, General Wavell and Air Chief Marshal Peirse visited Singapore and, with the exception of eight Hurricanes and eight Buffaloes, authorized the withdrawal of the fighters. Prime Minister Winston Churchill queried the move and stated that ninety more Hurricanes were en route to Singapore; promises notwithstanding, by 5 February the air defence of Singapore was reduced to fourteen Hurricanes of 232 Squadron RAF plus four naval Swordfish biplanes.

On that same day, 5 February, Air Vice-Marshal Pulford took the decision that as most of his command was in the process of leaving Singapore the best thing for him to do would be to depart for Batavia and put in train the urgently required reorganization of the scattered units at his disposal. Air Vice-Marshal Maltby would remain in Singapore for the time being to supervise the final stages of the evacuation of RAF personnel and equipment and then proceed to Batavia. On hearing of the decision Air Chief Marshal Peirse took exception to Air HQ leaving Singapore at that stage as it would give the wrong impression concerning British intentions for the colony, which he maintained could still be saved. What actually went through Pulford's mind at this time is uncertain but it is believed that he took Peirse's comments as a personal reproach from his superior for suggesting what amounted to the abandonment by Air HQ of both the Army and Singapore. Whatever his private thoughts, Pulford was thereafter determined to remain to the end.

By 9 February Japanese troops of the 5th and 18th Divisions were ashore on the north-west coast of Singapore Island, and with Pulford steadfastly refusing to leave, Maltby, on Wavell's orders, left the following day to take command of all British and Commonwealth air units in Java and Sumatra. Despite the heroic efforts of the pilots and ground crew of 232 Squadron they were in grave danger of being decimated by vastly superior numbers, therefore prior to leaving himself, Maltby gave orders for them to withdraw to Palembang. With their departure the air battles for Malaya and Singapore came to an end, battles in which the RAF had seen virtually its entire strength destroyed including 122 Buffaloes and forty-five Hurricanes. Japanese sources were quoted as putting their own losses at 512 aircraft.

With the situation rapidly deteriorating, by 13 February Pulford and his remaining staff had been allocated space in a small flotilla of boats. Finally persuaded by Lieutenant General Percival, Pulford agreed to depart and boarded a launch in company with forty or so others, but the launch was attacked by Japanese aircraft and beached on a bleak uninhabited island to the north of Banka. Two months later, starvation and disease having taken their toll, the survivors surrendered. Air Vice-Marshal Pulford was not among them.

With his forces driven within a perimeter around Singapore town, Percival informed his senior officers that there was little point to their remaining on the defensive; they either had to attack or capitulate. He favoured the former, his fellow commanders did not, and on the afternoon of 15 February he surrendered 62,000 British and Commonwealth troops to the 35,000 Japanese soldiers of Lieutenant General Yamashita's Twenty-Fifth Army. Winston Churchill called the fall of Singapore 'the worst disaster and largest capitulation in British history'.

Notes

1. The Sian Incident: in December 1936 Chiang Kai-shek was kidnapped by rebel Chinese army officers who attempted to persuade him to stop his campaign of repression against the communists, and instead combine his Nationalist forces with them in a united front against the Japanese. Chiang refused to deal with the rebels and while some were prepared to kill him,

others, including the communist leader Chou En-Lai, saw him as the only man capable of uniting the nation. Chiang was released and his Nationalists did unite, temporarily, with the communists to fight the invader.

2. TNA Air 2/7932, Report of Air Vice-Marshal Sir Paul Maltby, p. 1349.
3. TNA Air 2/7773, Report of Air Chief Marshal Sir Robert Brooke-Popham, p. 17 & Appx I.
4. *Ibid.*
5. *Ibid.*, p. 41.
6. *Ibid.*, Appendix J, p. 40.
7. *Ibid.*, p. 21.
8. Sakaida, Henry, *Japanese Army Air Force on the Attack* (Delprado Publishers, 2000), p. 11.
9. The Japanese operated two distinct and, for Allied observers, contradictory methods for the identification of aircraft types, consequently to make clear which type of aircraft was being referred to in dispatches the Allies gave most Japanese aircraft types code names – hence the Ki-43 became the 'Oscar'.
10. Hata, Ikuhiko, Izawa, Yasuho and Shores, Christopher, *Japanese Army Air Force Fighter Units and their Aces, 1931–1945* (Grub Street, 2002), p. 28.
11. Ford, Daniel, *Flying Tigers* (Smithsonian Institution Press, 1991), p. 60.
12. 'As we dived for the attack, I didn't want to launch my torpedo. It was such a beautiful ship, such a beautiful ship.' An anecdote related by Lieutenant Iki Haruki and quoted in Nicholson, Arthur, *Hostages to Fortune* (Sutton Publishing, 2005), p. 131.
13. Ismay, General The Lord, *The Memoirs of Lord Ismay* (Wm. Heinemann Ltd., 1960), p. 242. General Ismay also mentions having dreamed on the night of 9/10 December that *Prince of Wales* had been sunk and that he woke up in a cold sweat, only to receive the awful confirmation with the coming of morning.
14. TNA Air 2/7773, Report of Air Chief Marshal Brooke-Popham, p. 23.
15. *Ibid.*
16. TNA Air 2/7932, Report of Air Vice-Marshal Sir Paul Maltby, p. 1373.
17. *Ibid.*, p. 1411; also Probert, Air Commodore Henry, *The Forgotten Air Force* (Brassey's, 1995), pp. 57–8.

Chapter Two

Burma's 'Few'

I

No. 67 Squadron RAF, formed in Singapore April 1941 and transferred to Burma in October 1942, discovered on arrival at Rangoon's principal airfield, Mingaladon, that most of their Brewster Buffaloes were still in packing cases behind the south hangar. Three aircraft had been assembled by the personnel of No. 60 Squadron, whose aircraft had been retained in Malaya, so 67 Squadron's ground crew set to work immediately on the remaining thirty. Soon fully assembled aircraft were rolling out of the hangar at a rate of two per day, until by mid November the full squadron complement was both assembled and tested.[1]

The Brewster Buffalo was short and fat and being none too fast and none too manoeuvrable, soon became known none too affectionately as the flying barrel. Nevertheless, while they were no match for Japanese fighters, they would prove useful at bringing down enemy bombers. Maintenance seemed to be never-ending. Spot welds would break on the box section undercarriage, big end bearings would fail depositing white metal into scavenge filters, and on first assembly rivets were often discovered in fuel lines, fuel pumps and carburettors. At least one veteran of the squadron ground crew put this last down to sabotage by 'certain workers' in the United States.[2]

Three days after Pearl Harbor, and with every aircraft urgently needed in the air, the squadron received a signal from Air Headquarters grounding all their Buffaloes until checks were carried out on valve springs of the Cyclone engines. This required that each engine be stripped, checked, rebuilt, tested and passed fit, the major overhaul being completed within five days. On 16 December the squadron received another signal from Air Headquarters grounding the aircraft once again until the valve gear had been rechecked for another fault. Again engines

26

were stripped, checked and passed. Whether fighter, bomber, transport or reconnaissance, a squadron is not just its pilots and aircrew – it is the ground crew who keep the aircraft flying and in Burma they would have to do so in the face of almost insurmountable shortages of spares, tools and equipment of every kind.

A pilot making his approach to Mingaladon would see the three gravel runways of the airfield below him laid out like a sloping letter 'A' with the main runway, the east-west crosspiece, stretching beyond the airstrip that comprised the right leg. In mid December 67 Squadron were joined by 3 Squadron ('The Hell's Angels') of the American Volunteer Group, equipped with twenty-one Curtiss P-40B fighters. As these aircraft had originally been destined for the RAF they were often referred to by their RAF nomenclature – Tomahawk Mk IIAs. The AVG were assigned to the crosspiece runway at Mingaladon while 67 Squadron used the right-hand north-south runway, both squadrons being sub-divided into two flights with one flight at each end of its allotted runway. When the alarm sounded pandemonium broke loose as four flights took to the air, each from a different direction and meeting where the runways crossed. Strong nerves and good timing were required for the system to work but it got the fighters into the air quicker than any other could have done.

Although equipped with thirty-three aircraft 67 Squadron had but eighteen pilots, mostly 'green' New Zealanders without combat experience. With their aircraft passed operationally fit in late December these pilots entered a sharp learning curve when the squadron was ordered to carry out a strafing raid on the Japanese-held airfield at Girikham in Siam. Days later, on 23 December, Mingaladon experienced the full force of the JAAF's response as sixty Mitsubishi Ki-21 Sally heavy bombers approached, dividing their attention between the airfield and Rangoon. The raid over Mingaladon lasted no longer than a few minutes but in that time 67 Squadron's thirty-three combat-ready Buffaloes were reduced to eleven, the remainder being destroyed on the ground together with three Tomahawks. Some one hundred or so airmen and civilians died, their 'bodies hanging forlornly in the telegraph wires and scattered like so many crumpled bits of rag around the field'.[3] A number of Buffaloes from 67 Squadron and Tomahawks of the AVG did get airborne and between them shot down five bombers over the airfield for the loss of two Buffaloes and a Tomahawk. 67 Squadron pilot 'Ketchil' Barge claimed one bomber, getting so close in the process that oil from the stricken 'Sally' sprayed all over his windscreen, obliging the Kiwi to find an unoccupied piece of sky, remove one flying boot and a sock, slide back the canopy, stand up in the cockpit and lean out to wipe the windscreen clean with the sock.[4] Engaging the interlopers with a will the AVG claimed three more bombers over Rangoon for the loss of another Tomahawk. On the ground, work began immediately to cannibalize the wrecked aircraft while the Japanese returned to Siam also somewhat chastened by their losses.

By dawn on Christmas Eve, 67 Squadron had fourteen Buffaloes operational, the AVG twelve Tomahawks. With both squadrons forced to scratch around among wrecked aircraft for usable spare parts, the AVG encountered a particular problem in the shape of an alarming shortfall of ammunition for the wing guns of their aircraft. With some foresight Chennault had based a detachment at Toungoo and since the AVG mess hall at Mingaladon had not survived the raid, the mess supervisor drove the 350-mile round trip overnight, returning on the morning of the 24th with 70,000 rounds of 7.92 mm ammunition and two replacement pilots.[5] By mid morning that same day no Japanese had materialized over Rangoon and the Buffaloes took off for another raid on Girikham, shooting up a ceremonial parade at the airfield and strafing a troop train on their way home.

On Christmas Day the Japanese were back – sixty-three Ki-21 Sally heavy bombers and a sprinkling of Mitsubishi Ki-30 Ann light bombers, escorted by twenty-five Nakajima Ki-27 Nate fighters. Fourteen Buffaloes and fourteen Tomahawks – the AVG ground crew having resurrected another aircraft – took off to intercept. The bombers once again divided their attention between Mingaladon and Rangoon, losing five of their number and five fighters at a cost to the air defence of four Buffaloes and two Tomahawks.

It being Christmas, 67 Squadron had salted away a capacious barrel of beer with which to celebrate – fifty gallons, or half a gallon per man! The beer nestled alongside Christmas dinner in the cookhouse, which received a direct hit. Miraculously the barrel survived but the blast turned the beer sour and dinner on Christmas Day 1941 comprised hard biscuits and half a mug of water. The raid also seems to have broken the spirit of many of the Burmese residents of Rangoon and for days thereafter thousands of refugees streamed past Mingaladon on their weary way north.

The Japanese saw the old year out with a temporary change of tactics, despatching a couple of bombers with fighter escort at various times during the day, upsetting the routine on the ground and working on frayed nerves in the process. Rest during the night was ruined by singleton Japanese intruder aircraft droning across the airfield on an hourly basis strafing anything and everything as they went. Without night fighters there was little the RAF or AVG could do about these nuisance raids, and that too shortened tempers and drove home the precarious nature of their situation.

Over at the AVG end of the base, Oley Olsen, Commander of 3 Squadron AVG, faced with a steady whittling down of his command, urgently requested Chennault to withdraw them to Kunming. Chennault would have liked nothing better than to consolidate the AVG in China but Chiang Kai-shek would hear nothing of it, understandably insisting that 'his' air force assist in keeping the Burma Road supply line open. Chennault did relieve The Hell's Angels, however, pulling them back to Kunming and replacing them at Mingaladon with 2 Squadron (The Panda Bears).

From the moment that Japanese invasion forces appeared off Singora it must have been apparent that not only Malaya and Singapore were in grave danger of invasion, but that Burma, the lynchpin of the Burma Road, must be a prime target. Beyond that India itself might also be at risk.

On 12 December 1941, Air Vice-Marshal D.F. Stevenson found himself appointed to command the air forces in Burma and in possession of a promise from the Air Ministry to reinforce his command with four fighter squadrons, six bomber squadrons and one reconnaissance squadron, the object being to halt the Japanese in Burma should Malaya and Singapore fall.

Stevenson arrived in Rangoon on 1 January 1942 and spent his first week in Burma assessing his command and the tasks that it faced. Both prior and subsequent to the Air Vice-Marshal's arrival, overall command of the RAF in Burma was a moveable feast that seems, when taken in conjunction with a number of indicators, including the fate of Force Z, to reveal a lack of clarity and singleness of purpose among the higher echelons of Britain's political and military leadership with regard to operations in the Far East. Initially organized as Burgroup under C-in-C India, RAF Burma became 221 Group under the command of AOC Far East. On 15 December 1941, 221 Group found itself transferred back to the command of C-in-C India, just weeks later being re-designated again, this time as Norgroup under the command of General Wavell, Supreme Commander South-Western Pacific Command based in Java. To complicate matters, for administrative purposes Norgroup remained under C-in-C India. Following the fall of Java, Norgroup once more reverted completely to the command of C-in-C India.[6]

On inspection Stevenson found that in early January 1942 the air garrison of the country comprised the two fighter squadrons at Mingaladon. The only other air forces present were the de Havilland Moth biplanes of the Communication Flight of the Burma Volunteer Air Force and the personnel of No. 60 Squadron RAF, whose aircraft were

29

still in Malaya. As Stevenson assessed his tiny command, the planned reinforcement of Burma with six bomber squadrons was cut to three and that only on the assumption that Blenheim aircraft would become available with which to re-equip 60 Squadron. As things were to turn out there would never be sufficient aircraft. What did arrive during January and early February were the Blenheim Mk IVs, personnel and 'pack up' (tools and equipment etc.) of No. 113 Squadron RAF, plus the Blenheim Mk IVFs of No. 45 Squadron RAF, but without either personnel or 'pack up'.

Spares and tools for all types of aircraft were in chronically short supply, a factor which led to the sidelining of otherwise perfectly combat-ready aircraft for want of minor repairs, a situation in its turn leading to cannibalization in order to keep a force of some sort in the air. Initially there were no Repair and Salvage Units (RSU) or Air Stores Parks (ASP) anywhere in Burma and when No. 60 RSU and No. 39 ASP did finally turn up they had no equipment.

On the face of it the one bright spot in an otherwise gloomy scenario concerned airfield development and construction. Works carried out on behalf of the RAF by the Burmese Government had been to a high standard, with most bases having one or two all-weather runways plus accommodation and ancillary equipment. A serious airfield problem did exist however and that concerned their location.

In order to counter the possibility of an enemy air force based in China and neighbouring Siam the main line of airfields ran northwards from Victoria Point, on the southern tip of the Tenasserim Peninsula, up the valley of the Sittang, through Toungoo, Heho, Namsung, and finally to Lashio in the north, a distance of around 800 miles. To the east and south-east of this line jungle-covered mountains almost impossible to traverse stretched away to the Siamese border – an exceptionally poor area in which to attempt to place RDF stations and the telephone communications with which to warn the airfields of approaching enemy aircraft. A more strategically sound programme would have placed the airfields along the valley of the Irrawaddy with forward RDF stations and communications in the valley of the Sittang. The reason for poor airfield siting probably lies rooted in the chopping and changing of control of the RAF referred to above. Utilizing the valley of the Sittang was a decision taken by Far East Command based in Singapore, where Burma held a very low priority and where in any event the staff would have little detailed knowledge of the terrain. Had the RAF remained the responsibility of C-in-C India, whose air staff would necessarily be more familiar with the topography of Burma, the implications of such a plan would have been recognized immediately. Nevertheless what was done was done and to try to make the best of the poor positioning the RAF drew up plans for early warning radar comprising three chain RDF stations, two COL stations to track low-flying aircraft, and two GCI stations. An attempt was also made to develop a telephone system across the Karen Hills and the Salween Valley, and requests were passed to India for the necessary personnel and equipment to man thirty-five W/T posts. Despite these good intentions, with the commencement of the air war over Burma there existed just one RDF set in the whole of the country, a COL unit languishing at Moulmein where its arc of observation was ineffective. The set was subsequently moved to Rangoon and from there to Magwe as the situation demanded. No spares of any kind existed for the set although superhuman efforts on the part of the technicians kept it working effectively until it left Rangoon.

II

On 5 January 1942, four days after Stevenson's arrival in Rangoon, the 5th *Hikoshidan*, JAAF, transferred from Formosa to Bangkok to replace 3rd *Hikoshidan*. The 5th, under the command of Lieutenant General Hideyoshi Obata, was a combat-experienced, well-equipped and highly capable unit comprising the 8th, 14th, 31st, 50th, 62nd and 77th *Hikosentai* plus the 4th and 10th *Hikodan Shireibu* each of which brought with it a reconnaissance *chutai*. The 5th was tasked primarily with the destruction of opposing air forces; only units of the 10th *Hikosentai* being assigned to ground support after the Japanese Fifteenth Army began its invasion of Burma at the end of the month.[7]

Air raids on Rangoon had begun during December but now Obata increased the pressure, ordering the combined fighter and bomber *chutai* of the 4th and 10th *Hikosentai* to seek out and destroy the Allied Air Force at its bases around the capital. During the course of January Allied Photo Reconnaissance and other sources put Japanese air strength within close range at something over 150 bombers and fighters, or an effective readily available offensive force of some 100 or more aircraft. As reinforcements arrived during the ensuing weeks this total rose to over 200 aircraft, or an offensive force of around 140, ranged against Burma's two fighter and one bomber squadrons – some 53 aircraft as at 14 February.[8]

Difficulties imposed by the location of airfields in the Sittang valley now became apparent as an early warning equivalent to at least 50 miles flying time was required in order to get defences primed and fighter cover in the air. Fitted with long-range tanks Japanese fighters were capable of a combat radius of over 500 miles and would sweep in at low level strafing airfields, damaging and destroying aircraft and equipment, all too often catching defending fighters on the ground as a result of the lack of an effective chain of RDF stations. The efforts of the Burma Observer Corps (using the local public telephone system) and the relocation of the single COL RDF unit to Rangoon went some way towards mitigating this deficiency.

Having made himself familiar with his small but (hopefully) growing command, Air Vice-Marshal Stevenson saw his main priority as the defence of Rangoon with its vital docks and airfields. To inflict as high a casualty rate as possible on the enemy Stevenson proposed to lean forward (his phraseology) with his fighters by basing them at advanced airfields along the Tenasserim Peninsula at Moulmein, Tavoy and Mergui. From these bases the enemy air force would be attacked whenever and wherever found while his bombers attacked roads, railways and airfields. Ground support for the Army would also have to be undertaken but enemy air attacks on northern Burma would have to go unchallenged unless significant reinforcements were forthcoming.

Desperately short of bombers, Stevenson ordered the Blenheims of 113 Squadron RAF to attack Bangkok, the principal Japanese base in Thailand, on 7 January the very night of their arrival. As with much of the aircraft reinforcement he was to receive, the Blenheims had already seen action in the Middle East and were still fitted with desert fuel filters and ferry tanks. Nevertheless they were prepared in double quick time by the ubiquitous 60 Squadron personnel, who also supplied crewmen for two aircraft for the 700-mile round trip. The Blenheim did not carry a particularly heavy bomb load with which to attack built-up areas, 1,000 lb (434 kg) internally plus 320 lb (145 kg) externally, however, in all 11,000 lb of explosives and incendiaries were dropped on the docks in the centre of the city and a number of fires started. Following the raid the squadron was withdrawn north to Lashio to enable detailed aircraft inspections to be carried out following the long flight from the Middle East. Not for the first time or the last, the problem of lack of spares raised its head and it was not until 19 January that the Blenheims were fit for action once more.

In compliance with Stevenson's strategy 67 Squadron had two of its Buffaloes pushed forward to Moulmein, while two more were based 30 miles to the north at Zayatkwin. In mid January the JAAF carried out one of its regular singleton raids across Mingaladon, the aircraft strafing the airfield and flying off south. Two Buffaloes, piloted by Battle of Britain veteran and Flight Commander Colin Pinckney, plus a Sergeant Pilot, responded and gave chase. The attack, however, was a trap and the two RAF aircraft were 'bounced' by seven enemy fighters. Pinckney ordered the Sergeant Pilot to return to Mingaladon while he took on the Japanese single handed, and in the ensuing dogfight is believed to have accounted for three before being shot down himself.[9]

Toward the end of January 67 Squadron's flying flights were all moved to Zayatkwin, but one flight quickly found itself moved back to Mingaladon as a crisis developed in the land war. A build-up of Japanese ground forces along the Siam-Tenasserim border necessitated the evacuation of the southernmost airfields at Mergui and Tavoy on 18 January, the invasion of Burma beginning eleven days later with an advance by the Lieutenant General Iida Shojiro's Japanese Fifteenth Army through Tenasserim, its objective Rangoon. Ground forces defending in Burma at this time were both outnumbered and outgunned, amounting to 1st Burma Division being deployed in central Burma and 17th Indian Division defending the line of the Salween River and Rangoon, both under the overall command of Lieutenant General T.J. Hutton. With commendable alacrity, arrangements were put in place to plan air support each evening at a general staff and air staff conference at Air Vice-Marshal Stevenson's Headquarters. A useful pointer for future operations was provided by Stevenson and Hutton themselves, who met each morning and evening to dovetail ground and air operations. Priority necessarily went to the front line unit, 17th Indian Division, and an Air Liaison Officer was attached with communications established via W/T and telephone.

Commanded by Major General 'Jackie' Smyth, 17th Division soon found itself hard pressed and made numerous requests for bombers to make up for its deficiency in artillery. However, providing a foretaste of the problems to come, close support bombing in Tenasserim posed a number of difficulties, principally the distinguishing of friend from foe in the dense jungle, a dilemma complicated by the favoured Japanese tactic of outflanking defensive positions and creating a fluid combat area lacking an easily definable front line. The quandary in which the RAF found itself was compounded by reports from forward army positions around Kawkariek detailing apparently indiscriminate Japanese bombing of jungle areas and the adverse effect that this was having on the morale of British and Commonwealth troops. In an attempt to bolster morale by showing that the enemy were also subject to bombing raids Stevenson ordered attacks on jungle areas believed to contain Japanese units, despite the possible risk to friendly troops.

Units of the Japanese Fifteenth Army invested Kawkariek on 20 January, and the RAF attacked a JAAF forward air base at Mesoht with a mixed force of bombers and fighters, a number of aircraft being damaged or destroyed on the ground. With Allied troops pulling back from Kawkariek, Blenheims sortied against the Japanese-held airfields at Raheng and Mesarieng on 21 and 22 January, dropping some 6,000 lb of bombs on each raid. The JAAF was not idle during this time and launched a heavy fighter-supported bomber raid on Moulmein; however Allied fighters covering an outgoing Blenheim raid intercepted the Japanese formation and in the battle that followed claimed to have shot down seven bombers and nine fighters.

While appreciating the need for ground support, and accepting the use of fighters in this role when suitable targets presented themselves, Stevenson still saw his principal operational requirement as the maintenance of air superiority over Rangoon. Once this was lost the port and associated bases and supply dumps would be subjected to very heavy bombing as would the line of communications to 17th Division. As a consequence the Allied fighter force was for the most part kept concentrated in the Rangoon area where it achieved considerable success despite its diminutive size.

En route for the Middle East the personnel of No. 17 Squadron RAF found themselves diverted to Burma, arriving at Mingaladon on 16 January without any aircraft. Having spent a frustrating time cooling their heels the first of their fighters – three Hurricane IIBs – arrived on 23 January from the Middle East. As with much of the limited supply of aircraft that turned up in the Far East during these dark days, these Hurricanes were by no means new. Long and arduous service already having been experienced in the Western Desert, in any other theatre but Burma/India the aircraft would have been declared 'clapped out' and scrapped. Among the many and varied difficulties with which ground and air crew had to contend, the Hurricanes were discovered to be still fitted with tropical air filters for desert conditions, reducing top speed by about 30 mph and adversely affecting their rate of climb. The aircraft nevertheless had useful firepower via their twelve machine guns as opposed to the usual eight, but even this raised a problem as the 17 Squadron armourers calculated that the weight of the extra guns further reduced speed and manoeuvrability to such an extent that any improvement in firepower was cancelled out by the difficulty encountered in actually being able to bring the guns to bear – in all probability these fighters had been used in the ground support role in the desert. Consequently, along with all the other repair and maintenance jobs required to make the aircraft combat ready, four machine guns were removed from each. Inevitably spares and tools for the Hurricanes were as hard to come by as for any other Allied aircraft and it was only with the invaluable assistance of local British Rangoon Railway engineers, who made specialized tools for the squadron, that the aircraft were kept flying at all. Motor transport was also virtually non-existent and had to be obtained from local car dealers. On hearing of the shortage the AVG also happily obliged in exchange for a number of 17 Squadron's ground crew. To further complicate matters the Hurricanes arrived fitted with non-jettisonable 90-gallon long-range fuel tanks under each wing which the squadron asked to be allowed to remove for speed/manoeuvrability reasons similar to those surrounding the extra guns; however, given the notoriously 'short legs' of the Hurricane and the limitations such a deficiency imposed upon Air Vice-Marshal Stevenson's plan to attack enemy aircraft wherever and whenever found, the AOC at Mingaladon refused.

Shortly after their arrival the three Hurricanes were scrambled to intercept incoming Japanese bombers and fighters. With the AVG already in the fray the Hurricanes attempted to climb to join in, but getting to 10,000 feet with long-range tanks fitted took an inordinately long time to achieve, and before gaining the necessary height the RAF aircraft were jumped by ten Japanese Ki-27 Nates. In short order two Hurricanes were forced to break off the engagement and land, the third attempting to continue the fight until it too was forced to land, so badly shot up that it had to be scrapped for spare parts. In this engagement over Mingaladon Major Toyoki Eto, commander of the 1st *Chutai*, 77th *Hikosentai*, claimed as his tally three Allied fighters shot down plus one probable.[10] Back at Mingaladon strong representations were made to the AOC who, albeit reluctantly, agreed to the removal of the long-range tanks.

With the arrival of Hurricanes for 17 Squadron Air Vice-Marshal Stevenson felt able to develop a more coordinated approach and agreed with Jack Newkirk, Commander of 2 Squadron AVG, a mutually supportive role with Hurricanes and Tomahawks fighting in tandem. The AVG pilots now had considerable combat and flying experience, while a number of 17 Squadron pilots, particularly the flight commanders, had fought the Luftwaffe in Europe. Tactics were similar to those employed in Europe with one significant difference, to counter the greater agility of the Japanese fighters the most successful method was not to engage them in 'turn-for-turn' dogfights, which the Allied pilots were unlikely to win, but instead to attain height for a diving attack. This gave the Tomahawks and Hurricanes the initial advantage of height and sun, the dive being followed by a rapid half roll or aileron turn before regaining height to repeat the manoeuvre.

Enemy fighter-escorted bomber raids would be attacked as soon as they were located, however as a counter measure the JAAF adopted a strategy of sending fighter formations of between forty and sixty aircraft at height in advance of the bombers, hoping to draw up the Allied fighters and shoot them down before the bombers could be engaged. On these occasions Allied aircraft would fall back on Rangoon and wait for the enemy fighters to either drop down to deliver ground attacks, or turn for home.

Despite the fact that Japanese aircraft operated without flame dampers, and initially sortied with navigation lights burning, night interception of their raids proved fraught with difficulties. Neither Tomahawks nor Buffaloes were equipped with suitable RDF or illuminated instruments, in addition to which their pilots were not trained for night operations, although from time to time the attempt was made, generally with poor results. The arrival of 17 Squadron, including on its roster a number of pilots trained for night flying, went some way toward addressing the problem and it was agreed that they would try an interception on the occasion of the next 'bombers' moon' (the Japanese rarely sortied on moonless nights). The opportunity arose on the night of 27 January and two Hurricanes piloted by Battle of Britain veterans Squadron Leader C.A.C. 'Bunny' Stone and 'Jimmy' Elsdon took off into a clear night sky, Stone patrolling above 20,000 feet, Elsdon somewhat below. Their first hint of targets approaching turned out to be the dull thud and orange shell bursts of distant anti-aircraft fire, and it was some time before Stone noticed what appeared at first to be a moving star until realization dawned that what he saw were the engine exhausts of two Japanese bombers approaching Mingaladon somewhat below him at around 9,000 feet. As the Squadron Leader put his Hurricane into a dive a gunner in one of the bombers opened fire, but was quickly silenced when the Hurricane's eight Browning machine guns responded. Stone quickly turned on the other enemy aircraft and fired into it until it burst into flames and rolled over into a dive, his tracer bullets passing over Elsdon, who had also spotted the bomber, in the process. The 17 Squadron pilots claimed both aircraft destroyed although Stevenson only mentions one in his report.[11] Buoyed by their success the Hurricanes made two additional night interceptions, shooting down enemy bombers on each occasion, however with the limited resources available and pilots required to be in a constant state of readiness in daylight hours, it was not possible to put patrols up every night.

Further north at Toungoo, No. 1 Squadron IAF arrived 1 February equipped with twelve Westland Lysanders. These were slow, unwieldy monoplane army cooperation and reconnaissance aircraft, activities for which the squadron had trained. In the early hours of the morning following the squadron's arrival the 5th *Hikoshidan* commenced a series of four raids on Toungoo using between six and fifteen bombers, inflicting considerable damage, although luckily the Lysanders escaped unscathed. No. 1 Squadron's Commanding Officer, Squadron Leader Majumdar, did not feel disposed to take this attack lying down and with the coming of daylight had his Lysander fitted with bomb racks enabling the aircraft to carry two 250 lb bombs, one under each wing. Escorted by two Brewster Buffaloes, Majumdar took off on 2 February and headed across the border into Siam, bound for the Japanese-held airfield at Mae-Haungsaun, where the JAAF attack was believed to have originated. Flying in low Majumdar attacked the airfield's only hangar, which contained an aircraft, scored two direct hits and returned to Toungoo. The following day No. 1 Squadron repeated the attack, this time with all twelve Lysanders fitted with bomb racks, causing damage and disruption to the enemy held airfield. For this raid the Lysanders flew unescorted, relying on camouflage and their ability to fly at treetop height to keep them from the attention of patrolling Japanese fighters. On completion of this second raid the Lysanders flew on to Heho in northern Burma, losing only one aircraft on the way, the Indian pilots attributing their success to skills acquired flying over inhospitable country along India's North-West Frontier. Assisted by elements of 28 Squadron RAF flying Lysander IIs, No. 1 Squadron subsequently raided Japanese-held bases at Chiengmai and Chiangrai, also in Siam. On 5 February the squadron was ordered south to Mingaladon to fulfil its army cooperation role in Tenasserim, but did not miss any opportunity for further bombing raids, carrying out forty-one sorties against Japanese airfields and direct support targets.[12] Such was the dearth of reconnaissance aircraft that during the second week of February the squadron was split up, one flight remaining at Mingaladon, one flight returning to Toungoo, and the remainder, together with Squadron Leader Majumdar, despatched to Lashio to carry out reconnaissance operations on behalf of the Chinese Army in northern Burma. Also carrying out reconnaissance operations from Mingaladon were two Blenheim Mk Is of No. 3 Flight IAF.

III

As January drew to a close and the situation on the ground in Tenasserim steadily worsened the small force of RAF Blenheims, usually around six operational aircraft, plus whatever fighters could be spared from the defence of Rangoon, were required to keep up a series of attacks on Japanese aerodromes, motor transport and lines of communication. In three days of raids commencing on 24 January, the Blenheims dropped a total of 42,100 lb of bombs, yet despite this and the best efforts of 17th Indian Division, Japanese ground forces kept up their relentless advance and by 30 January were attacking Moulmein, which had already been subjected to 'softening up' attacks by the JAAF. This being a significant Allied air base 5th *Hikoshidan* devoted some effort towards its destruction, sending in an initial attack by nine fighters on 3 January followed up in subsequent weeks by daylight raids utilizing fighter-escorted formations of up to twenty-seven bombers, interspersed with night attacks by pairs of bombers. During this period 5th *Hikoshidan* simultaneously carried out small-scale operations against Rangoon.

Having decided that the retreat of opposing ground forces might profitably be hurried along by increased attention from the air, the JAAF put into operation another short-term change in tactics by switching their bombers from airfield assaults to a ground-support role and for four days beginning on 8 February blasted Allied infantry positions. Moulmein duly fell to Japanese ground and air attack and by 15 February 17th Indian Division had withdrawn to a line along the Bilin River. Such Allied bombers and fighters as were available kept up attacks on enemy infantry positions plus river craft, batteries, landing stages, railway stations, barracks and stores. Around 70,136 lb of bombs were dropped in an attempt to slow the Japanese advance, with much of the bombing carried out at low level for maximum results.

On 17 February Japanese infantry drove home fierce attacks on the Bilin River line and by the following day they were across, 17th Division once more being obliged to withdraw. On 20 February Lieutenant General Hutton gave instructions to Major General Smyth to fall back behind the Sittang and by 22 February the establishment of a new defensive position on the right bank of the river, covering the bridge by which the division would withdraw, was being attempted against stiff opposition from enemy ground and air forces. Japanese artillery could now clearly be heard in Rangoon and as the crow flies units of the Fifteenth Army bivouacked less than 5 miles from Mingaladon.

The day before, 21 February, reconnaissance at last located what appeared to be a good target for air attack in the shape of a large motorized column comprising 300 or more vehicles on the road between Bilin and Kyaikto. Air Vice-Marshal Stevenson pulled all available fighters from the defence of Rangoon and ordered them, together with his remaining bombers, to attack. Twelve Tomahawks of the AVG strafed the column at 1630, and eight Hurricanes at 1640, followed by bombing runs from the Blenheims, direct hits being observed and fires reported amongst the motor transport and in the village of Kyaikto. Whether there was ever a Japanese column close to the target area given to the Allied air forces is still the subject of controversy, however it appears certain that 17th Indian Division was subjected to several incidents of 'friendly fire' from the RAF and AVG at this time, causing what was described as 'numerous' casualties. Air Vice-Marshal Stevenson carried out an enquiry into the allegations and failed to reach a conclusion as to their validity, however, bearing in mind the nature of the terrain, he considers that it was 'not improbable' that mistakes were made, which is about as close as he might be expected to get to an admission of error in an official report.[13] As if attacks from its own air forces were not enough for the division to contend with as it struggled to reach the Sittang, it was also forced to endure concentrated raids from up to ninety fighters and twelve bombers of 5th *Hikoshidan*. This disastrous day was, however, only the precursor to an even greater misfortune about to befall the Allied troops.

In its arduous retreat 17th Division had lost much of its materiel including, crucially, most of its radio equipment. With the road from Mokpalin to the Sittang Bridge crammed with Allied motor transport, infantry units scattered through surrounding jungle attempting to beat off determined Japanese attacks, communications at best haphazard and intermittent, the view from Divisional Headquarters appeared desperate. Fearing that the bridge might be captured intact Major General Smyth ordered it destroyed, and at 0500 on 23 February it was blown, trapping half the division on the wrong side of the river with all the divisional artillery and most of its transport. The Japanese lost no time in moving in to destroy the remnants. Not only was the blowing of the bridge premature it was unnecessary, for while the British and Commonwealth troops, with their reliance on motorized transport, needed the Sittang Bridge to cross the river, the Japanese, living off the jungle and captured Allied supplies, in the main carried their much lighter loads on mules and did not need the bridge at all – they simply marched a short distance upstream and forded the river without difficulty.

With its only defence force effectively destroyed the situation now facing Rangoon was perilous in the extreme. In the week leading up to this disaster, in fact since the capture of his forward air bases at Mergui and Tavoy, Air Vice-Marshal Stevenson had become convinced that the forces available for the defence of Burma were unlikely to be able to hold the Japanese Fifteenth Army for anything like long enough for substantial ground and air reinforcements to arrive. He further believed that in his capacity as Air Officer Commanding it was his responsibility to develop contingency plans to save what could be saved of his command – at that time the only Allied air force in existence between the Japanese and the Middle East – for the defence of India.

On 12 February Stevenson telegraphed ABDACOM suggesting that in the event that Rangoon might be captured plans needed formulating as to the fate of the air forces in Burma. With Rangoon in Japanese hands no reinforcements would be forthcoming and as a consequence the air force would wither away as casualties took their inevitable toll. In Stevenson's opinion the most logical step was for the air defence of Burma to move into India where RDF cover, spares and replacements would be available, and from where bombers could support army operations in Burma. The alternative was for the Air Force to remain with the Army as it carried out its stated intention to retreat generally northwards in the direction of China, where no air early warning system existed and where aircraft would be constantly open to surprise attack on the ground. Additionally in China itself there were no facilities for operating RAF bombers and fighters. Stevenson received no reply to his message.[14]

Following the further Japanese advances already referred to, on 18 February Lieutenant General Hutton also telegraphed ABDACOM notifying them that the evacuation of Rangoon had now become a distinct possibility. This message was reinforced by an additional communication from Stevenson outlining the three courses open to him as he saw it:

1. Air forces to remain with the Army as it withdrew towards China. In these circumstances the RAF units would become a wasting force since heavy losses for a small return would be inevitable and reinforcement difficult if not impossible.

2. Withdraw the air forces to India as soon as Rangoon was closely threatened.

3. Leave a mixed force comprising a Hurricane squadron, a Blenheim Flight and an Army Cooperation Flight, and withdraw the remainder of the force to India.

Stevenson received no reply to this message either, and here it seems that the problem of who controlled the RAF at any given time rears its head once more. General Wavell subsequently commented that receipt of Stevenson's telegrams was subject to considerable delay, by which time RAF Burma had been transferred from ABDACOM back to C-in-C India. Wavell went on to state that Air Vice-Marshal Stevenson had appended a proviso stating that if no response was forthcoming he would take action himself, consequently as far as ABDACOM were concerned 'no reply was therefore necessary'.[15] Since Stevenson appears to have been unaware of these vital changes to his line of communication it seems astonishing that neither General Wavell, nor C-in-C India, nor their respective staffs, saw fit to notify him, thereby leaving the Air Officer Commanding at the 'sharp end' in a vital theatre of the war in limbo.

At a meeting held at Government House in Rangoon on 20 February, Lieutenant General Hutton outlined plans that he proposed to implement for the evacuation of Rangoon and the establishment of Rear Headquarters at Maymyo. Stevenson again attempted to contact ABDACOM, but receiving no reply agreed with Hutton that when the Rangoon airfields appeared lost the bulk of the air forces should be withdrawn to India, while keeping two airfields operational in Burma, at Magwe and Akyab. Temporary airstrips would need to be constructed in the Rangoon area to provide what fighter and bomber support could be given. Stevenson then organized what would remain of his command along the lines of option 3 in his telegram of 18 February. At Magwe in upper Burma this comprised a mixed Wing, designated Burwing, made up of one Hurricane squadron, one Blenheim squadron, the AVG squadron and half an Army cooperation squadron. Akyab would also host a mixed wing, designated Akwing, to be made up of one Hurricane squadron, one bomber squadron and one General Reconnaissance squadron, the initial intention being that these wings would be built up and supplied from India.

Despite being far from perfect in respect of runways and facilities – for example dispersal arrangements were poor and there were no blast protection pens for the aircraft – Magwe was selected as it lay behind two lines of the Burma Observer Corps, one down the valley of the Salween towards Rangoon, the other down the valley of the Irrawaddy. Early warning would be further reinforced by removal of the single COL RDF set from Rangoon to Magwe should the necessity arise. The size of Burwing was based upon the amount of maintenance existing in the country as at 20 February, Stevenson's staff estimating that there would be sufficient for three months. Akyab was selected as it had the necessary all-weather air strips and was still open to access from the sea, making supply from India less of a problem; however no road or rail connections existed between Akyab and Magwe, which also had no direct connection to India, the only roadway, from Manipur in the north, not having been completed. Putting the plan into operation Stevenson still had no contact with ABDACOM; however, on 19 February he did receive a personal telegram from Air Vice-Marshal Sir Patrick Playfair, AOC India, informing him that Air Headquarters had prepared a plan for the withdrawal of his command to India. It must have been some comfort to know that not everybody had forgotten Burma. The following day Stevenson requested that transport aircraft be sent to begin a shuttle service between Magwe and Akyab for the evacuation of an estimated 3,000 air personnel, the majority of whom were in the Rangoon area. Transportation of personnel and equipment from Akyab to India would be by sea and air.

Set to become the outstanding revelation of the campaign for Burma, in February 1942 Allied air transport was, like everything else, in lamentably short supply, the outbreak of hostilities with Japan finding India Command operating a grand total of two serviceable Douglas DC2 aircraft. Belonging to 31 Squadron RAF, these aircraft were put into operation between Calcutta and Rangoon carrying urgent stores and evacuating personnel,[16] however in January 1942 one of these invaluable transports was destroyed during a Japanese raid on Mingaladon.[17] 31 Squadron, probably the most experienced air transport squadron in the RAF at the time, recalled its remaining DC2s from operations in the Middle East and at the end of February was despatched to Akyab to set up the shuttle service to Magwe.

On 21 February the Burmese Postmaster General informed Air Vice-Marshal Stevenson that in view of the imminent fall of the city the public telephone system in Rangoon would cease operating at 1800 that day. Since the Burma Observer Corps used the public telephones much of the early warning available to Mingaladon, Zayatkwin and associated airfields in the area of the capital would be rendered inoperative leaving just the single RDF set – in Stevenson's words 'worn out and of the wrong kind' – with which to detect incoming Japanese attacks. RAF personnel were immediately despatched to man the observer centre at the Central Telegraph Office in order to maintain early warning of some kind, limited though it was.

With Army Rear Headquarters established at Maymyo supply dumps were located up-country towards the Mandalay/Maymyo area, Stevenson being under the impression that the initial line of withdrawal would be along the 150-mile Prome Road, although whether the Army would continue into China or link up with the Manipur Road and fall back towards India was not clear. The Prome Road created more problems for the air arm as all their airfields were further to the east, straddling the Burma Road along the valley of the Sittang. The main transportation route, the railway line to Mandalay, also wound its way along the valley of the Sittang before turning north to Myitkyina and north-east to Lashio. For the air arm to effectively support the Army's retreat a number of rough and ready 'kutcha' (dirt) airstrips had to be cut into the hard paddy fields around Mingaladon and Zayatkwin, and to the north and west along the valley of the Irrawaddy to Prome. The locations of these temporary airstrips were kept as secret as possible and with the coming of night front-line aircraft from Mingaladon and Zayatkwin would be dispersed to surrounding 'kutcha' runways, rotating those used in an effort to offer some protection against the very real possibility that the dwindling Allied air force might be destroyed completely in surprise attacks. RAF Rear Headquarters opened at Magwe on 22 February, forward Headquarters remaining at Rangoon for the time being. In order to establish command and control in what was soon certain to develop into a highly fluid situation Stevenson established 'X' Wing, a mobile Headquarters with a picked staff and as good a system of communications as could be provided with the limited resources at hand, the unit under the command of Group Captain Noel Singer. 'X' Wing was tasked with maintaining air superiority over Rangoon until demolition works at oil installations, docks, power stations and other vital areas could be completed, and thereafter to fall back with, and maintain air superiority over, remaining ground forces until they reached Prome.

As testament to the capabilities of the outnumbered and outgunned Allied air force the 5th *Hikoshidan* was forced to repatriate its 14th *Hikosentai* to Japan due to severe losses and to upgrade its remaining Ki-21 Sally Mk I bombers to Mk IIs.[18] Nevertheless with Japanese ground forces forging ever closer to the Burmese capital, on 24–25 February the JAAF mounted a concerted effort to wrest air superiority from the Allied air forces.

Having located a build-up of JAAF forces at Moulmein, on the 24th, Tomahawks of the AVG escorted by Hurricanes of 17 Squadron carried out a strafing raid on the airfield, reporting a number of enemy aircraft damaged or destroyed. The JAAF quickly responded, 5th *Hikoshidan* employing an estimated 166 bombers and fighters in an attempt to smash its troublesome opposition. No doubt as a reminder of happier times several of the temporary airfields around Rangoon were given the names of well-known whisky brands of the time, two of these being John Haig and Highland Queen. 25 February dawned misty but that did not stop the Japanese, who mid morning put in a full-scale attack on Mingaladon. With most of 67 Squadron at Magwe and 17 Squadron carrying out a raid on river transport on the Salween, defence of the airfield fell to the AVG. Dispersed to John Haig, in true Burma fashion Tomahawks roared into the air from both ends of the strip simultaneously, but it was still only six aircraft in two flights of three against many times that number. From that engagement and several later in the day the AVG claimed a total of 24 aircraft shot down, bringing Allied claims for the two days to 30 destroyed plus 7 probables, the majority falling to the AVG. Whether or not this number was accurate is largely immaterial as the JAAF took the hint and stayed away from the Rangoon warning zone, a radius of some 40 miles from the city centre, until the city was evacuated and its attendant airfields were in Japanese hands. The Allied air forces also suffered casualties and from a high point of forty-four combat-ready Hurricanes and Tomahawks on 17 February, was reduced to less than ten by the 28th, the remainder being grounded through lack of spares and maintenance or shot up in air battles. In order to keep the JAAF on the defensive bombing raids were carried out on their airfields, but here also the number of bombers available would depend largely upon the spares situation at any given time and see-sawed between five and sixteen aircraft.

In the midst of an almost unmitigated tale of woe for Allied troops in Burma, on 27 February they did enjoy one priceless piece of good fortune in the shape of the arrival, aboard one of the last Allied transport ships to dock at Rangoon, of 7th Armoured Brigade – The Desert Rats. This experienced, battle-hardened unit was – unusually for reinforcements to the Far East at that time – fully equipped and was to prove invaluable in extricating British and Commonwealth forces from Burma in some sort of order.

IV

With Allied air forces just about holding their own and the situation on the ground in rapid decline, early March saw two important command changes take place. On the 3rd, Air Marshal Sir Richard Peirse replaced Air Vice-Marshal Playfair as AOC India, and on the 5th, General Sir Harold Alexander replaced General Hutton as GOC. Alexander had combat experience during the First World War and by 1937 was the youngest general in the British Army. He was also experienced in handling extremely difficult situations, having been placed in command of the British Expeditionary Force during the Dunkirk evacuation. He would need all his skill and experience in the weeks to come. Following on the heels of a visit by General Wavell, now C-in-C India, Alexander arrived at Magwe on 4 March, immediately flying down to Rangoon in order to join the remainder of 17th Division at Pegu, where they were engaged in trying to halt Japanese attempts to sever the Army's line of retreat. The new GOC, having witnessed the dire military situation, ordered the evacuation of Rangoon and the withdrawal of the Army northward along the Prome Road before it could be cut. As Fifteenth Army pressed forward its attempts to complete the destruction of 17th Division, the JAAF maintained considerable air activity over the immediate battle area, combined with attacks on Maymyo, Toungoo and Bassein. Remarkably the Rangoon area remained left to its own devices, enabling the first stages of the military evacuation to proceed relatively unhindered, together with completion of demolition works – all the more noteworthy since operations by the Burma Observer Corps in the area were by now ineffective, the RDF station had been removed to Magwe and the only early warning of air attack that the city possessed was a single Hurricane circling the area by day.

Thanks to the untiring efforts of the ground crews the number of combat-ready Hurricanes had risen to twenty, but that was about it, the AVG being down to four serviceable Tomahawks at Magwe alongside eight remaining Buffaloes of 67 Squadron which were earmarked for withdrawal to Akyab. Despite the paucity of bombers available, in operations from Magwe, Highland Queen and John Haig, the first week of March saw 96,800 lb of bombs dropped on enemy troop concentrations, riverboats, trains and transport columns. By 6 March the Hurricane force, elements of 17, 135 and 136 Squadrons, stood at fifteen aircraft, and with demolition charges and the final evacuation of Rangoon set for that night, Mingaladon and Zayatkwin were evacuated and 'X' Wing removed to Zigon, a 'kutcha' strip from which air cover would be controlled for the initial phase of the Army's withdrawal northwards.

Air operations on 7 March were hindered by hazy conditions made worse by a pall of smoke from burning oil installations in Rangoon rising to some 15,000 feet and drifting northwards, but despite the difficulties one extremely risky task was undertaken. When Mingaladon had been abandoned the previous day two serviceable Hurricanes were left behind. These aircraft were desperately needed and at Magwe two RAF pilots were selected to retrieve them, the problem being how to get them there. The answer appeared to be the Lysanders and when Squadron Leader Majumdar of No. 1 Squadron IAF called for volunteers to fly down to Mingaladon, Flight Lieutenant Raza and Flying Officer Rajendra Singh stepped forward. With the Hurricane pilots in their rear cockpits the Lysanders took off and made their way down to Mingaladon, now in imminent danger of capture by the Japanese. Fortunately no ground troops materialized but two Japanese reconnaissance aircraft flew low over the airstrip as Hurricanes and Lysanders made ready to leave, which they did just in time, returning safely to Magwe.[19]

On the ground two further pieces of luck now attended the British and Commonwealth forces. In the first, the local Japanese commander in the Rangoon area, having succeeded in establishing a roadblock across the Prome Road, misunderstood his instructions and removed his forces, thereby allowing Allied troops to move quickly northwards without having to fight their way along the road. In the second piece of good luck Lieutenant General William Slim was seconded to Alexander as a Corps Commander. In time Slim would command all ground forces in Burma and come to be recognized alongside Montgomery as one of the finest officers that Britain produced during the Second World War.

Zigon was hard on the Hurricanes, the rough surface of the airstrip causing tail wheels to break at an average rate of one in five landings – with no certainty that they could be repaired. Despite this, Magwe being too far north for the Hurricanes to be able to cover the retreat, twelve to eighteen sorties per day were carried out until 11 March when 'X' Wing was withdrawn to Magwe and disbanded, to be replaced by Burwing under the command of Group Captain Seton Broughall and comprising 17 Squadron (Hurricanes), 45 Squadron (Blenheims), the remnants of the AVG squadron, a few Lysanders of No. 1 Squadron IAF and the RDF unit.

Air Vice-Marshal Stevenson moved his headquarters to Akyab on 12 March and formed Akwing, having days before been informed by Air Marshal Peirse that he was now responsible not only for air support of the Army in Burma and the two mixed wings at Magwe and Akyab, but also for the air defence of Calcutta, Asanol and Tatangar in India, the oil installation at Digboi in Assam, plus for good measure reconnaissance and bombing raids from India into Burma and along the Bay of Bengal. Since Akwing initially comprised 135 Squadron equipped with obsolete Hurricane Mk Is and a solitary Mk II, a General Reconnaissance Flight and a small air communications detachment, Stevenson must surely have allowed himself a moment or two's solemn reflection on what he was supposed to carry out these new responsibilities *with*. It was hoped to bolster Akwing with Blenheims for 113 Squadron as soon as aircraft became available, and Hudsons for 139 GR Squadron when they too were available, but this was nothing like enough and in any event the Air Vice-Marshal had been here before – hopes and promises were one thing, actions were another. As for the servicemen, if Magwe was nothing to write home about, Akyab was even worse, being described as 'a den of vice and depravity ... drunken Lascar seamen lurched out of the bars along the waterfront. Brawls were frequent and knives had been known to strike deep into human flesh.'[20] On 17 March Stevenson departed for Calcutta to establish his new headquarters, his command once again re-designated 221 Group.

RAF attempts at the secret dispersal of aircraft succeeded up to a point and the JAAF spent several fruitless days searching for its quarry on the airfields along the Burma Road, however the deception did not last for long and on 9 March a fast, high-flying Mitsubishi Ki-46 Dinah, on a photographic reconnaissance mission for the Fifteenth Army's 33rd Division, then in pursuit of Alexander's Burma Army along the banks of the Irrawaddy, discovered the Allied air build-up at Magwe. With substantial reinforcement in the shape of the 7th and 21st *Kokutai* (Air Groups) expected in the coming days, Lieutenant General Obata opted to delay offensive operations until the destructive impact of his entire force could be brought to bear, and in the hope and expectation that more aircraft would arrive at Magwe in the meantime and provide him with an opportunity to deliver a final crippling blow to enemy air capability in Burma.[21]

Allied intelligence estimated that some 400 aircraft were available to the JAAF for operations over Burma, although not unusually for intelligence services they had managed to produce something of an over-estimate. Nevertheless the scratch Allied air force was undoubtedly faced by many times its number and by mid March some 260 Japanese aircraft were believed to be in Burma itself. On the evening of the 20th air reconnaissance by a Blenheim of 45 Squadron discovered a concentration of fifty or so enemy aircraft of various types at the former Allied airfield at Mingaladon. Upon receiving their report Group Captain Seton Broughall at Magwe decided that this was a target too good to miss. Quickly organizing his limited resources Broughall put together a raid comprising ten Hurricanes of 17 Squadron and nine Blenheims of 45 Squadron, which took off at dawn the next day, the two groups making their separate ways south and ordered to rendezvous at 25,000 feet just west of Mingaladon. The Hurricanes arrived on schedule and circled Mingaladon for some minutes but of the Blenheims there was no sign. Noticing activity on the airstrips as Japanese fighters prepared to take off to intercept, Squadron Leader Stone decided he could wait no longer and ordered his fighters to follow him in a low-level attack. The Hurricanes could manage a tidy turn of speed in a dive and at some 400 mph roared down towards their target, to be met by flak from ex-British Bofors guns that had not only been left undamaged but also fully armed – a bitter pill indeed! A number of Hurricanes peeled off to attack the old AVG dispersal from the north-east while Squadron leader Stone took the remainder and attacked the main runway from the west. During these attacks sixteen enemy bombers and fighters were claimed destroyed on the ground. As the Hurricanes swept up and away the Blenheims arrived to deposit their total load of 9,000 lb of bombs with stick adaptors on and among the Japanese aircraft parked beside the runways. While still some 70 miles from Mingaladon the Blenheims had been intercepted by eighteen Japanese fighters and had to fight their way to Mingaladon, make their bomb runs, then fight their way back, claiming two enemy aircraft shot down and four damaged for no loss to 45 Squadron, although all their Blenheims were comprehensively shot up.[22] Incredibly their only aircrew casualty was one wounded pilot. A number of Hurricanes were also badly damaged but made their way back to Magwe, Squadron Leader Stone having to stop off at Prome to have a bullet hole in the oil tank of his Hurricane's Merlin engine plugged.[23]

The raid on Mingaladon was counted a great success but in order to mount it all Allied aircraft save the worn-out Hurricanes at Akyab were concentrated at Magwe. This could not have been better for Lieutenant General Obata who had put together an attack force of nine combat *Hikosentais* and a plan calling for them to converge on Magwe from six airfields in two countries. Before Group Captain Broughall could put into operation an intended second raid 5th *Hikoshidan* struck with devastating force against a Magwe airfield that was by now badly exposed. One Observer Corps line remained, stretching southward to Toungoo and Prome, reporting through Mandalay and backed up by a chain of posts on the railway line between Pyinmana and Kyaukpadaung which reported directly to the Magwe operations room over an RAF W/T link. The only other early warning system was the RDF unit, which as mentioned was of the wrong type and in any event its arc of observation was to the south-east leaving the approach from the west around to the north-east of the base bereft of early warning of any kind. At 1300 on 21 March a Ki-46 Dinah approached Magwe for a final reconnaissance and two Hurricanes were scrambled to intercept, which they failed to do. By 1323 a formation of twenty-one Ki-21 Sally bombers escorted by fighters approached from the west while Magwe was in the process of scrambling its remaining fighters, four Hurricanes and six Tomahawks, in response to early warning of another attack coming in from the south-east. Outnumbered by weight of attack from two directions the Allied fighters did their best and claimed four enemy aircraft, but the bombers got through and dealt a significant blow to Magwe – and that was only the beginning. Over the next twenty-four hours attack after attack swept across the airfield, the JAAF utilizing an estimated 230 fighters and bombers to drop some 200 tons of bombs. Follow-up attacks on Akyab commenced on 23 March and by the 27th the Allied air force in Burma had to all intents and purposes ceased to exist, although through no fault of the pilots or ground crew. From the end of January fighter pilots were uniformly kept at two-minute readiness from dawn until dusk – a period of eight weeks in which they flew and fought to the point of collapse. Ground crews likewise worked round the clock to keep aircraft in the air. The skill, determination and

48

courage were there to match their opposite numbers in the JAAF – what they needed was up-to-date equipment of suitable quantity and quality to enable them to get on terms. The question for their leaders was where was it going to come from?

Notes

1. Helsdon Thomas, J., *Wings Over Burma* (Merlin Books Ltd., 1991), pp. 16–17.
2. J.W. Loosemore, in correspondence with the author.
3. *Op. cit.*, Note 1 (above), pp. 19–20.
4. *Op. cit.*, Note 1, p. 20.
5. Ford, Daniel, *Flying Tigers* (Smithsonian Institution Press, 1991), p. 137.
6. TNA Air 2/7787, Report of Air Vice-Marshal D.F. Stevenson, p. 2.
7. *Japanese Monograph No. 64* (The Library of Congress, Washington DC), p. 10.
8. *Ibid.*, pp. 6, 21 & 22.
9. *Op. cit.*, Note 1, p. 23.
10. Hata, Ikuhiko, Ozawa, Yasuho and Stone, Christopher, *Japanese Army Air Force Units and their Aces, 1931–1945* (Grub Street, 2002), pp. 192–3.
11. Cotton, Squadron Leader M.C. 'Bush', *Hurricanes Over Burma* (Titania Publishing Co., 1988), p. 173; and TNA Air 2/7787, Report of Air Vice-Marshal D.F. Stevenson, p. 8.
12. Gupta, S.C., *History of the Indian Air Force 1933–1945* (Combined Inter-Services Historical Section India & Pakistan, 1961), p. 77.
13. *Op. cit.*, Note 6, p. 11.
14. *Op. cit.*, Note 6, p. 12.
15. Air 2/7787, covering letter from General A.P. Wavell attached to Air Vice-Marshal Stevenson's report.
16. TNA Air 41/37, *Air Supply Operations in Burma 1942–1945*, p. 1.
17. Franks, Norman L.R., *First in the Indian Skies* (The RAF Collection in conjunction with 31 Squadron Royal Air Force Association, 1981), p. 77.
18. *Op. cit.*, Note 7, p. 23.
19. *Op. cit.*, Note 12, p. 84.
20. *Op. cit.*, Note 1, p. 33.
21. *Op. cit.*, Note 7, p. 11.
22. Initially reported as being Navy Zeros, the Japanese force probably included a number of Nakajima Ki-43 Oscar fighters then becoming available. Unlike the Nakajima Ki-27 Nate, the JAAF's principal fighter at that time, the Oscar had a retractable undercarriage for improved performance, which also gave it a profile similar to the Zero. It is also possible that they may have been Nakajima Ki-44 Tojos, although only some forty or so of the 1A were ever produced and not many would have been available in March 1942. A more powerful version of the Tojo became available in larger numbers from late 1942.
23. *Op. cit.*, Note 6, p. 17; see also Note 11, p. 195.

Chapter Three

The End of the Beginning

I

As if March 1942 had not been bad enough for the Allies in South East Asia, the end of this desperate month also saw a serious seaborne threat develop. Following their crushing naval victories at Pearl Harbor, the Java Sea and the destruction of Force Z, the Imperial Japanese Navy held sway from the Pacific to the Indian Ocean, and quite apart from the situation in the Far East, elsewhere the news was grim. German armies planned massive new attacks in Russia, the battle for Britain's vital sea lanes across the Atlantic hung in the balance, and in the Mediterranean the combined efforts of the Luftwaffe and the Regia Aeronautica turned the diminutive island of Malta into the most bombed area on earth. Much of Britain's supplies and reinforcements for her hard-pressed army in North Africa already traversed the Cape of Good Hope to make the journey through the Suez Canal to Alexandria, but should Malta fall the Mediterranean would be denied to the Royal Navy completely and the long voyage around the Cape would be the Eighth Army's only lifeline, a lifeline that might easily be cut should enemy forces be able to operate from Ceylon (Sri Lanka), where they would also be in a position to sever seaborne connections to India and the Far East.

On 28 March Allied intelligence reported that Admiral Nagumo's First Carrier Fleet, comprising five large aircraft carriers, four battleships, two heavy cruisers, one light cruiser, nine destroyers, and attendant supply ships, was en route for Ceylon and would probably be in a position to launch air attacks from 1 April. It was Nagumo's Task Force that carried out the attack on Pearl Harbor and the fear at the time was that an invasion of Ceylon might be imminent, although it is now known that Nagumo's intention was in fact the destruction of British naval forces in the Indian Ocean to prevent any intervention they might make in the struggle for Burma. A side benefit, at a time when Gandhi was active in agitating for India's independence, would be a demonstration of British weakness and Japanese invincibility. A large convoy of Japanese transports was also at sea bearing substantial reinforcements which they planned to run into Rangoon under cover of the sortie by the First Carrier Fleet.

To counter Nagumo's approach C-in-C Eastern Fleet, Admiral Somerville, divided his forces into two groups, Group A comprising a battleship, two aircraft carriers, four cruisers and six destroyers, and Group B comprising four old battleships, an aircraft carrier, three cruisers and eight destroyers. With his carriers equipped with outdated Swordfish and Albacore biplanes Somerville was in no position to take on the First Carrier Fleet with its 300 or so state-of-the-art monoplane fighters and bombers, but despite being under strict orders not to risk his ships he needed to locate the enemy both to maintain his own security and that of Ceylon. Having searched for Nagumo without success, by 2 April Somerville's two groups were heading westward to Addu Atoll to refuel and replenish, and while passing to the south of Ceylon the C-in-C detached four ships to the island, the cruisers *Cornwall* and *Dorsetshire* to Colombo and the carrier *Hermes* accompanied by the destroyer *Vampire* to Trincomalee.

On Ceylon itself the RAF had its own Group Headquarters, No. 222 under the newly appointed Air-Vice Marshal J.H. d'Albiac, and had available three fighter squadrons, the recently formed No. 258 plus Nos 30 and 261 which had flown in from the carrier *Indomitable* early in the month. All three squadrons were equipped with Hurricanes, a total of fifty serviceable aircraft. In addition the Fleet Air Arm (FAA) had on the island two squadrons equipped with two-seater Fairey Fulmar navy fighters, a reasonable aircraft although with a maximum speed of 247 mph and a service ceiling of 21,500 feet, outclassed by the Japanese Navy's Zero with a maximum speed in excess of 300 mph and a service ceiling of 35,000 feet. As regards bombers the only aircraft available were the fourteen Blenheim Mk IVs of 11 Squadron with, crucially, no torpedo bombers on hand save a few Fleet Air Arm Swordfish and 273 Squadron's virtually useless Vickers Vildebeests. An urgent request for Bristol Beauforts with which to rectify the shortfall was rejected by the Chiefs of Staff.

An added complication for the Allies was the presence in the Port of Calcutta of some 250,000 tons of merchant shipping which – with the only Allied heavy ships in the area the Royal Navy units far to the south with Somerville – would in effect be bottled up in the Bay of Bengal for as long as Nagumo's fleet remained in the Indian Ocean. This large concentration of Allied merchant ships had to be dispersed, either in convoy with the minimal fighter and bomber escort available plus any naval escorts that the small Royal Indian Navy might be able to provide, or scattered into the Bay of Bengal. Both options carried with them inherent difficulties since convoys were open to attack by surface ships and scattered merchantmen were easy pickings for submarines and aircraft, however, Admiral Nagumo's decision to detach a cruiser force to raid along the Indian coast focused minds on the adoption of a plan to scatter the merchantmen as the least worst alternative. In order to give the merchant ships the best possible chance the RAF needed to deal with the principal source of Japanese intelligence, a fleet of nine, rising to thirteen, four-engine long-range flying boats based at Port Blair in the Andaman Islands, which had been captured by Japanese forces on 23 March. The only aircraft with the range to make the round trip to Port Blair – and even then a refuelling stop at Akyab would be required – were the three remaining Hudson bombers of 139 Squadron based at Dum Dum airfield, Calcutta. The Japanese were believed to have developed the Port Blair airstrip and installed fighter defence so any raid would be extremely hazardous, nevertheless two Hudsons made the attempt. Flying in at low level and finding the Japanese flying boats moored in lines the bombers carried out a number of mast-height runs strafing the craft using their turret guns. Three flying boats were sunk and many more damaged. Days later the sortie was repeated and with the Japanese flying boats still moored in lines, two more were sunk and damage inflicted on the remainder. On this occasion the Hudsons were attacked by Japanese fighters and one bomber failed to return, but the enemy reconnaissance force remained inactive for many months thereafter.

Admiral Somerville's fleet arrived at Addu Atoll on 4 April; at 1605 that same day a Catalina of 413 Squadron piloted by Squadron Leader L.J. Birchall located the Japanese fleet some 360 miles south-east of Ceylon, and radioed in the position before being shot down. Somerville realized that having been discovered Nagumo would take the earliest opportunity to launch an air strike against Colombo and ordered *Cornwall* and *Dorsetshire* to rendezvous with Group A, which sortied from Addu Atoll at around midnight.

On the morning of 5 April eighty-four Japanese bombers escorted by thirty-six Zero fighters approached Colombo, but once again lack of adequate radar equipment meant that the interlopers were not spotted until they were virtually over the city itself. Despite this Nos 30 and 258 Squadrons got thirty-six Hurricanes in the air and 803 Squadron FAA joined in with eight Fulmars. In the ensuing dogfights the Allied aircraft, unable to gain height over their opponents due to the lack of warning, came off worst losing fifteen Hurricanes and four Fulmars at a cost to the JNAF of perhaps five or so aircraft – but for Nagumo there was also disappointment as he failed in his intention to catch Somerville's force in Colombo and inflict a Pearl Harbor-style defeat on it. Japanese reconnaissance did however locate *Cornwall* and *Dorsetshire*, both of which were sunk in air attacks at around midday.

With the Japanese attack in progress the small strike force available to Air-Vice Marshal d'Albiac also took to the air, but without success. Six FAA Fairey Swordfish torpedo bombers became involved in the attacks on Colombo and were all shot down, while 11 Squadron was given incorrect coordinates for the Japanese fleet and its Blenheims were despatched in the wrong direction.

Nagumo tried again on 9 April, this time launching his aircraft against Trincomalee. Catalina reconnaissance aircraft had located the Japanese fleet 400 miles east of Ceylon the day previously and Somerville again ordered all ships to disperse to sea. As the JNAF fighters and bombers swept in they were this time successfully located by radar while still 90 miles out, enabling the defence force – seventeen Hurricanes and six Fulmars – to gain height and utilize the dive and turn tactics necessary to stand any chance against the superior manoeuvrability of the Japanese aircraft. Considerable damage was inflicted on the naval dockyard and airfield but around twelve Japanese aircraft were believed destroyed. Having left port most ships escaped unscathed but *Hermes* – with her aircraft ashore she was virtually defenceless – *Vampire*, the corvette *Hollyhock* and two tankers were sighted and all were sunk.

11 Squadron was again ordered to attack and this time received the correct coordinates. At 1025, in an extremely risky operation undertaken in broad daylight without fighter cover – all available fighters were engaged over Trincomalee – the squadron's nine Blenheims attacked Nagumo's flagship, the carrier *Akagi*. Under attack from defending Zeros the bombers came in at 11,000 feet and straddled but failed to hit the carrier, losing five aircraft in the process including that of the Commanding Officer, Squadron Leader Ault. The remaining four aircraft, all badly damaged, limped back to Ceylon.

Although Nagumo had failed to catch the bulk of the Eastern Fleet he had inflicted serious losses and Somerville withdrew his remaining ships to East African waters until reinforcement or a more propitious moment should arrive. Satisfied with that, Nagumo withdrew. The British naval and air forces had received a mauling at the hands of the Japanese but Ceylon, the strategic lynchpin, was safe. On the debit side, however, under cover of Nagumo's action the Japanese reinforcement convoy entered Rangoon unhindered.

II

Following the crushing JAAF attacks on Magwe the AVG exercised its right not to have to operate from airfields at which inadequate warning existed, and on 23 March withdrew its three remaining Tomahawks to Loiwing. The RAF at Magwe now mustered 17 aircraft – 6 Blenheims and 11 Hurricanes – all airworthy but none combat ready due to lack of spares or damage from enemy attack. These aircraft were flown out to Akyab in the hope that they might survive long enough to be withdrawn to India to refit, although most of the Hurricanes were subsequently destroyed.

The intention at this time was still not to abandon Magwe but to build up its early warning systems and bring in replacement bomber and fighter squadrons with which to cover the Army's withdrawal. This intention does not seem to have been grasped by personnel on the ground, who deserted the airfield en masse leaving quantities of equipment and a number of aircraft which should have been removed, repaired or destroyed. As a result of this somewhat hurried exodus arrangements had to be put in hand to salvage as much as possible from Magwe, and in the period leading up to its capture by the Japanese some three weeks later several successful attempts were made by RAF personnel to retrieve spares, bombs, ammunition and aviation fuel. As it happened Lieutenant General Slim was present during the attacks on Magwe and later reported the anger felt by army personnel at what was seen to be the unseemly haste of the air force departure. It should also be said that he went on to record the quite exceptional achievements of the tiny Anglo-American air force in facing its juggernaut opponent up to that point, but for all that the ill-feeling at the time is probably understandable given the parlous situation that the Army faced.

In order that he might be kept 'on-side' during these dark days of the war with Japan, Generalissimo Chiang Kai-shek was appointed Supreme Allied Commander in the China Theatre with the US Army's Lieutenant General Joseph W. 'Vinegar Joe' Stilwell, who arrived in China February 1942, appointed Allied Chief of Staff and deputy commander in China under Chiang. Some weeks after Stilwell's arrival the Chinese Fifth Army, on the Southern Shan front to support British and Commonwealth troops and protect the Burma Road, suffered a serious defeat that allowed Japanese forces to advance quickly towards Lashio. Although most of his staff officers were air lifted out, Stilwell chose to remain with the Chinese on their five-week trek back into China, behaviour that gleaned much favourable comment from the press in the United States but did not display a particularly intelligent grasp of military priorities by a senior theatre commander.

Although Burwing still existed as an organization, in view of the lack of resources available and the speed of the Japanese advance, C-in-C India decided not to re-equip the command and opted instead to concentrate on the defence of India. Burwing personnel assisted the limited operations that were possible from Lashio and Loiwing, and were then withdrawn to China to provide British refuelling parties at Chinese air bases. For its part, having achieved a crushing victory over its adversary, 5th *Hikoshidan* switched elements of its offensive power to ground support, assisting the 56th Division in its encirclement of Toungoo and supporting 33rd Division as it pursued retreating British and Commonwealth troops northwards along the Irrawaddy.[1] Viewed from the other side of the hill, General Slim felt that the JAAF missed a trick by devoting not enough of its now virtually unopposed strength to these army cooperation sorties and too much to carrying out heavy raids against civilians in towns and cities, which did little to delay the retreating Allied armies.

RAF transport operations between Akyab and Magwe continued until the end of March when 31 Squadron was forced to move back to Dum-Dum airfield. As the relentless Japanese advance continued this vital transport squadron dropped supplies and medical stores to both military personnel and civilian evacuees, carried reinforcements into Magwe, Shwebo and Myitkyina, and returned with battle casualties. Civilian refugees were airlifted out if space allowed. Inevitably 31 Squadron suffered from the same problems as the rest of the Allied air forces. Despite airframes and engines being thousands of hours' flying time over their safe limit, corners were cut on major inspections in order to keep the vital DC2s in the air, one engineering officer reporting that inspections were pointless in any event since there were no spares for replacements. Things were tried that would in normal circumstances turn any self-respecting ground or air crewman's hair white. Differing types of engine and propeller would be fitted to the same aircraft and it became commonplace for DC2s to fly with a 550 HP engine fitted to the port wing and a 700 HP engine to the starboard. Once again the ground crew – who in 31 Squadron could also be called upon to double as air crew – were the unsung heroes of the hour, performing miracles on a routine basis to keep aircraft in the air. Thankfully April did see some reinforcement to add to the strength in the shape of three C47 Dakotas donated by American businessmen.

In March 1942 Major General Louis Brereton USAAF arrived in Assam to take command of what was to become the principal US military unit in the China-Burma-India theatre, the nascent Tenth Air Force. Brereton brought with him eight B17 heavy bombers which immediately found themselves pressed into service as transports, such was the dearth of aircraft available for this vital role. During March, in a foretaste of what was to come, the B17s transported a fully equipped battalion of the Inniskilling Fusiliers from India to Magwe and on return trips brought out 425 civilian refugees. In April ten USAAF C47s arrived from Africa and were put to work ferrying in a total of some 2,000 tons of rice, salt and medicine from India to retreating Chinese troops, returning with wounded personnel and civilian refugees. The fresh American involvement was welcome although Britain and the United States had deeply differing priorities which needed somehow to be meshed, for the time being at least. For Britain the coming campaigns were to regain her Far Eastern Empire – a proposition to which the United States was fundamentally opposed and had no intention of devoting US man-power and materiel. America's only interest in India/Burma was to keep supplies flowing to Chiang Kai-shek, but for that they needed the assistance of the Colonial power – Britain. Brereton's arrival also brought with it one turf war, over who was to command what US forces, and started another. In a continuance of a disagreement that had been rumbling on for some time in Washington, Brereton argued that the Tenth was responsible for general security and that he as commander on the ground had the right to decide how, when, and to what purpose the aircraft under his command were to be employed. Since, as mentioned, the most pressing reason for US involvement in India/Burma at all was the maintenance of a supply route to China, Air Corps Ferrying Command countered that transport to China must take precedence over combat operations and that they should therefore have the final say. The War Department attempted to smooth ruffled feathers with a complicated solution that put Stilwell in command of the Assam–China route, Brereton the trans-India route, and left the War Department itself with final responsibility for deployment of aircraft and supply.

The arrival of Lieutenant General Stilwell had also fuelled a local row over allocation of Lend-Lease supplies. Chiang Kai-shek believed the authority to be his, Chennault constantly demanded more for the air forces under his command, and Stilwell pitched in demanding the lion's share for the Chinese ground forces. The placing of Chennault's American Volunteer Group under Stilwell's overall command resulted in an uneasy relationship between the two headstrong Americans. Stilwell fervently believed that he could re-forge China's armies, generally held to be venal and of little military value, and use the revitalized force to defeat the Japanese in Burma. Chennault equally passionately believed that the quickest and most cost-effective way to beat Japan was with air power. While paying a certain amount of lip service to Stilwell's ideas Chiang Kai-shek had no intention of removing patronage and corruption from his armies since that was how he controlled them. The Generalissimo consequently tended to back Chennault.

With the fall of Rangoon the destination for Lend-Lease supplies to China switched to Karachi on the west coast of India (now Pakistan), and Calcutta on the east coast. Thereafter they would be taken on tortuous train journeys involving several different railway lines with different gauges, each of which demanded a time-consuming nightmare of loading and unloading, until arrival at Assam Province in north-eastern India. From there they were flown in the main by USAAF transports via Myitkyina to Chungking. Having snuffed out supply to China by road from Rangoon, the Japanese were equally determined to extinguish supply by air via Myitkyina and a major effort was put into the capture of the base, which fell on 8 May – but if the Japanese hoped this would cut Chiang Kai-shek's lifeline once and for all they were to be disappointed.

The amount of supplies initially fell dramatically but did continue by air utilizing a more hazardous northerly passage from Ledo over the Himalayas to Chungking – a daunting flight that came to be known as 'The Hump' route, pioneered by Lieutenant Colonel William D. Old USAAF, in April. Transport aircraft of the time were pushed to design limits and beyond, take-offs from Dinjan in Assam requiring laden aircraft to reach an altitude of 7,000 feet within fifteen minutes and climb to 16,000 feet to cross the Himalayas themselves. Treacherous cumulonimbus cloud formations topping the peaks would force aircraft up to 18,000 feet or more to avoid the potentially fatal battering that would be experienced flying through them. According to one RAF veteran, flying 'The Hump' in the monsoon, 'one could take off from Dinjan straight into cloud with torrential rain, thunderstorms and icing and not see the ground again for maybe 32 hours at Kunming.'[2]

Getting supplies and ammunition to the troops at the front was and is a basic necessity of warfare, but with conflict on a global scale the shortage of transport aircraft was becoming a major headache for Allied leaders to rival the shortage of ships. In March 1942 the prime source of transports, the USAAF, had available 216 aircraft for its entire war effort. Of these 139 were assigned to plans already in the making for the invasion of Europe, fifty-seven to Air Ferry Command, and none to the China airlift. In desperation a proposal was put forward to convert fifty B24 bombers into transports for China, but the Operations Planning Division in the War Department objected on the grounds that every available bomber would be needed for the prime task, the forth-coming campaigns in Europe. The US Administration considered that by comparison China was an unimportant side-show, but in February, under intense diplomatic pressure from the Chinese, President Roosevelt ordered the requisitioning of twenty-five civilian C47s, and the following month 100 pilots from the USAAF reserve were called up to provide crews for the airlift.

Despite the disasters at Magwe and Akyab, air support for the retreating Allied armies did not halt completely. In addition to vital transport operations, in the eight weeks between 21 March and 20 May when General Alexander's Burma Army finally reached Imphal and comparative safety, 58 raids were undertaken – 13 by the USAAF, 45 by the RAF – and virtually all by bombers as the only fighters available, the Curtiss Mohawk Mk IVs of No. 5 Squadron RAF based at Dinjan, did not have sufficient range.

What has been termed the longest retreat in British history had been a nightmare for Alexander's army. At Mandalay the crush of refugees and military personnel was so acute that smallpox became rife, and cholera spreading rapidly through polluted water sources claimed 600 lives per day. For those struggling to survive in what in normal times was a beautiful and important cultural and religious centre, it must have seemed that not only disease but disaster itself had become contagious. Fires started during a Japanese air raid on 3 April quickly spread, one bomb scoring a direct hit on the fire station. In the ensuing firestorm three-fifths of the town was gutted and hundreds of Burmese died, either in the fires or drowned when they were blown into the moat around Fort Dufferin. Of the original 25,000 combat troops who started the retreat less than half remained to fight their way out.[3] Things were no better for Stilwell and the Fifth Army, and despite the valiant efforts of the USAAF transports already described, following their defeat the Chinese suffered grievously from starvation and cholera as they struggled back to Yunnan.

During the retreat of the British & Commonwealth and Chinese armies the USAAF evacuated 4,499 persons, the RAF 4,117 persons, and the China National Aviation Corporation – 55 per cent of which was owned by the Chinese government, 45 per cent by Pan-American Airlines – reputedly close to 10,000 persons. Additionally 109,652 lb of supplies were dropped to civilian and military personnel.

With the coming of the first monsoon of the war 5th *Hikosentai* adopted what was to become a regular 'standing down' procedure, reducing the number of offensive operations and withdrawing much of its combat strength to the Malay Peninsula to undertake a series of training exercises.[4] Nevertheless operational sorties of one sort or another were still necessary and on 29 April, Warrant Officer Yoshito Yasuda flew fighter escort for transports ferrying paratroops to Lashio for a planned attempt to cut off retreating Chinese that in the event did not take place due to inclement weather. Encountering engine trouble Yasuda made a forced landing in dense jungle terrain and was fortunate to be rescued by natives, subsequently making his way 120 km back to base in three days. Quickly returning to duty Yasuda became involved in an incident that resulted in the death of one of the most successful JAAF aces of the war. It may be remembered that the personnel of 60 Squadron RAF languished for some time at Mingaladon awaiting aircraft which, having been destroyed in the air battles for Singapore, never materialized. Withdrawn to Magwe in February, squadron personnel were dispersed following the debacle there, reformed at Lahore in March and equipped with Blenheim Mk IVs. On 22 May a single Blenheim from the squadron, piloted by Warrant Officer Martin Huggard, carried out a low-level attack on Akyab and turned to make its way back across the Bay of Bengal to India. Led by Lieutenant Colonel Tateo Kato, Commander of the 64th *Hikosentai*, four newly arrived Nakajima Ki-43 Oscar fighters took to the air in pursuit of the bomber, which Huggard flew low over the sea, forcing pursuing aircraft to attack from above and expose themselves to fire from the twin 0.303 in (7.7 mm) machine guns manned by Sergeant 'Jock' McLuckie in the power-operated dorsal turret. As each fighter in its turn caught up with the bomber and carried out a swooping attack, each, including that of Warrant Officer Yasuda, suffered damage that forced it to withdraw. Last to attack was Lieutenant Colonel Kato and this time McLuckie's return fire was particularly accurate, the Oscar being badly damaged and crashing into the sea. With a claimed eighteen combat victories to his credit Lieutenant Colonel Kato was the most celebrated ace in the JAAF and on his death was awarded a citation and posthumous promotion to Major General.[5]

With the Allied air forces largely destroyed or in disarray, strength and dispositions for 5th *Hikoshidan* during the 1942 monsoon were as follows:[6]

Unit and location	Aircraft, number and type
Hikoshidan Shireibu	Commanding Officer's aircraft, 2 liaison, 2 transport aircraft plus Signals and Navigational Aid aircraft.
4th *Hikodan Shireibu*, Toungoo.	Commanding Officer's aircraft, 2 liaison aircraft, HQ Flight Platoon, HQ Signals Platoon.
50th *Hikosentai*, Singapore.	Upgrading equipment to 30 Nakajima Ki-43 'Oscar' fighters.

8th *Hikosentai*, Toungoo & Moulmein.	Seven Mitsubishi Ki-46 Dinah reconnaissance aircraft plus seven Kawasaki Ki-48 Lily light bombers.
7th *Hikodan Shireibu*, Sungei Patani.	Complement similar to 4th *Hikodan Shireibu*, above.
12th *Hikosentai*, Alor Star.	25 Mitsubishi Ki-21 Sally heavy bombers.
98th *Hikosentai*, Sungei Patani.	25 Mitsubishi Ki-21 Sally heavy bombers.
64th *Hikosentai*, Mingaladon (under the direct command of Divisional HQ).	25 Ki-43 Oscar fighters.
12th *Hikodan Shireibu*, Singapore.	Complement similar to 4th *Hikodan Shireibu*, above.
1st *Hikosentai*, Singapore.	25 Ki-43 Oscar fighters.
11th *Hikosentai*, Singapore.	25 Ki-43 Oscar fighters.
81st *Hikosentai* (minus one company), Leku.	7 Mitsubishi Ki-46 Dinah reconnaissance aircraft.

Training undertaken involved exercises for a planned post-monsoon attack on Calcutta plus improvements to aerial combat and ground support techniques.

Important changes now took place in the organization of the JAAF which, hitherto, had depended on the *Hikoshidan* (air division) as its principal organizational unit, an integral part of, and taking orders from, the Army. The Imperial High Command quickly appreciated, however, that the vast territorial acquisitions made by Japanese force of arms would now require defending – a long-term task quite different to the 'blitzkrieg' tactics required to conquer territories ill-prepared to defend themselves. To meet the challenge, in June 1942 three new *Kokugun Shireibu* (Air Army Headquarters) came into being as follows:

- 1st Air Army Headquarters, Tokyo.
- 2nd Air Army Headquarters, Hsingkiang.
- 3rd Air Army Headquarters, Singapore.

Two additional Air Army Headquarters subsequently came into being, the 4th in New Guinea at the end of 1943, and the 5th in Nanking early in 1944. 5th *Hikoshidan* remained the principal operational unit in the China/Burma/India theatre but now came under the control of 3rd *Kokugun Shireibu* in Singapore.

The new headquarters found itself confronted with a number of problems in the Burma area of its responsibilities. Immediately following the expulsion of the British and Commonwealth Army from Burma, 5th *Hikoshidan* estimated that only fifteen airfields were in operable condition, as a consequence of which a programme of repair and construction was immediately put in place and by August 1943 some 100 were reported ready for the approaching combat season.

Operations involving heavy bombers of 7th *Hikodan Shireibu* in particular brought to light difficulties with the defensive armament of their aircraft, necessitating the return of many of the *Hikoshidan*'s bombers to Kagamigahara in Japan during the monsoon to re-equip with automatic cannon. Responsibility for repair and supply within Burma fell to 15th *Rikugun Kohu Sho* (Air Repair Depot) based at Bangkok and its subordinate unit at Rangoon, work being carried out at both locations to increase the availability of combat-ready aircraft.

For the Allies, June 1942 dealt a severe blow to USAAF attempts to get 'The Hump' route to China fully operational. In the Middle East, following the fall of Tobruk to Rommel, Britain's Eighth Army was pushed back almost as far as Cairo and the Afrika Korps seriously threatened the Suez Canal. In response, despite having been in India for a mere three months, Major General Brereton was ordered to the Middle East to assist the British with all available bombers and to take with him all necessary personnel for his headquarters, plus any transport aircraft required. Brereton was also authorized to commandeer any India-bound cargo and equipment passing through the Middle East, and a squadron of light bombers earmarked for China was placed instead under his command. A furious Chiang Kai-shek ordered Stilwell to get a firm commitment from Roosevelt that the China Theatre was a necessary field of operations for the United States, and after some prevarication the US President promised 500 aircraft for the Tenth Air Force by early 1943, plus 100 transports for 'The Hump' and Lend-Lease equipment for Chinese divisions. In August 1942 Stilwell's air advisor, Brigadier General Clayton Bissell, was named commander of the Tenth Air Force and Sino-American relations settled down for a time.

III

Conditions for the Allied troops in India were to be a revelation – and not an entirely pleasant one! In Burma the climate from October to March was generally agreeable but in India the same dry season was oppressively hot, and the early months of 1942 particularly so. Calcutta residents said that nothing like it had been known for eighty years or more and people died in the streets of the city in unheard-of numbers, their bodies lying uncollected. Out on the airfields where blast pens were being built to protect the aircraft, work was only possible until 10.00 am. At Allahabad 200 of 700 airmen became victims of heat exhaustion, their temperatures rocketing to as much as 108 degrees. If left untreated, half an hour at that temperature would leave the victim dead or permanently insane. Disease was rife – cholera, malaria, infectious jaundice, dengue fever, dysentery, foot-rot, dhobi itch, prickly heat – and then there were eye-flies and the myriad varieties of insects to contend with. Taken from a little later in the war the following comments by Warrant Officer F.A. Galea, a veteran of several squadrons based in India/Burma, will nevertheless help to bring home the day-to-day life faced by soldiers and airmen totally unused to and unprepared for such conditions:

> The billet I shared with mixed members of mixed crews housed eight. On a raised concrete platform stood a rice thatched timber and plaster rectangular hut boasting a wooden door and wooden windows (no glass). The roof was lined with a layer of sheeting that gave the rats privacy. From the ceiling were two or three swinging punkas that wafted a breeze in the heat of the day. A length of rope attached to each led through a wall and was kept in motion by a punka wallah seated in an outdoor shelter pulling a rope. Poor beggar. If he dozed off a bellow from inside shattered his peace.
>
> Besides daily doses of mepacrin (anti malaria) tablets, also salt to replace losses, a constant programme of anti cholera injections was in place. Outbreaks of dysentery occurred. If affected one became helpless.
>
> I recall waking one night to find a colony of bed bugs emerging from the cracks in the wooden charpoy (bed), so out came the kerosene and brush.
>
> We each employed a hungry lizard to patrol our nearby wall to scoop up the constant inroad of creepy crawlies. Eventually the fattened fellow fell off the wall. A skinny replacement cost 2 annas (16 annas = 1 rupee).
>
> On one predetermined monsoon day clouds of ants of numerous species emerged. They would fill the air, mate, shed their wings and scuttle off to build a colony. With the coming of DDT we would de-ant a billet by squirting a dose into known tunnels. After a couple of hours one could easily sweep up a bucketful of ants.
>
> One member of my hut had an old springless gramophone and a few Mario Lanza records. We would take turns revolving the records by hand and pour out the sound effects.
>
> Returning to base after an op we would approach our containers of flying rations, shake furiously, open smartly to eject the scrambling cockroaches, then get stuck into the bully-beef assortment. We all had tweezers to remove foreign bodies from bread – clearly visible if we held it up to the light.
>
> Packs of wild hunting dogs frequently raced through the camp at night. An experience quite foreign to the English countryside.[7]

If the men hoped that the coming of the rainy season would bring relief from the heat they were wrong. The heat continued and so did the work, the men now having to carry out their tasks in an unrelenting stinging downpour, cope with the customary dearth of spare parts and inadequate tools and go to bed exhausted to find camp beds and blankets sodden with no means to dry them. Meals were repetitious and mostly uncooked. The enlisted man's pet relaxation – a cigarette – became ruined by mould, everything in the tents smelled of mildew and even the writing paper was too sodden to write home and bellyache. When a storm passed the heat did not, and in the interval waiting for the next storm to arrive moisture hung damp and choking in the air. And yet the men made a go of it – they were not dragged into the slough of despond either by the conditions or the drubbing they had received at the hands of the Japanese.

To help maintain their morale the men also noticed that a trickle of essential equipment had now started to arrive – Air Stores Parks, Maintenance Units, Repair and Salvage Units, Wireless Units, unglamorous but essential. Gradually the necessary back-up for a resumption of the air campaign began to materialize, firstly along the front line in Bengal, Assam and Manipur and subsequently stretching back to rearward areas – the beginnings of a supply and maintenance system that would have some strength in depth and avoid the sidelining of perfectly operable aircraft for want of a few spares.

Sorting out the problems of the air arm had barely scratched the surface, however, and on his arrival in New Delhi to take up his post as AOC India and Ceylon, Air Marshal Sir Richard Peirse was scathing about both the number and quality of the Air Headquarters personnel that he encountered. In India the RAF had always been the poor relation of the Army, dependent on the Indian military budget for funding and subject to Army tactical control over operations that amounted to little more than flying outdated aircraft to support ground operations against restless tribes along the North West Frontier. Consequently AHQ traditionally had very little to do beyond rubber-stamping Army instructions, but now, in the space of four short months, this ramshackle 'cushy billet' found itself dropped uncomfortably into the hot seat of a state-of-the-art industrialized war in which the Army would rapidly come to appreciate that it quite literally could not operate without air support.

Peirse set to work on the mammoth task of bringing RAF India up to speed in the minimum possible time. His first undertaking was to greatly expand the command structure by creating several new Group

Headquarters through which control of the expanding air force could be maintained, these were:

- No. 225 at Bangalore to take charge of the whole of peninsula India.
- No. 227 at Lahore responsible for all training in the command, including that of the Indian Air Force.
- No. 226 at Karachi, responsible for supply and maintenance.

The two original Group Headquarters, No. 222 at Colombo and No. 1 (Indian) at Peshawar (responsible for the North-West frontier) remained in being although No. 1 became 223 Group.

The principal area of contact with the Japanese, however, was in the north-east where Air Vice-Marshal Stevenson had reformed 221 Group. Stevenson kept responsibility for bomber and reconnaissance operations while another new Group, 224, assumed control of the area's fighters. Both Peirse and Stevenson held grave concerns over the difficulties inherent in operating effective command over these two groups from their headquarters at Delhi, 850 miles distant, and as a consequence Peirse took the bull by the horns and without consulting the Air Ministry in London announced the formation of a new advanced Air Headquarters Bengal, based at Calcutta in close proximity to the local army, navy and civilian command centres. On hearing the news the Air Ministry took umbrage at this innovative piece of free thinking and informed the Air Marshal in no uncertain terms that his new headquarters was unnecessary for the force available in India as presently constituted. A heated exchange of messages ensued culminating with Peirse putting his case to Chief of the Air Staff, Sir Charles Portal, and London despatching Inspector General of the Air Force, Air Chief Marshal Sir Edgar Ludlow-Hewitt, to India to assess the situation on the spot. Ludlow-Hewitt duly reported that all Air Marshal Peirse's command changes were fully justified and there the matter rested, with Peirse having established a priceless precedent to command on the spot as he saw fit.[8]

As the front in Burma collapsed and the enemy drew ever closer only sixteen all-weather airstrips existed in the whole of India, not one radar unit – even Burma had *one*! – and the only observer posts were on the wrong side of this vast country in the north-west. So it was that in this eventful and critical month of March 1942 an ambitious plan to spend £50 million building 215 new airfields gained top priority. Drawing up the plan was one thing, implementing it was another for India lacked the infrastructure, industrial base and skilled labour with which to carry it forward. Not just airmen then, but technicians, plant and equipment, required importation from the UK or USA, all subject to the availability of scarce shipping resources for which, as with everything else, the Far East languished at the bottom of the priorities list. Despite all the problems 148 airfields were ready by November 1942, 83 with all-weather runways of over 1,600 yards, 60 fair-weather strips and 5 standard runways.[9] By the end of 1942 the number of radar units was well on the way to fifty-two in India and Ceylon, allied to seven filter rooms for the coordination of plots. This, accompanied by the formation of an Indian Observer Corps network around the principal port of Calcutta, greatly improved prospects for early warning.[10]

Back in the bustling month of March 1942, in addition to putting in train the building of new airfields, the Chiefs of Staff in Whitehall also appreciated that, while Britain and the United States had agreed to concentrate on the defeat of Germany first, something must be done to reinforce India. In RAF terms this amounted to a target of sixty-four squadrons plus one(!) transport squadron and one Photographic Reconnaissance Unit. Although aircraft would start to be made available the Far East would remain lodged firmly at the bottom of the list of priorities as far as quality was concerned, being for the most part the recipient of much-used types now obsolete in Europe. A call went out for long-range heavy bombers with which to strike back at the Japanese, C-in-C India General Wavell being openly critical of the vice-like grip that Air Chief Marshal Sir Arthur Harris, AOC Bomber Command, kept on the 'heavies' for the almost exclusive purpose of bombing German cities. Harris had warned Admiral Sir Tom Phillips not to be too hidebound in his belief in his preferred weapon, the big-gun battleship, but the Air Chief Marshal himself now inclined to a myopic view, believing that using heavy bombers to pound German cities could win the war almost unaided. Nevertheless Sir Charles Portal effectively put an end to the argument by pointing out that no useful purpose would be served by sending significant numbers of heavy bombers to India at the present time as the facilities to service and maintain them simply did not exist.

Despite the wrangling much-needed reinforcement was sent in the form of Wellington medium bombers which, despite being phased out in Europe, had proved their worth in the Middle East and would do so again in India/Burma. The first squadron equipped with these aircraft, No. 215 RAF, arrived in April, followed by No. 99 in October, the two subsequently being formed into 175 Wing at Jessore, north-east of Calcutta. With Spitfires and other types replacing Hurricanes in Europe a sizeable reserve of these robust aircraft now existed and conversion into Hurribomber fighter-bombers for India began, the intention being to use them in an army ground-support role, a concept also successfully proven in the Middle East.

In September 1940 the British Purchasing Commission had placed a substantial order for the US-built two-seat Vultee Vengeance dive-bomber and a number were now shipped to India, No. 82 Squadron RAF being equipped with this aircraft in November 1942, Nos 45, 84 and 110 Squadrons by the end of the year, together with two squadrons of the Indian Air Force.

On completion of its retreat from Burma, the Army came to rest along a line of defence between the Chindwin and Brahmaputra rivers extending from Chittagong, west of the Arakan, north-eastwards through Imphal and Kohima in Manipur State. This line afforded ground supply of sorts, but, as the Japanese intended, no means of making an advance back into Burma over land. The Japanese reasoned that this mountainous country had never been invaded from the west owing to the exceptionally difficult terrain to be encountered, and were further convinced that there was no danger that the status quo might be due for a change. They did not perceive air transport to be a feasible option, and neither did the Allied commanders, with one exception.

Together with most of his colleagues, General Wavell, C-in-C India, believed that only two possibilities existed to retake Burma – an invasion from the sea through Rangoon, or striking across the mountains with the invasion force building a supply road as it progressed. Transport aircraft were not considered, but Air Vice-Marshal A.C. Collier, Air Officer Administration, AHQ India, commenting on an Air Staff planning paper also ignoring the third alternative, wrote on 14 July 1942 that:

> It is surprising to see no mention of transport aircraft for the solution of supply problems during the initial stage of an advance into Burma. In my opinion, the success or failure of operations ... in this communicationless (sic) area would depend very largely on the intelligent use of transport aircraft.[11]

It would take some time for the notion to take root, not only because the scale of supply that would be required had never previously been attempted, but because air supply itself was such a novel idea to the Chiefs of Staff that Britain did not in fact produce any military transport aircraft of its own and would be required to obtain them from the United States.

Elsewhere, despite the monsoon, a small-scale but nonetheless hazardous air-supply operation did take place. Following the fall of Myitkyina the only Allied garrison in Burma itself was at Fort Hertz in the far north of the country. A small party of British personnel, including a number of women, reached this isolated outpost without food or arms, and the job of provisioning them fell to 31 Squadron. Starting on 9 May air drops continued until a decision was taken that despite the restricted nature of the available airstrip, the Fort should be evacuated. A number of attempts during early June were frustrated by bad weather but finally, on 13 June, 31 Squadron got a Dakota down and successfully evacuated twenty-three people.

With the collapse of the Allied armies some 400,000 refugees attempted to escape from the advancing Japanese, some by sea from Akyab to India, many through Imphal, and others through the Hukawng valley to Ledo. All these refugees, in varying stages of distress, had to be supplied or, where possible, transported out of Burma by air. With the onset of the monsoon the Hukawng valley route in particular became a death trap, the only escape across the mountains in this region being a narrow track that quickly became impassable. Through all of this terrible period 31 Squadron RAF and the transports of the USAAF flew incessantly, regardless of any but the most severe weather conditions, dropping food and medical aid to those below.

Discovering that Fort Hertz had not been taken by the Japanese, India Command conceived the idea of developing the airstrip there as an emergency landing-ground on 'The Hump' route from India to China, and using the Fort to raise and train guerrilla bands to harass the Japanese. Accordingly an advance party of two British army officers and nine men were parachuted from a Lockheed Lodestar on 13 August, followed one week later by a colonel, a wireless operator and a wireless transmitter, disgorged from an Audax that landed at the airstrip. By 24 August the strip had been extended to 1,000 × 50 yards and was prepared to accept transport aircraft, ready for a 31 Squadron Dakota to make a trial landing while bombers from the RAF and USAAF bombed nearby Myitkyina to keep Japanese heads down. By 10 September a 197-strong garrison was in place, dependent entirely on supply from the air by a detachment of 31 Squadron based at Dinjan.

IV

By the time the 1942 monsoon blew itself out the situation along the Burma/India border had stabilized to some degree, but did not offer too much comfort to the Allies. It has been said that the Japanese had the dry zone, the plains, and the healthiest part of Burma, while the Allies had the mountains, malaria and the monsoon. With the grain of Burma running essentially north to south the Japanese were able to supply their armies along the roads, railways and river valleys leading from Rangoon. The British and Commonwealth Army, by contrast, lay astride the northern end of those same river valleys but with yet higher mountains to the rear separating it from its supply bases in India.

Primarily there were three potential areas of contact with the Japanese (see map p. xv):

1. To the south-west in the Arakan (the most suitable place for an Allied advance as the coastal plain could be reached by sea for much of its length).
2. The middle front around Imphal.
3. The river valleys north of Mandalay.

Each area was to receive its share of attention from the protagonists in the years to come, the Allies having the most to lose since any deep penetration by Japanese forces along any of the three battlefronts could spell disaster for the whole line. For the Allies the problem was always one of supply. Even if they did manage to penetrate the Japanese lines how would they get food, ammunition, reinforcements and so on to the front and get the wounded out?

All through the monsoon the Allies had been making probing ground attacks along the Burmese littoral, including Akyab, and in the Chindwin Valley. The principal benefit was experience. Using this experience combined with – and hampered by – military thinking of the time that maintained large-scale supply of an army on the move could only be carried out either by land or sea, General Wavell proposed to mount an offensive in the Arakan. During the same period the Imperial High Command in Tokyo were making plans of their own for the Burma front, and on a larger scale than those of their opponents. General Terauchi, based in Singapore and commanding the Japanese Southern Area, was instructed to reconnoitre the front from Imphal to Akyab, the intention once again being to cut the supply line to China, this time by means of an advance into Assam and eastern India to deny 'The Hump' route airfields to the Allies.

To support the impending ground offensives the protagonists moved their air forces closer to their respective front lines, the Allies from Calcutta to the Arakan front, and 5th *Hikoshidan* principally to Meiktila, Toungoo and Meimyo. As a result of Allied air raids on their forward airfields the Japanese bombers were subsequently moved back to Siam and the Malay Peninsula at night, moving forward at dawn to carry out their raids then retiring back to their rear bases to repeat the process the following dawn. The JAAF also carried out offensive operations and during December launched a substantial raid on Ti Sukia to interrupt American supply efforts to China over the Himalayas.

The JAAF had planned a major air assault on Calcutta immediately following the monsoon but several factors combined to force a delay – transportation difficulties during the monsoon meant that neither aircraft nor ancillary equipment were in position on time; intelligence reports noted the build-up of Allied air and ground forces along the Arakan front necessitating re-assignment to ground support operations; and finally difficulties were being experienced with new engine exhaust flame dampers developed for the heavy bombers. Until the dampers could be made to work effectively night operations by the JAAF were problematical but not impossible. During the full moon period in December a number of small-scale night raids were made on Calcutta and went largely unchallenged as the RAF had moved most of its fighter squadrons across the Bay of Bengal to Chittagong to support the Arakan offensive. Some twenty-three raids were made in total with a maximum number of eight aircraft taking part, yet the raids engendered the same fearful response in the Bengalis as in the Burmese before them, some 1.5 million hurriedly leaving Calcutta for the surrounding countryside. Following the fall of Rangoon Calcutta had become a prime target for the JAAF, the teeming city with its port facilities opening into the Bay of Bengal now the principal Allied supply base in the India/Burma theatre. Despite having to postpone the large-scale raid planned, the JAAF nuisance raids began to have an undreamed of effect, the mass exodus of the population causing the city to grind slowly to a halt, piles of uncollected rubbish rotting in the streets and the resultant stench raising fears of plague. A number of fighters remained in the area but were not fitted with radar for night interceptions. Exhaust damper problems with the Japanese bombers might have made interceptions possible but, as with the 17 Squadron sorties over Rangoon earlier, it was essential for fighter pilots first to be trained in night-fighting techniques. The fact that no fighter cover was present must have done much to exacerbate civilian concerns.

Something needed to be done urgently and both General Wavell and Sir Richard Peirse (now Air Chief Marshal), sent urgent telegrams to the Chiefs of Staff requesting night fighters with state-of-the-art interception equipment. The ideal allocation would be Bristol Beaufighters and for once the Far East got the equipment it needed. Using many components from its stablemate the Beaufort torpedo-bomber, the Beaufighter was a twin-engine two-seat fighter with a powerful punch (including 20 mm cannon) and a range of over 500 miles. Because of the silence of their Hercules engines Beaufighters became known as 'whispering death' from their ability to appear unheralded at treetop height.

The first Beaufighters to arrive in India were the Mk VIFs of the re-formed 27 Squadron stationed at Armarda Road, 130 miles south-west of Calcutta. These aircraft arrived in November but were not fitted for night fighting. Nevertheless, following service and air tests, the aircraft were passed combat ready and on Christmas Day 1942 carried out the first Beaufighter operation against the Japanese. The target was Toungoo, which the JAAF utilized as a bomber base for operations against Calcutta and the Arakan front, but the raid did not go entirely to plan. The selected aircraft flew across the Bay of Bengal to Feni and then on to Toungoo, sweeping unannounced across the airstrip damaging several enemy bombers before a malfunction caused their cannons to jam. The aircraft returned to Armarda Road and two days later tried again against He-Ho in the southern Shan States of eastern Burma. Again a malfunction caused the guns to jam and the raiders returned empty handed. This time the squadron was moved to the RAF Maintenance Unit at Kanchrapara, north of Calcutta, for a complete overhaul of their aircraft armament. The problem was traced to too much tension on some cannon links, preventing the affected cannon shell releasing from its link when reaching the cannon breech.[12]

The response to the urgent messages from Wavell and Peirse was to despatch a flight of three night-fighter-equipped Beaufighters from 176 Squadron RAF, then based in the Middle East, to Dum Dum airfield. On the night of 15 January a Beaufighter piloted by Flight Sergeant Pring intercepted three Japanese bombers and shot them all down in a matter of minutes, local newspapers trumpeting the pilot's success the following day with the headline 'Pring Prangs Three'. Four nights later a Beaufighter piloted by Flying Officer Crombie, an Australian, intercepted four bombers and shot down two plus a possible third. During the engagement Crombie's aircraft took a number of hits which caused an engine fire and resulted in both he and his navigator having to bail out to land in the swamps of the Hooghly River. The two aviators then had to walk for three hours chest deep in water before reaching dry land, but the Beaufighters' success brought an end to raids on Calcutta for the time being and much relieved Bengali citizens returned to the city in droves.

Prospects for the Allied offensive in the Arakan appeared good. Intelligence reports indicated that the Japanese had only four divisions in the whole of Burma, one in the far north-east facing the Chinese in Yunnan, two on the Assam front facing Imphal, and the 55th Division in western Burma of which only one regiment plus a few additional units were based in the Arakan itself. The offensive had limited objectives encapsulated in the capture of Akyab for its airfields and the control the island held over the estuaries of the two main rivers in the area, the Mayu and the Kaladan. The assault, by units of XV Corps commanded by Slim, would move down the Mayu Peninsula, which stretches southward for some 90 miles from Cox's Bazaar before tapering to a point rather like an exclamation mark, with Akyab Island the full stop. Along the spine of the peninsula runs the Mayu Range, a jungle-covered ridge from one to two thousand feet high extending to within approximately one thousand yards of the Bay of Bengal on the western side and to the Mayu River on the eastern side.

Hamstrung as he was in terms of overall resources General Wavell nevertheless had a card up his sleeve that he proposed to play in conjunction with the assault by XV Corps. In March 1942, Wavell summoned Lieutenant Colonel Orde Wingate to India and instructed him to draw up plans for a guerrilla campaign behind Japanese lines in Burma. Wingate had been born in India to parents who were Plymouth Brethren, although while serving in Palestine, where Wavell had become acquainted with him, Wingate himself became a committed Zionist, apparently with something of a Messianic aura about him. The new Special Forces commander appears to have been a complicated personality, in Slim's words 'a strange, excitable, moody creature, but he had fire in him'.[13] Wingate was inspirational to his men, irascible, unconventional and demanding of complete loyalty from his subordinates while not believing himself hampered by any such commitment to his own superiors. His training methods and tactics have been roundly criticized by fellow military men and yet there is no doubting that the two operations that he set in motion, while falling far short of their objectives, did achieve much in terms of the all-important morale of the British and Commonwealth soldiers by showing them that the Japanese could be confronted and beaten in the jungle terrain that they appeared to have made their own.

Wingate was authorized to train a guerrilla force of brigade strength drawn from units of the British and Commonwealth Army, Wavell's original intention being to use it in conjunction with XV Corps in the Arakan. However it became apparent that the Chinese also planned an advance from Yunnan into northern Burma and the decision was taken to use Wingate's 'Chindits' in cooperation with that advance,[14] since penetrating attacks on both flanks simultaneously would pose the Japanese maximum problems.

Many delays hampered the opening of the First Arakan campaign and it was not until mid December that Major General W.L. Lloyd's 14th Infantry Division began its 90-mile advance along both sides of the Mayu range. Initially the advance went well and by January 1943 motorized patrols had penetrated almost as far as Akyab, at which point a ten-day delay caused by unseasonably heavy rain washing out tracks by which supplies were transported to the front allowed Japanese reinforcements to arrive and counter-attack.

5th *Hikoshidan* delegated 4th *Hikodan* to the ground-support role, plus, when the 55th Division went over to the attack in February, all other available aircraft not operationally engaged against the Allied air forces. Harrying operations were also carried out against Allied air bases at Feni, Silchar, Cox's Bazaar and Dohazari.

Air Vice-Marshal T.M. Williams replaced Stevenson as AOC Bengal Command in January 1943 and immediately established a close rapport with the Army, General Slim commenting that Williams 'was an inspiring commander for his own Service and an understanding and unselfish colleague to us ... Bill Williams was the man who laid the foundations of the air supremacy we later gained, and on which everything else was built.'[15] RAF support for the First Arakan campaign fell to 224 Group operating from airfields around Chittagong and comprising five Hurricane squadrons, a Mohawk squadron, three Blenheim squadrons and a Lysander flight. In addition to ground support for the Army the fighter squadrons were also required to mount air defence for Chittagong. With Japanese infantry again making use of infiltration tactics through thick jungle RAF bombers were obliged to attack unseen objectives during daylight hours. Areas to be attacked would be indicated by map references supplied by the Army, or picked out by smoke shells. Aircrew disliked these operations as it meant bombing one area of jungle indistinguishable from any other, but the Army welcomed the raids.

A native of Essex, Flight Sergeant Les Brazier trained as an RAF Wireless Operator and following an eventful sea journey to India in late 1942 found himself posted to a forward position on the Arakan front as part of 167 Wing, 224 Group. As he discovered, the Japanese were not the only problem to be encountered:

> After arriving at the dirt strip which was the RAF base at Ramu, and which housed two squadrons of old Hurricanes, I was transferred to the Operations 'Room' a couple of miles away in a copse in the jungle. This radio unit consisted of about thirty personnel, under canvas ... The unit was mobile and most of the personnel had to be able to drive so that we could move everything quickly and at short notice.
>
> Our work consisted of keeping contact at quarter hour intervals night and day with about fourteen Wireless Observer Units each having three unlucky chaps [a wireless operator, driver and cook] sent out to a map location in front of our troops, to report aircraft and other enemy movements to us and to our HQ at Chittagong. We frequently lost contact with WOU units never to be heard of again. They were probably overrun

by the Japs ... All reports received by us were passed to the Ops Room for action as necessary in scrambling our fighters or reporting to the Army. Our shifts were fairly exhausting, being a watch system of two operators each shift, 8 am to 1 pm, 1 pm to 6 pm, 6 pm to midnight, and midnight to 8 am.

The cooks did their best with mostly bully beef, which was POURED out of large tins, as we had no refrigeration!!, hard tack biscuits, rice, rice and rice and sometimes sweet potatoes. Plenty of certain kinds of fruit, as we were in a mango glade and large delicious mangoes dropped on our tents night and day with loud plops ... Occasionally pineapples would arrive. We also had delivered four or five cattle which were kept in a corral and from time to time the cooks would go out, lasso one animal, drag it to the side and poleaxe it. So we had fresh meat as well as the local chickens, goat or buffalo meat acquired from local natives who were pleased to be able to trade profitably with British units ...

Our biggest problem was water. We commandeered a local Hindu bathing tank (a large pool or pond dug by the locals) which had hitherto been used for bathing, water, toilets and the rest. This water was boiled by the cooks for a minimum of twenty minutes then heavily chlorinated and this we drank as chlorinated tea (char). All our drink and food tasted heavily of chlorine especially the rice, which to this day I eat only under sufferance! Despite all the precautions most of us suffered from the 'screamers', as it was jocularly known, on a three week cycle. Our latrines consisted of a slit trench behind a canvas screen ... with a horizontal pole about three feet high to hang on to. The pole did on the odd occasion collapse with some dire results! Personal washing and hygiene was also a problem. Heath Robinson constructed showers in the open with a bucket with holes in the bottom, tilted after being filled with water with a complicated string arrangement ...

Disease was a great problem ... Malaria, dysentery, stomach problems, venereal disease, and skin problems accounted for a great many casualties. I personally was lucky in that I was one of the few who did not contract malaria or indeed any other medical ailments other than skin and tummy upsets. We all had to take mepachrin of course on a daily basis which tended to turn one's skin yellow.[16]

The JAAF hoped to catch the Allied air forces on the ground at Chittagong as they had at Magwe and Akyab, and while early warning was initially poor sufficient radar equipment did arrive for defending fighters to be given the distance from which enemy formations approached, but not the height. One technical innovation that Japanese fighters had was the telescopic sight, which gave their pilots extremely accurate aim for their guns but blinded them to anything outside the view through the sights. In one incident Battle of Britain veteran Wing Commander Frank Carey landed at an airfield immediately prior to an incoming Japanese attack. As enemy bombers pounded installations

Carey again took off and was immediately 'bounced' by six JAAF fighters, which the RAF pilot then proceeded to lead in a frantic chase a few feet above the ground before lifting delicately over a small hill which the Japanese pilot immediately behind failed to see and into which he buried his aircraft. Following a similar incident involving Flying Officer Roy Gray the tactic became accepted as a means of last resort.[17]

607 Squadron arrived at Alipore on 25 May 1942 having journeyed from the UK. In June the squadron was equipped with Hurricane Mk IICs and in December 1942 found itself despatched to support the First Arakan campaign. Flight Sergeant Alex 'Paddy' Calvert hails from Northern Ireland and recalls the squadron's arrival:

> The RAF in their wisdom decided that ground staff maintenance men etc would no longer move forward with the pilots but rather would remain in situ as servicing echelons and apply their skills to the next squadron to arrive ... However someone had to go with the air crew and take along their servicing records etc to the next station and see to it that the servicing echelon there properly carried out squadron maintenance and duly signed the necessary documents ... I was the person chosen to accompany the air crew and was with them right through to the surrender of the Japanese, a delegation of whom came to Rangoon.[18]

Also with 607 Squadron was Flight Lieutenant Wilfred Goold, an Australian destined for an eventful couple of years during which he became one of the more successful pilots in the India/Burma theatre:

> Early in December the Japs put on a 100+ raid on Chittagong. Our early radar was pretty hopeless and we were scrambled when they were over us. It was a very one sided affair and our squadron was severely mauled.
>
> On December 20 we were escorting Blenheims to Magwe and I was one of three acting as top cover. I was watching the bombers approach the strip when I felt this banging and saw whisps across my wings. Looking up into my rear vision mirror I saw this Jap right on my tail. I thought, 'this is it', so I threw everything into the corner [pushed the foot pedal to one side and the joystick into the same corner], pushed the throttle through the gate [emergency acceleration] and down I went, hotly pursued by this character. Somehow he didn't nail me again, and when I hit the tree tops I was really moving and rapidly outpaced him. I was in a dilemma; I had to turn back, so I steep turned to face him, only to see that he had turned also. I gave him a long burst, out of range, I might add, but I saw one of his legs [landing wheel and its undercart – the Japanese fighter may well have been a Nakajima Ki-27 Nate with fixed spatted undercarriage (author)] fall. I didn't wait or pursue the attack as we were still in the precincts of Magwe and I wanted to get out. I wasn't sure if I had any damage, so headed for home and arrived very much a relieved pilot. Later the Blenheims confirmed my action, and I was credited with one destroyed.[19]

As the fighting intensified and Allied infantry were forced back, 224 Group found itself entirely committed to the ground-support role at critical junctures. With the Japanese transporting supplies and ammunition by such roads and tracks as were available between central Burma and Akyab, a major assault by the Wellingtons of 221 Group and B17s of the USAAF attempted to disrupt the traffic, while fighters attacked water-borne transport. Wilfred Goold and 607 Squadron were again involved:

> During January we carried out extensive sweeps and I caught a 20 seater transport near Meiktila, which I destroyed. Another day we did a rhubarb [intruder operation looking for enemy] up the Irrawaddy River and caught a 3 decker Mandalay River steamer which we beached and set on fire. Further up stream we had been warned of the Japs stringing a wire hawser across the river. Fortunately I spotted it early enough and straffed the gun post. A bit further up we cornered some storage barges, which we destroyed. It was a rather successful day![20]

The stresses and strains of war come in all kinds and affect the participants in different ways. Wilfred Goold experienced a particular sort but his 607 Squadron compatriot Alex Calvert endured an entirely different kind:

> I got news that my brother in the RNVR was missing believed dead and I simply lost my head. I volunteered to take a squad, one of each trade, to a forward position closer to the Japanese front lines so that our pilots could stop and refuel etc on the way home from a strike as they could not make the complete sortie on one tank of fuel.
>
> This little strip was called Lewe (pronounced Lee-Wee) where Liberators took us with tool kits etc and followed with loads of 40 gallon drums of 100 octane fuel.
>
> After some time there the rains came and the Squadron Commanding Officer Squadron Leader Pegg flew over and dropped a note to say 'operation over, destroy all and make your own way back'.
>
> The distance was in excess of 150 miles so we split up and set off in pairs and walked most of it, just getting the odd lift.
>
> I can recall arriving at the C.O.'s tent in vest and short pants, boots, no socks, no cap, standing to attention in front of him not daring to salute (no cap) and saying, much to his surprise and amusement, 'reporting for duty, Sir!'[21]

Despite the war being more than twelve months old these fighter and bomber raids in support of the Arakan campaign of 1942–3 were the first opportunity to come the way of the Allied air forces to mount a concerted large-scale operation against the Japanese and although they had their successes enemy ground forces once again pushed forward, until by 11 May 1943 Allied troops were back where they had started.

Valuable experience in air/ground support was gained while deficiencies in equipment had once more been underlined, but by far the most negative effect of the campaign was on the morale of the Allied forces, once again bested by their tough, resilient opponent.

Notes

1. *Japanese Monograph No.64* (The Library of Congress, Washington DC), p. 14.
2. Franks, Norman L.R., *First in the Indian Skies* (RAF Collection in conjunction with 31 Squadron Royal Air Force Association, 1981), p. 102.
3. *Wings of the Phoenix* (HMSO, 1949), p. 10.
4. *Op. cit.*, Note 1, p. 12.
5. Hata, Ikuhiko et al., *Japanese Army Air Force Fighter Units and their Aces 1931–1945* (Grub Street, 2002), pp. 271 & 215; also TNA Air 2/7787. Report of Air Vice-Marshal D.F. Stevenson, p. 19; and *op. cit.*, Note 1, p. 27.
6. *Op. cit.*, Note 1, pp. 27–8, estimated as at July 1942.
7. Warrant Officer Galea, in correspondence with the author.
8. Probert, Air Commodore Henry, *The Forgotten Air Force* (Brassey's), pp. 122–3.
9. Gupta, S.C., *History of the Indian Air Force 1933–1945* (Combined Inter-Services Historical Section India & Pakistan, 1961), p. 90.
10. *Op. cit.*, Note 8, p. 113.
11. TNA Air 41/37, *Air Supply Operations in Burma 1942–1945*, p. 4.
12. Innes, David J., *Beaufighters Over Burma* (Blandford Press, 1985), p. 41.
13. Slim, Field Marshal Viscount, *Defeat Into Victory* (Pan Grand Strategy Series, 1999), p. 162.
14. Wingate's chosen brigade sign was the chinthe, a mythical beast that stands guard outside the religious buildings of Burma. The word became mispronounced as 'chindit' and the name stuck.
15. *Op. cit.* Note 13, p. 132.
16. Flight Sergeant Les Brazier, in correspondence with the author.
17. *Op. cit.* Note 3, p. 26.
18. Flight Sergeant Alex Calvert, in correspondence with the author.
19. Flight Lieutenant Wilfred Goold DFC, in correspondence with the author.
20. *Ibid.*
21. *Op. cit.* Note 18.

Chapter Four

The Flight of the Phoenix

I

The official title for Wingate's 'Chindits' was the 77th Indian Infantry Brigade, and bearing in mind the hardships almost certainly to be endured, the brigade counted among its number, few of whom were volunteers, some surprising choices. The 13th Battalion the King's Regiment (Liverpool), for instance, had been sent to India for internal security duties and was made up of personnel with the high average age of thirty-three years. By contrast the 3rd Battalion, 2nd Gurkha Rifles comprised for the most part under-age soldiers with inexperienced officers and NCOs, the unit falling victim to the practice of posting Indian Army officers with experience or potential to Europe or the Middle East. Wingate himself had never fought in jungle conditions and was scarcely qualified to formulate brigade training, although that is what he did.

If there were problems with the brigade there were also problems with their proposed mission. Initially the Chindits were to be used in conjunction with the XV Corps assault in the Arakan, then in conjunction with a Chinese attack in northern Burma which was subsequently cancelled. Despite this General Wavell decided that Wingate's brigade should go forward from Imphal as planned in an attempt to disrupt Japanese communications and raise as much trouble for the enemy as they could. As General (later Field Marshal Viscount) Slim has pointed out, the raid was in fact familiar to military history as the cavalry raid in strength on enemy communications which, to be successful against a resolute opponent such as the Japanese, should ideally be mounted in conjunction with a main attack elsewhere.[1] Wingate's operation differed from the cavalry raid of old in one vital respect however – it would be supplied from the air. Jungle tracks might easily be cut by storms or the enemy, 'So,' said Wingate, 'bring the goods like

Father Christmas, down the chimney.'[2] The brigade numbered some 3,200 men which Wingate structured into eight columns of about 400 men each, organized along the lines of an infantry company but with the essential addition of an RAF officer and two radio operators per column with which to call in air support. The columns took mules for transportation of their immediate needs and being without wheeled vehicles were designed to operate completely independently and go where they might in the jungle, making their location by the Japanese a difficult proposition and in effect turning established Japanese tactics back on them. When Wingate needed the columns to concentrate for a particular operation he would contact them by radio. An innovation destined to cause problems was Wingate's notion that when faced by enemy in strength the columns should disperse into the jungle to reform later at a predetermined rendezvous point. In the confusion of actual battle conditions, briefing everybody on the rendezvous point proved extremely difficult to organize and on one occasion a column dispersed when faced by no more than an enemy patrol which it should easily have overwhelmed.

In February the Chindits crossed the Chindwin in two groups, the northern group of five columns and Wingate's Headquarters making for the Shwebo–Myitkyina railway and beyond that the Irrawaddy; the southern group of two columns – due to sickness and casualties of one sort or another one column had to be broken up as replacements for the remaining seven – crossed some 35 miles to the south and made for the same objectives.

RAF transports for the operation were the DC2s and C47s of 31 Squadron and the Hudsons of 194 Squadron, newly formed around a kernel of 31 Squadron personnel that included the squadron Commanding Officer, Wing Commander Alec Pearson, a former 31 Squadron flight commander. Both squadrons operated detachments from Agartala for the Chindit raid and for the first time supplies were dropped by night and day, both particularly hazardous undertakings as the infantry columns pressed further into enemy territory. Approaching the Myitkyina railway the unarmed transports were beyond fighter range and had to fly on alone.

Aircrew of the transports were understandably learning new skills as they went along, and occasionally some supplies went astray. On the night of 16 February over 10 per cent of the total dropped became lost in marsh and forest, however at least some of the blame went to the infantry columns, who, as the official report dryly puts it, 'took very little trouble to observe and recover distant parachutes while local villagers showed great celerity'.[3] This incident, it should be noted, occurred in the early stages of the operation. As the Chindits got deeper into enemy territory examples of missed supplies became very rare.

Areas into which supplies would be dropped were large paddy fields, the occasional jungle clearing and on occasion even mountainous country where a large enough plateau and clear approach existed. Inevitably, since the process of air supply was being learnt 'on the hoof', there were problems. The situation on the ground might not permit a drop at a particular time, W/T communications were not always perfect and weather conditions occasionally, although rarely, intervened. Two particular problems grew in importance as the raid progressed. W/T sets inevitably became damaged or were abandoned for one reason or another, leaving the column uncontactable, allied to which aircraft from the two squadrons were never available in sufficient enough numbers to be able to keep track of the scattered groups. As a result all the columns in their turn suffered some degree of privation, on occasion for days at a time. In an effort to overcome the W/T problems a detachment of No. 2 Squadron IAF, equipped with Hurricanes, was despatched from Ranchi to Imphal, arriving on 13 April, their task to reconnoitre the area of the raid in an effort to locate Chindit groups which might otherwise be unable to make contact. Operations commenced on 15 April and involved flying at treetop height to pinpoint positions, whereupon they would return to base to lead transport aircraft to the appointed location. The IAF Hurricanes were fitted with long-range fuel tanks to enable them to reach out to the limits of the raid, sorties often taking three to three and a half hours. The detachment remained in operation until 26 May when it was withdrawn having flown 148 sorties of which 70 were contact, 60 tactical – strafing river craft, trains and Japanese ground troops – 15 photographic, 2 offensive and 1 escort reconnaissance. During one sortie an IAF Hurricane flying over the Chindwin attacked a small Japanese patrol and saved the life of a wounded Gurkha infantryman lying on the riverbank nearby.

No means of bringing the wounded out existed during this first Chindit operation, consequently most had to be left behind in the jungle, the fortunate ones with money to buy supplies from the natives, the less fortunate with no more than a bottle of water, a pistol and a hand grenade. Their fate if they fell into the hands of the Japanese would not be pleasant and it does not take much imagination to appreciate what the pistol was for. Occasionally, however, it did prove possible to evacuate wounded, in one instance thanks to a particularly skilful piece of flying by a 31 Squadron crew. During early April, 31 Squadron received eight more Douglas C47s – a larger development of the DC2 – by which time the Chindits were on their way back toward Allied lines. During the course of a supply sortie on 11 April aircrew noticed on the ground the message *Plane land here* written in strips of parachute silk. The aircraft attempted a landing but was thwarted by the restricted nature of the jungle clearing. On returning to base the pilot, David Lord, reported that a landing might be made if the Chindits marked out a runway of sufficient length over firm ground and cleared away any obstructions. Radio contact was made with the group in question, who advised that they had a number of wounded unable to make the 200-mile trek to safety and unless they could be flown out would have to be left to the dubious mercies of the jungle and the Japanese. Instructions were given for the preparation of a suitable landing ground and on Tuesday, 13 April, two C47s flew out to make the attempt. En route the aircraft were advised that there would not be as many wounded as expected and one returned to Agartala. The remaining aircraft, piloted by 31 Squadron veteran Flying Officer Mike Vlasto, and crewed by Jamaican Sergeant Frank Murray, Canadian Sergeant Jack Reeves and Sergeant Charles May, continued until Vlasto spotted marked out below *Land on white Line. Ground there VG.* Vlasto first circled the Dakota to parachute out the supply load, and then took the aircraft in for a landing. The strip was 800 yards long, a good forty yards shorter than recommended, and a strong tail wind blew toward the unforgiving teak forest at the far end. As soon as the aircraft touched the uneven strip Vlasto braked hard and pulled up at the edge of the cleared area. In twelve minutes seventeen sick and wounded Chindits were taken aboard and the C47 was airborne once more, on its way back to Agartala. The remainder of that particular Chindit column made their way to Fort Hertz, arriving three weeks later to be flown out to India.[4]

By June 2,182 Chindits of the original number had returned, although such had been the privations of the operation that only some 600 or so were ever fit for active service again.[5] Of the 1,000 or so missing, approaching 450 were battle casualties and 210 were captured, of whom 168 died or were killed by the Japanese. The Chindits marched for over 1,000 miles and penetrated some 200 miles eastwards into enemy territory, blowing up bridges and destroying cuttings on the Mandalay–Lashio railway line, although they did not manage to cross the Irrawaddy. Much of the damage inflicted on the enemy was quickly repaired, the casualty rate was high, and in purely military terms the results were not considered sufficient for the resources employed. However, the raid cannot be considered in just those terms for there was a dramatic quality to it that was picked up by the world's press and the Army was quick to exploit the opening given. With skilful manipulation the story went around the world that British troops had entered the Japanese jungle domain and beaten them at their own game. Morale in the British and Commonwealth Army, at rock bottom following First

Arakan, picked up noticeably and by these highly important markers the raid was a resounding success. Wingate himself, promoted to Major General and a Churchill favourite – the Prime Minister believing he should command the army in India – went on to plan a much larger incursion into Burma.

The Army may not have felt that it gained much in military terms from the raid but the RAF drew two important lessons from the experience:

1. The answer to the by now familiar Japanese tactic of envelopment to cut off Allied forces lay in air supply, enabling ground troops to ignore land lines of communication which had been proven time and again to be all too vulnerable.

2. Some effective means of rescuing the sick and wounded would be vital for future campaigning, whether raids or full-blown battles. The answer lay in the development of an air evacuation service and since strips of 8–900 yards in length were not always practical, light aircraft capable of landing and taking off in confined spaces would be required.[6]

To support the first Chindit expedition the RAF flew 178 supply-dropping sorties, of which a mere nineteen had to be aborted. Over 300 tons of supplies were dropped to the columns, almost entirely free of interference from the JAAF who, not for the last time, completely failed to understand the crucial importance of air transport.

In addition to supplying the Chindit operation, 31 and 194 Squadrons had to maintain their other transport duties, and in the six months from January to June flew 717 sorties dropping 949 tons of supplies in the Chin and Naga Hills, 154 tons in north Burma and 63 tons to Fort Hertz, utilizing an average of ten aircraft between them. Destinations for supply drops included Sumprabum, Fort Hertz and Chinese-American units in the Hukawng valley. Eventually the constant effort began to take its toll on men and aircraft and it was agreed between AHQ Bengal and the Tenth Air Force that the USAAF would take over responsibility for the Hukawng Valley.

The air transportation of supplies continued throughout the monsoon period, and up to mid November 1,059 sorties delivered 2,930 tons to the Army, the principal recipients of air supply being Allied military units and civilians in the Chin Hills and Chinese-American forces in north Burma. Fort Hertz also continued to be maintained by air and in addition to supplies troop reinforcements were also flown to wherever they were needed. This considerable effort was primarily the responsibility of 31 Squadron.[7]

The lessons learned during the Chindit expedition and subsequent transport operations during the monsoon inevitably reflected the

81

substantial problems encountered. It was quickly realized that air transport required not just aircraft and air crew but an extensive support network of administration and equipment on the ground, plus training and experimentation in the use of transport aircraft. This last was put in hand at the Airborne Forces Research Unit, a multi-service formation based in the Punjab. In time the work of this unit combined with experience gained from continuing operations to produce ground-breaking results.

II

On 'The Hump' route to China the USAAF had its own problems. Sixty-two C47s were promised by December 1942 of which 15 were destroyed, 4 retained by Brereton in the Middle East, and many of the remaining 43 regularly sidelined by the all-too-familiar problem of lack of spares. Communications were at best basic and the weather routinely atrocious, one pilot reporting that 'the present system is if you can see the end of the runway, it's safe to take off.'[8] Aircraft refuelling was carried out for the most part by native labourers pumping fuel by hand from drums. Supplies getting through to China over the Himalayas were minimal and the problem seems to have been not just one of lack of equipment but a continuing clash of personalities. Stilwell commanded 'The Hump' route but as an old-style infantry officer appears to have had little faith in air transport, Chennault claiming that both Stilwell and Tenth Air Force Commander, Bissell – whose comments were oddly negative for a career air force officer and pilot – held the system in contempt. Such bellicose rumblings as these should be taken in context as Chennault and Stilwell held divergent opinions on a number of issues, but there does seem to have been an element of truth in them. December did see a streamlining of the rather unsatisfactory mixed command structure previously referred to, when Air Transport Command assumed command of the trans-Himalayas route 'to work in close harmony with the Theater commander but not to be under his control so far as the conduct of the operation is concerned'.[9] The basis for this decision was the American priority for keeping China supplied as opposed to becoming embroiled too deeply in military operations. ATC was a transport command pure and simple and was less likely to be 'side-tracked' by military operations than Stilwell, the theatre commander; even so command of the India-China Wing of ATC was given to Colonel Edward H. Alexander, Stilwell's air officer. The ATC objective was transportation of 4,000 tons per month across the Himalayas for the first eight months of its control of the route. A slow increase did manifest itself but fell short of expectations:

December 1942	1,227 tons
January 1943	1,263 tons
February 1943	2,855 tons
March 1943	2,278 tons
April 1943	1,910 tons
May 1943	2,334 tons
June 1943	2,382 tons
July 1943	3,451 tons[10]

These figures represent gross tonnages from which were deducted between 383 and 651 tons per month, dependent upon the weight of fuel required for the return flights from India to China.

Having hopefully straightened out their internal command problems, and prodded unceasingly by Chiang's representatives in Washington – which on occasion included the formidable Madame Chiang – the US Administration was now brought face to face with the scarcity of transport aircraft and the fact that the majority of those at present in use over 'The Hump' were ex-civilian aircraft which struggled to gain the altitude required to clear the Himalayan peaks. ATC Headquarters duly put in place a programme to send 50 Curtiss C46 Commando aircraft to Assam during the course of 1943, plus 50 Consolidated C87s (a Liberator variant) and 24 Douglas C54 Skymasters as soon as practicable. Deliveries fell behind schedule but in early April thirty C46s left for Assam carrying 250 personnel – pilots, co-pilots, maintenance men, and so on, for the new aircraft. All personnel, particularly aircrew, would be of inestimable value as those already in theatre had been working around the clock, and many suffered the debilitating effects of acute fatigue.

The C46 had an airliner lineage so thirty of the new pilots were temporarily requisitioned from Northwest Airlines and TWA for training purposes. Flying the aircraft trans-America and flying the aircraft across the Himalayas were two entirely different propositions however, and the service pilots who were required to perform the latter did not take to the aircraft, nicknaming it 'Dumbo' and counting it as great a hazard to life and limb as the unforgiving terrain and the weather. Technical problems also manifested themselves – serious malfunctions with the hydraulics (at least one USAAF mechanic referring to the aircraft as 'a plumber's nightmare'), plus fuel system defects and, bearing in mind the weather conditions to be encountered in India/China, an unfortunate tendency to leak like a sieve in heavy rain. Nevertheless with its service ceiling of 22,000 feet and range of 1,800 miles, every C46 making the flight to China had one undeniable advantage – its ability to carry 4 tons of supplies in its cargo compartment, well in excess of the Douglas C47 Dakota.

In addition to increasing the allocation of aircraft to 'The Hump' airlift the US Administration also ordered ATC to increase the tonnage transported to 7,000 tons by July 1943 and 10,000 tons monthly by the following September. Of that total the Fourteenth Air Force was initially given a priority allocation of 4,700 tons per month for a planned air offensive, Stilwell 2,000 tons per month to equip Chinese ground forces for a projected campaign along the Salween River, with anything in excess of these amounts to be split between air and ground forces at Stilwell's discretion. Of course whether or not the 10,000 ton lift could be achieved and maintained remained to be seen.

A perennial problem in Assam, as elsewhere, was airfields, construction of which was ultimately the responsibility of General Wavell, C-in-C India. During the winter of 1942/43 India-China Wing ATC operated from three airfields in northern Assam, Chabua, Sookerating and Mohanbari, the latter two of which had neither runways, taxiways nor hardstanding, and therefore had to be abandoned with the coming of the monsoon. Both Bissell and Stilwell made representations to the British authorities to have outstanding works completed promptly, and Colonel Alexander went as far as suggesting that Washington take the matter up with Churchill in person. As recounted elsewhere the British were themselves struggling with a shortage of qualified personnel, both engineering and administrative, and problems with the quality of work of a number of local contractors.

'The Hump' route lay open to Japanese attack at both terminals, India and China, and also where it crossed northern Burma. Fighter defence in China was provided by the Fourteenth Air Force, which came into being in March 1943 having grown from the American Volunteer Group via the China Air Task Force. The Fourteenth was commanded by the now Major General Chennault, once more of the USAAF. Initially the new formation operated fifty-six P40 fighters and eight North American B25 Mitchell bombers from its main base at Kunming. Included on its roster were a few AVG pilots although most decided that regular army 'bull' and rates of pay were not for them and left when their contracts expired in July 1942. Air Defence in Assam was the responsibility of the India Air Task Force (IATF) under Brigadier General Caleb Haynes, activated in October 1942 with nine squadrons. Of these four were heavy and three medium bomber units, leaving the command short of fighters. None of the squadrons were combat ready and to add to the difficulties imposed by a lack of fighters, early warning for the Assam airfields was negligible.

Following its practice established the previous year, the 1943 monsoon saw 5th *Hikoshidan* withdraw to rear areas to repair and consolidate. During December 1942 both the 12th *Hikodan* and the 14th *Hikosentai* were transferred to the Solomon Islands as part of what was to become a regular process for the Japanese of weakening their air forces in Burma in order to strengthen the Pacific front. In this respect it is worth bearing in mind that in June 1942 the US Navy achieved a considerable victory over the Imperial Japanese Navy at Midway, destroying the four Japanese aircraft carriers present, shifting the balance of naval power in the Pacific and obliging the Japanese to draw JAAF units into that theatre in an attempt to make up the losses.

Despite the desire to repair and recuperate, Allied air activity kept 5th *Hikoshidan* occupied, fighter units being detailed to the protection of sea transportation and the defence of Rangoon, while elements of the bomber strength were despatched to patrol the sea lanes around Sumatra and to act as anti-submarine convoy escorts.

During the 1943 monsoon the units, strength and location of 5th *Hikoshidan* were as follows:[11]

Hikoshidan Shireibu, Rangoon.

4th *Hikodan Shireibu*, Toungoo.

50th *Hikosentai* upgrading to twenty-seven Type II Nakajima Ki-43 Oscars (with armour protection for the pilot but still only partially self-sealing fuel tanks). Units at Mingaladon and Singapore.

8th *Hikosentai*, twenty-seven Kawasaki Ki-48 Lily twin-engine light bombers. Units at Toungoo and Sungei Patani.

7th *Hikodan Shireibu*, Sungei Patani.

64th *Hikosentai*, thirty Type II Ki-43 Oscars at Mingaladon and Sungei Patani.

12th *Hikosentai*, fifteen Mitsubishi Ki-21 Sally heavy bombers based at Medang and Savan (Sumatra).

98th *Hikosentai*, fifteen Mitsubishi Ki-21 Sally heavy bombers at Patang.

81st *Hikosentai* (Headquarters Reconnaissance), fifteen Type II Mitsubishi Ki-46 Dinah reconnaissance aircraft.

21st *Hikosentai*, twelve Nakajima Ki-44 Tojo fighters based at Sungei Patani.

Aircrew replacements arrived via Air Headquarters in Japan or through the Southern Army Field Air Replacement Unit based at Rangoon. Some training for unskilled crewmen was put in place but 5th *Hikoshidan* evidently believed that the best training was to be had in battle conditions and sent new recruits out on operations as soon as possible.

Appendix 1 provides a snapshot of the Allied air forces as at June 1943 and shows a considerable improvement in terms of numbers at a time when there had been a corresponding weakening of the JAAF, but, although the situation was improving, many aircraft types were still obsolete compared to the European theatre. There was still a long way to go before the air arm would be in a position to provide effective cover for substantial ground operations – particularly with regard to the all-important transport aircraft.

With the withdrawal of many JAAF units to bases beyond the reach of the medium bombers available, in May AOC-in-C Sir Richard Peirse switched attention to 'Lines of Communication' targets such as roads, railways, the military transit camps at Prome and Taungup, and Rangoon. For these targets the twin-engine Beaufighter and the single engine two-seat Vengeance dive-bomber proved highly successful. Like so many aircraft the Vultee Vengeance did not initially take to the dank humidity of Burma/India and hard work was needed by maintenance units and ground crew to sort out the problems. In time, however, fitted with British 0.303 (7.7 mm) machine guns in the rear cockpit to replace the original unreliable American weapons, the Vengeance proved itself an extremely effective aircraft in the hands of RAF and IAF squadrons. In fact so successful was the Vengeance and so urgent the requirement for dive-bombers and ground-attack aircraft that a number of pilots were put straight onto operations without the formality of undergoing a conversion course. They trained themselves in action. Beaufighters also excelled in the ground-attack role, strafing roads and railways, and setting fire to the oil installations at Yenangyaung. During the Allied exodus from Burma five sizeable river steamers, each able to transport large bodies of troops or tow hundreds of tons of supplies in barges, were left along the Irrawaddy. Beaufighters now accounted for four of these boats, leaving their hulks burning on river sandbars. After two or three months of monsoon storms roads became flooded and impassable and large tracts of the country reduced to waterlogged swamp. At this time the Japanese were obliged to switch to water transport, providing tempting targets for Beaufighters and Hurricanes, which duly took the opportunity to destroy 182 motorized river craft and sampans, and around 2,000 smaller craft in the Arakan and on the Irrawaddy. To put this loss into perspective a sampan carried three days' supplies for seventy soldiers, and the building of just one such craft took twenty men a month.

Despite being pretty well obsolete and marked down for early replacement the Blenheims continued in operation for the time being, and far from cursing their temperamental charges the ground and air crew redoubled their efforts to keep their aircraft in the air. The squadrons themselves became famous for their good-humoured camaraderie and were sought after as postings regardless of the venerable age of their aircraft.

Night bombing raids by Wellingtons and Liberators were made more hazardous as a result of the navigational aids fitted to the aircraft being far below European standards, navigators often having to calculate their course by the stars, which were not always visible. The Allied commanders' decision, in contrast to their opponents, to continue air operations where possible during the monsoon imposed yet more difficulties. Aircraft crashed in the mountains or were lost in the jungle, and of the 111 crewmen from the twenty-seven aircraft that came down in the Indian Ocean and Arabian Sea, only sixty-nine were rescued. Burma propped up the bottom of the list of priorities for Air-Sea Rescue crews and equipment as for everything else. The effort had its beneficial effects, however, for Japanese aircraft were kept back in Siam and Allied army bases and airfields were free from attack as a result. USAAF Liberator attacks on shipping and attacks by both the RAF and USAAF on Rangoon made use of the port a very hazardous undertaking.

III

In June 1943 General Sir Claude Auchinleck, an old hand in the sub-continent having had a successful army career there pre-war, replaced Wavell as C-in-C India. The post was by this time mostly administrative but Auchinleck showed considerable energy in ensuring the adequate training of troops, and mobilizing India's resources.

Signals and communications proved to be almost as much of a problem for the Allied air forces during the 1943 monsoon as hitherto. The exceptionally long distances involved, the wide dispersal of squadrons and the usual shortages of suitable equipment meant that landlines were largely impractical. One squadron kept in contact with its Wing HQ entirely by W/T, with all the disadvantages and time delays that system's dependency on Morse code inevitably brought with it. Typex machines were one method of speeding up the W/T process but between June and November 1943 only seventy-eight units were received for the entire command, consequently the tried and tested – and painfully slow – method of referral to book cipher was the order of the day.

Landlines and communications were the responsibility of four Indian Air Formation signals units and all were heavily committed, one in Ceylon, two in the Bengal area, with the final unit left to cover the whole of the remainder of India. By November two additional units were raised and trained, one more for Bengal and one for southern India, but a shortage of trained Indian operators prevented their full implementation.

Coordination of the signals effort along the crucial Bengal front was an imperative and to achieve this plus bring closer and more effective supervision of maintenance and administration of the system, three Signals Wings, Nos 180, 181 and 182 were formed to operate from Calcutta, Imphal and Chittagong respectively, their principal duties being the administrative and technical control of all early warning equipment, permanent W/T and D/F stations. An immediate improvement was noticed, the Imphal area doubling its efficiency while on 20 October an air raid on Chittagong was detected at the previously unheard of range of 115 miles.

A network of some seventy Air Ministry Experimental Stations equipped with radar stretched from the Assam–Burma border south to Akyab, and continued on to cover Calcutta and coastal areas that might be subject to attack. Forward of the stations in Eastern Bengal were the Wireless Observer Units, with posts across the Manipur Road and southward through the Chin Hills as far as the Arakan Hill tracts. These units were in the process of replacement by Indian Mobile Wireless Observer Companies manned by personnel employed on Observer Corps duties in and around Calcutta, Vizagapatnam and Madras. Reports flowed through a number of filter rooms:

- Imphal, Chittagong and Calcutta covering Bengal.
- Vizagapatnam, Madras and Trincomalee covering the Eastern seaboard.
- Cochin and Bombay covering the Western seaboard.

Ground-to-air communication improved but was still greatly hampered by shortage of equipment. Thirteen Direction Finding stations were established on the trans-India reinforcement route, while a number of fighter stations were equipped with Very High Frequency Radio Transmitters. Shortages were apparent, however, in the supply of aircraft Ground Control Interception equipment necessary for operations rooms to direct fighters on to hostile formations. With approximately half the required units available care had to be taken that for each section of two fighters one should be fitted with the necessary apparatus.

With the impending arrival of modern bombers to swell the command, experience with the operation and maintenance of their specialized communications equipment in the difficult climatic conditions to be encountered was needed. To this end No. 1577 Flight was formed and equipped with the Avro Lancaster and Handley Page Halifax but the inevitable shortages of equipment meant that development of advanced radio aids to navigation, submarine detection and precision bombing remained in the overloaded 'pending' tray.[12]

A number of circumstances led to a reduction in usage of the venerable Blenheims, which were in any event in short supply. Vultee Vengeance squadrons, training since the beginning of the year, began to achieve operational status in addition to which a substantial reserve of Hurricanes accelerated the switch in roles from the Hurricane as fighter to the 'Hurribomber' fighter/light bomber, a move made more practical toward the end of the monsoon when Spitfires at long last began to appear in India in some numbers. As a result Blenheim Squadron Nos 11, 34, 42, 60 and 113 RAF converted to Hurricane Mk IIC fighter/bombers, while Nos 607, 136 and 615 Squadrons RAF converted from Hurricanes to Spitfire Mk VCs, which entered service in Europe at the end of 1941. Wilfred Goold recalls the inevitable ups and downs when 607 took delivery of their new aircraft:

> On September 25 a bunch of us flew to Karachi in a Short Empire flying boat, it took 11 hours and 55 minutes. Having assembled our new 'planes we then flew back to Alipore without any hitches, only to find on arrival that we couldn't fly the Spits as some clown in Area Headquarters had consigned all the spares back to the Middle East because he 'knew we didn't have Spitfires in this area'! In October the Squadron flew to an Air Fighting Training Unit at Armarda Road to get used to the Spitfire in combat roles. Armarda Road was a place where only the best was accepted. It was staffed by experienced operational pilots; the Chief Instructor was Frank (Chota) Carey, DSO, DFC Bar, DFM, Bar and so on.
>
> We spent about 14 days doing all sorts of attacks, and we felt very comfortable with our new 'planes.[13]

Flight Lieutenant Goold here mentions the refresher courses in gunnery and tactics at Armarda Road headed by Group Captain Frank Carey, a highly experienced pilot deservedly credited with much of the exceptional improvement in the standard of RAF and IAF fighter pilots in the Burma campaign. Group Captain Carey and his team were constantly engaged in a battle of wits to counter changes in the tactics of the enemy and improve those of the Allies.

A fully equipped and operational Beaufighter Mk VI Squadron, No. 89 RAF, arrived from the Middle East and celebrated by shooting down a JAAF reconnaissance aircraft within days. Newly formed within India Command, No. 211 Squadron RAF was also equipped with Beaufighters. Lack of available aircraft meant that only one heavy bomber squadron, No. 355 RAF equipped with Liberators, was formed within the command between June and November.

Hurricane Mk IIBs found a vital new niche as Fighter Reconnaissance aircraft, Nos 135 and 261 Squadrons RAF taking on this role plus No. 5

Squadron, which had been equipped with Hurricane Mk IID 'tank busters' but re-equipped due to a lack of suitable targets in the India/ Burma theatre.

In March 1942 India was able to offer sixteen all-weather airfields of which only four were considered operational in all respects by the standards of the day, plus twenty fair-weather strips. By November 1943 the total had risen to 285 airfields plus fifteen under construction. Of these an impressive 140 were complete in all respects, 64 had one all-weather runway prepared, and a further 71 could provide fair-weather strips plus dispersals and domestic/technical accommodation in varying stages of readiness. A number of airfields were constructed on behalf of the USAAF airlift to China and by November 1943 thirty-four all-weather airfields plus eleven fair-weather strips had been handed over, in addition to which facilities were offered at a number of RAF airfields. The airfield construction programme was a mammoth undertaking costing some £50 million and brought to light a number of difficulties, notably a shortage of heavy construction equipment, engineers and supervisors. Work sub-contracted to civilian construction companies was not always up to standard and everywhere delays were experienced due to poor communications or inadequate control. Despite the problems by the end of the 1943 monsoon the Allied Air Forces in India were in a position to continue their rapid expansion in the knowledge that suitable bases existed from which to operate.[14]

On the far side of the hill the JAAF also busily repaired and constructed airfields. As the Allies retreated through Burma destruction of the country's industry and infrastructure, including airfields, had taken place to the extent that on the final withdrawal of the Allied armies the JAAF estimated that only fifteen to eighteen airfields were in operable condition. By August 1943 that total had risen to 100.[15]

During 1942 the Imperial Japanese Army and the JAAF in Burma received the bulk of its supplies by sea more or less without hindrance, but by 1943 Allied attacks on sea lanes had grown in intensity until the JAAF estimated that less than one third of the resupply required actually arrived, leading to an inevitable diminution of strike power. Japanese transportation within Burma was chiefly by rail, but again Allied air raids were greatly disrupting the service and necessitating a switch to road and air, 4th Motor Transport Company designated to the former and 11th Air Transport Unit designated to the latter by 5th *Hikoshidan*.[16]

A welcome but temporary reverse of the draining away of units from 5th *Hikoshidan* occurred towards the end of the year, reinforcements arriving in the shape of the 33rd and 204th Fighter *Hikosentai*.[17]

90

IV

On 5 August 1943 Winston Churchill set sail from London to Halifax, Nova Scotia, aboard the *Queen Mary* for the first Quebec conference with President Roosevelt. In addition to the Chiefs of Staff, among the high-powered notables accompanying the Prime Minister,[18] those representing the India/Burma theatre were Brigadier A.W.S. Mallaby, Director of Military Operations in India, and Brigadier Orde Wingate. Wingate had arrived in London that same day to report to the Chiefs of Staff, but on being invited to dine with Churchill, and making a highly favourable impression, was invited to join the British delegation to relate his experiences and recommendations to the Americans. Mrs Wingate, then living in Scotland, had a surprise conversation with a member of her local constabulary and was hurriedly whisked down to London for an entirely unexpected voyage to Canada in the company of her husband and the Prime Minister! Wingate himself had brought precious little but the worn uniform that he stood up in and was duly kitted out in naval battledress aboard ship.

The principal reason for the impending Conference was to settle details of the Overlord plan for the invasion of Europe, but during the preceding voyage time was also devoted to the vexed question of South East Asia. Several military plans had been proposed, Churchill favouring an amphibious assault on the tip of Sumatra (code-named Culverin). The Chiefs of Staff, however, did not feel that the resources were available for such a plan – practically all the landing craft available, for instance, would be required for Overlord – and the proposal was not included for presentation to the Americans on this occasion. Nonetheless Churchill took the opportunity to put forward an idea that was destined to revolutionize the command structure in the Far East. The Prime Minster proposed to remove responsibility for the direction of military operations from C-in-C India to a separate Military Commander with his own staff. As has already been mentioned the post of C-in-C India was by this time for the most part administrative, but the burden carried was a heavy one. Auchinleck, the current incumbent, held responsibility for the command, organization and training of the entire British and Indian forces in theatre, for the internal security of a sub-continent with a population getting on for 400 million, and for preserving peace on the troublesome North West Frontier, in addition to which he shouldered the responsibilities of a Secretary of State for War on behalf of the Viceroy. Seen in these terms it is perhaps surprising that the decision was not taken sooner, and the Chiefs of Staff readily agreed.

At the Quebec Conference the formation of South East Asia Command was agreed, bearing overall responsibility for military operations in the Burma/India/China theatre with at its head Admiral Lord Louis Mountbatten. Mountbatten was a great-grandson of Queen Victoria and on entering the Royal Navy saw action during the First World War aboard Admiral David Beatty's flagship, the battlecruiser *Lion*. By 1937 he was promoted Captain and in June 1939 was given command of the destroyer *Kelly*, becoming Captain (D) of the 5th Destroyer Flotilla in September that same year. Mountbatten's career at sea was undoubtedly spectacular – in short order the *Kelly* had nearly capsized, been in collision with another destroyer, was mined once and torpedoed twice. Finally she capsized off Crete under full helm at 34 knots while under attack by German aircraft. Anxious for senior officers with undimmed offensive spirit, in April 1942 Churchill made Mountbatten Chief of Combined Operations with the rank of Vice Admiral, and a de facto member of the Chiefs of Staff Committee. At forty-three years of age Mountbatten was young for a position as important as Supreme Commander SEAC but he cut a dashing figure that appealed to both Churchill and to the Americans – an important consideration as he would have US forces under his command. The device chosen by Mountbatten to represent the new command was the phoenix, a fabulous bird of Arabian mythology that rose from the ashes of its own funeral pyre with renewed youth. The symbolism was self-evident and the device doubly appropriate as the coming campaigns could only be carried forward on the wings of the air forces.

Another vitally important Allied appointment took place in October 1943 with the appointment of General Slim to command of the newly formed Fourteenth Army, effectively giving him control of all Allied ground forces in the theatre, his task the re-conquest of Burma.

For the air forces Mountbatten's plans were to be bold and controversial, the new C-in-C proposing nothing less than the full integration of all RAF, USAAF and IAF units under a single unified command, with Air Chief Marshal Sir Richard Peirse as Allied Air C-in-C. General Stilwell, until that time in overall command of US Air Forces – and a well known Anglophobe – became Mountbatten's Deputy Supreme Commander while retaining his autonomous role in China. Once again the often stated US position – that they were only in India to supply the Chinese, not help the British reinstate Burma into their Empire – raised its head. Given the long-term US antipathy towards 'empires' in the military sense this was scarcely a surprising, or unreasonable, attitude for them to take, but it did place significant obstacles in the path of the unified air command that would provide the best means of beating the Japanese.

As thunderclouds from the argument replaced the waning monsoon, lengthy discussions between Peirse and Stratemeyer to try to resolve the problem came to nought, the American refusing to be budged from the position that he and Stilwell had adopted that there should be two parallel commands, not a single unified command. Mountbatten took up his position as C-in-C on 16 November and on 12 December issued the directive integrating the theatre air forces. Finding himself faced with threats from both Stratemeyer and Stilwell to go over his head to Washington, Mountbatten states that he 'read the Riot Act to both',[19] as a consequence of which the American generals agreed to carry out the directive but asked that their objections be passed to Washington, which Mountbatten did together with his reasons for refuting them. The new C-in-C SEAC believed himself to be on pretty firm ground as he had already sounded out General Marshall, US Army Chief of Staff, and General Henry 'Hap' Arnold, Commanding General of the USAAF. The American stance concerning Burma notwithstanding, the two senior US officers appreciated the necessity for the command structure to be as streamlined and uncomplicated as possible, and gave their unofficial backing. Official confirmation came on 4 January with Mountbatten's receipt of a letter from General Marshall confirming the approval of the US Joint Chiefs for the unified command, while retaining the right to transfer units from the Tenth and Fourteenth Air Forces should it become necessary. Given the lead by his superiors General Stratemeyer grasped the new realism, issuing a General Order which included the phrase 'we must merge into one unified force, in thought and deed neither English nor American, with the faults of neither and the virtues of both.'[20]

Mountbatten had been obliged to assert his authority at the outset of his command and did so, the integration of the Allied air forces proceeding as outlined below:

Air Command South East Asia
Allied Air Commander-in-Chief, Air Chief Marshal Sir Richard Peirse RAF.

Eastern Air Command (EAC)
AOC and second in command to Peirse, Major General G.E. Stratemeyer USAAF, his position in respect of the Allied air forces corresponding to that of General Slim's for ground forces. EAC was organized into the following groupings:

1. The Third Tactical Air Force commanded by Air Marshal Baldwin and subdivided into:
   (a) The American North Sector Force with responsibility for supporting Stilwell's Chinese and protecting the air ferry route over the Hump to China.

(b) 221 Group RAF under Air Vice-Marshal Vincent, with headquarters at Imphal and responsible for the support of IV Corps along the main central front.

(c) 224 Group RAF under Air Commodore G.E. Wilson with headquarters at Chittagong and supporting XV Corps along the Arakan front.

2. The Strategic Air Force, Brigadier General Davidson USAAF.

3. Troop Carrier Command, Brigadier General W.D. Old USAAF.

Stratemeyer established his HQ in a huge jute mill near Barrackpore, while Baldwin's Third TAF and Brigadier General Old's joint US-British Troop Carrier Command HQs were set up alongside General Slim's Fourteenth Army HQ at Comilla. To a considerable extent the three headquarters operated as a joint command centre, pooling intelligence, planners working together and perhaps most significantly, the three commanders and their principal staff officers living in the same mess. Slim reports that integration reached the stage where Americans adopted the tea-sipping habit and the British learned to make drinkable coffee![21]

By November 1943 approximately two thirds of theatre combat aircraft were British, the remainder American although the US proportion was increasing, notably in the area of transports. The USAAF had begun the supply of Chinese-American forces in north-east Burma with the 1st and 2nd Troop Carrier Squadrons, which in January 1944 were joined by two additional units, 27th and 315th Troop Carrier. During the winter of 1943/44 the RAF too built up its tally of transport units, Nos 31 and 194 also being reinforced by two additional squadrons:

- No. 62, previously operating Hudson Mk VI aircraft on bombing and general reconnaissance duties, converted to Dakotas in early January 1944.

- No. 117, a veteran transport outfit, arrived from the Middle East, initially operating DC2s but converting to Dakotas in July 1944.

194 Squadron, operating the Hudson Mk VI on internal trans-India operations since its formation, converted to Dakotas in February in order to take its place alongside 'parent' squadron No. 31, its previous duties being taken up by 353 Squadron.

An essential part of Mountbatten's approach was to be seen and heard by the men who would have to do the fighting. To achieve this he embarked on a tour of the military units of all nationalities, and Wilfred Goold describes one such visit by the Supreme Commander to 607 Squadron:

On December 16 Lord Louis Mountbatten arrived on our strip and I was one of four to escort his Mosquito over the forward areas. He gathered everyone around him and told us of his plans and then told us what he expected of us. There was no doubt this time; there was no turning back.

The informal 'gathering everyone around' appears to have been an essential part of Mountbatten's attempt to make sure that everyone felt included, from the C-in-C to the cooks and admin clerks, they were all in this together and they all had their essential part to play.

While command changes took place the air war continued. Operating from bases in Assam the 311th Fighter Bomber Group USAAF attacked targets in Northern Burma. On 25 November Major Yohei Hinoki of the 64th *Hikosentai* intercepted a raid and led the 3rd *Chutai* in an attack with their Ki-43 Oscars. In the ensuing dogfight Hinoki shot down the first North American P51 Mustang of the Burma campaign, the aircraft piloted by Colonel Milton, Commanding Officer of the 311th, who became a POW. Two days later Hinoki's 3rd *Chutai* intercepted an estimated fifty B24 Liberators plus thirty fighters, Hinoki claiming a P51, a P38 Lightning and a B24, but falling victim to another P51. Badly wounded, Hinoki managed to return to base but his right leg required amputation and he was repatriated to Japan to take up training duties.[22]

Spitfire Mk Vs at last began to appear in an operational role and much was expected of them. Up to this time the twin-engine Mitsubishi Ki-46 Dinah reconnaissance aircraft employed by the JAAF had flown with impunity over Allied territory, its service ceiling and maximum speed too much for Hurricanes and other Allied fighters. However, in November 1943 Spitfires from 615 Squadron RAF based at Chittagong shot down four Dinahs from the 81st *Hikosentai* in quick succession and the news spread rapidly through the entire Allied command, providing a tremendous boost for morale as it did so.

The unexpected loss of their reconnaissance aircraft was a blow to 5th *Hikoshidan* but also gave them some indication of the power and performance of the new Allied fighter. Despite losses in aircraft and experienced pilots 81st *Hikosentai* continued missions in the Calcutta area and reported a large concentration of some sixty merchant vessels in the harbour – a target too good to miss. Wary of the Spitfires the JAAF attack formations planned a route well to the south of the Chittagong airfields at which they were based, while 8th and 34th *Hikosentai* (20 and 15 light bombers respectively) accompanied by 50th and 33rd *Hikosentai* (27 and 20 fighters respectively), plus 5 Dinahs of the 81st *Hikosentai*, carried out raids in the Chittagong, Silchar and Feni areas to keep the new fighters busy and off balance.

607 Squadron was based at Ramu at this time, a dirt airstrip south of Chittagong, and Wilfred Goold remembers a pattern of almost daily 'scrambles' to combat these raids:

> The tactics we were using were similar to those used by the Luftwaffe against our Hurricanes i.e. height advantage, then diving in, attacking and regaining height. The Japs used what we called a 'Beehive' [aircraft flying in circles] from a basic height up to about 25,000 feet. They were very colourful, highly polished, except for about a dozen, who, we learned, were the 'aces', they flew in drab coloured Oscars.
>
> Our radar was very good so we were always in the top position, but they were so manoeuvrable that zip, and they were gone.[23]

With additional raids having being staged in the Imphal area for weeks beforehand to draw off Allied fighters, the primary attack on Calcutta took place on 5 December and involved units of both the JAAF and JNAF, operating in two waves from Burmese airfields at Magwe and Allanmyo:

JAAF

7th *Hikodan*, comprising:

12th *Hikosentai* (9 heavy bombers)

98th *Hikosentai* (9 heavy bombers)

50th *Hikosentai* (27 fighters)

64th *Hikosentai* (27 fighters)

33rd *Hikosentai* (20 fighters)

204th *Hikosentai* (20 fighters)

81st *Hikosentai* (2 Dinahs to drop quantities of streamers just prior to the raid to confuse Allied radar).

JNAF

28th *Hikotai* (Flying Unit) comprising 9 medium bombers and 30 Zero fighters.

The plan to evade the Spitfires worked and although the raid was picked up by Chittagong radar, of the sixty-five Spitfires and Hurricanes scrambled to intercept only one Spitfire made contact, shot down a bomber and force-landed on a sandbank out of fuel. At Calcutta itself the defending Hurricane Squadrons, Nos 67 and 146 RAF, were over-whelmed by the raid's fighter defence and lost eight aircraft – the JAAF believed that they were only attacked by about ten aircraft in total. When the second wave of the attack swept in the Hurricanes were caught on the ground refuelling and only a few night fighters were able to get airborne. Two Spitfire squadrons from Chittagong attempted to intercept the raiders as they returned, but were again unable to make contact.

The raid had been carefully planned and executed and was an undoubted tactical success for 5th *Hikoshidan*, who were jubilant at having got off so lightly. Nevertheless, to gain the range for the long southward leg to avoid Chittagong the bomb loads had been necessarily small, consequently the damage inflicted, while unwelcome, was not devastating. Three merchant ships and a naval vessel were damaged, fifteen barges set afire, and a number of dockyard buildings destroyed. By far the most damaging aspect of the raid was the 500 civilian casualties caused, followed as it was by an immediate exodus of the local population from the docks area.

Encouraged by their success the JAAF planned further raids on Calcutta but first, having attacked the port at the far south of the Allied positions, they switched their attention to the far north – the trans-Himalayas 'Hump' route to China. As part of the Calcutta attack plan fifty fighters and eighty light bombers from 4th *Hikodan* attacked Tinsukia airfield on 8 November to disrupt the China supply route and keep Allied attention away from Calcutta. Following the raid on Calcutta 4th *Hikodan* commenced a series of raids on 'Hump' airfields inside China with Tinsukia again being the target on 11 and 12 December, followed by Yungning in succeeding days. On 18 and 22 December Kunming received the attention of seventy fighters and bombers of 7th *Hikodan* plus around ten heavy bombers specially brought in for this attack on the principal 'Hump' airfield in China. JAAF fighters also attacked transports in flight over northern Burma and for a time as many as three per day were being destroyed, but the supply route remained in operation.

Without sufficient resources to attack all its potential targets in strength simultaneously the JAAF once again turned its attention to the south, this time to the bustling port of Chittagong – and the Spitfires they had thus far gone to considerable lengths to avoid. On Christmas Day 1943, 7th *Hikodan* attacked the port with an estimated twenty bombers and thirty fighters. As an illustration of the way in which Allied air strength had grown over the past year the defences were able to put up eighty Spitfires and Hurricanes, but the result fell far short of expectations. If the availability of aircraft was now not as pressing a problem, the shortage of radar and ground-to-air communications equipment with which to vector fighters on to attacking aircraft effectively – plus trained operators – most definitely was. The uncoordinated mêlée of Allied fighters posed much less of a threat to the disciplined JAAF formation than it should have done if properly controlled, and a tally of three bombers and two fighters shot down was disappointing.

One Spitfire pilot, John Rudling, developed a highly unusual method of attack. With his squadron newly equipped with Spitfires, Rudling was returning to base following what up to that point had been a fruitless sortie. Noticing enemy bombers in the distance, and despite his fuel being down to ten gallons, Rudling headed toward them and swooped in to the attack. Opening fire on a bomber, Rudling

> observed strikes on the enemy's wings when I suddenly realised I was going to collide. I broke sharply away above, feeling my aircraft hit the rudder of the bomber. I then proceeded down, thinking I had damaged my aircraft for any further attack, but it was all right, so I pulled up under another vic ['V' formation] of bombers, firing from underneath at the leader.[24]

A Japanese fighter attacked the lone Spitfire and hit the aircraft with five shells, damaging the oil tanks. Rudling watched the bomber with which he had collided spiral down into the sea then force-landed himself without flaps or brakes. The RAF pilot became so attached to the collision method for downing bombers when his ammunition had expired that he tried it on succeeding occasions, and it was not until his third attempt that he was himself, perhaps unsurprisingly, killed.

So far the Spitfires had shown promise but had not really been able to get to grips with their opponent, however that was about to change. On 31 December 1943 a substantial JAAF force comprising fourteen Ki-21 Sally light bombers and fifteen Ki-43 Oscar fighters, attacked a Royal Navy force that had been bombarding Japanese forces along the Arakan coast. Scrambling from an airfield in the vicinity of Chittagong, twelve Spitfires of 136 Squadron RAF intercepted and broke through the fighter cover to find the bombers flying in perfectly disciplined 'V' formation – a formation resolutely maintained by the Japanese as the RAF fighters shot them down, one by one. Having completely destroyed the bomber force the Spitfires set about the Japanese fighters and in a series of dogfights destroyed the majority of the typically brightly coloured Oscars, those that did survive limping home badly the worse for the encounter. One Spitfire was lost, the pilot having a lucky escape as he descended by parachute. An Oscar swept by and machine-gunned the helpless airman, but the Japanese pilot misjudged his approach and crashed into the ground. This was the first substantial victory that the RAF, and certainly the new Air Command South East Asia, had been able to achieve over the JAAF and was without doubt a turning point in the air war.

On 15 January the JAAF tried again, this time the intended target being Chittagong itself, however the plan was for three fighter sweeps of between twelve and fifteen aircraft apiece to attack the Arakan battle area to draw off defending fighters and leave the port open to the bombers. As early morning mist lifted the first attack materialized and the Spitfires were scrambled. The Japanese pilots might well have been smarting from a loss of 'face' stemming from their defeat at the turn of the year, as they appear to have adopted do-or-die tactics in their efforts to come to terms with their opponents; but fanatical courage was not enough. Sixteen Oscars were destroyed at a cost of two Spitfires. On 20 January the JAAF tried again, 35 Oscars engaging 24 Spitfires and losing 7 of their number for 2 RAF aircraft.

With these battles the RAF wrested air superiority from the JAAF for the first time in the south, but the Japanese did not let it rest there and introduced the Ki-44 Tojo in greater numbers to counter the Spitfire Mk Vs, coupled with new tactics. JAAF fighters would usually be painted in the ostentatious colour schemes of their particular *Hikosentai* but now a few appeared with either their aluminium skins highly burnished to a mirror-like finish, or alternatively painted jet black, both colour schemes designed to be observed with ease from a distance. A few of these decoys would fly well below more numerous camouflaged aircraft in the hope of trapping Spitfire pilots, who soon learned to be wary of such glittering prizes. Fortunately for the Allies the much improved Spitfire Mk VIII made its appearance and with its true air speed of 419 mph in Burmese conditions, plus a service ceiling of 41,000 feet and faster rate of climb than the Spitfire Mk V, the JAAF was check-mated again. To the north, however, the issue of air superiority was still very much in the balance and it was to this sector that the scene of action once again moved, with 5th *Hikoshidan* using its entire fighter strength to attack transport aircraft on the Hump route in the skies above Sumprabum in northern Burma.

While the battles were fought in the skies overhead, down below the ground crews worked unceasingly, stripping, polishing, repairing engines and air frames, working until all hours of the night to get aircraft ready for the next day's sorties. Medical records show that of the Allied ground crew that had been in Burma/India since the beginning, by early 1944 almost half had lost two stone in weight and three quarters of them had contracted malaria or dysentery, some several times.

Notes

1. Slim, Field Marshal Viscount, *Defeat Into Victory* (Pan Grand Strategy Series, 1999), p. 163.
2. Quoted in *Wings of the Phoenix* (HMSO, 1949), p. 31.

3. TNA Air 41/37, *Air Supply Operations in Burma*, p. 5.
4. Franks, Norman L.R., *First in the Indian Skies* (The RAF Collection in conjunction with 31 Squadron Royal Air Force Association, 1981), pp. 93–4.
5. Ismay, General The Lord, *The Memoirs of Lord Ismay* (Wm. Heinemann, 1960), p. 305.
6. *Op. cit.*, Note 3, p. 7.
7. *Ibid.*, p. 9.
8. Koenig, William, *Over the Hump, Airlift to China* (Pan/Ballantine, 1972), p. 45.
9. Memo for Commanding General, USAAF, from Colonel C.R. Smith, subject India-China Ferry Operations, dated 13 October 1942. Quoted in *The Army Air Forces in World War II*, Volume VII, W.F. Craven & J.L. Cate (eds) (The University of Chicago Press, 1958), p. 120.
10. *Ibid.*, p. 123.
11. *Japanese Monograph No. 64* (Library of Congress, Washington DC), pp. 32 & 49.
12. TNA Air 2/7907, Despatch on Air Operations 21st June to 15th November, Air Chief Marshal Sir Richard E.C. Peirse, pp. 38–9.
13. Flight Lieutenant Wilfred Goold DFC, in correspondence with the author.
14. *Op. cit.*, Note 9, p. 43.
15. *Op. cit.*, Note 8, pp. 17–18.
16. *Op. cit.*, Note 9, p. 18.
17. *Ibid.*, p. 52.
18. Also aboard, but not in connection with India/Burma, was Wing Commander Guy Gibson of 617 'Dam Busters' Squadron. Air Chief Marshal Harris had appealed to Churchill to take Gibson with him by way of an enforced rest for the young flyer.
19. Portal Papers, File 12, Correspondence with Supreme Commander SE Asia, E1, quoted in Probert, Air Commodore Henry, *The Forgotten Air Force* (Brassey's, 1995), p. 150.
20. *Op. cit.*, Note 2, p. 42.
21. *Op. cit.*, Note 1, pp. 211–12.
22. Hata, Ikuhiko et al., *Japanese Army Air Force Fighter Units and their Aces 1931–1945* (Grub Street, 2002), p. 199.
23. *Op. cit.*, Note 11.
24. *Op. cit.*, Note 2, p. 44.

Chapter Five

Crescendo

I

The spring and summer of 1944 saw the ground war in India/Burma reach its peak as both sides, rested and reorganized, clashed to decide the issue once and for all in South East Asia.

With plans for an amphibious landing shelved due to a lack of landing craft and other essentials – all of which were required by the Allies for D-Day in Europe – General Slim planned, in conjunction with the Chinese, a series of advances along the entire Burma front but with the principal attacks mounted on the two flanks, north and south. In the north the US-trained Chinese troops of Lieutenant General Stilwell's Northern Combat Area Command would combine with Chinese Nationalist forces in an advance from Yunnan to capture the Hukawng Valley and the vital airfield at Myitkyina. This would allow the airlift to move southward via Myitkyina thus avoiding the Himalayas, and facilitate the completion of the Ledo Road from Assam to Kunming in China. Such had been the impression created by Wingate at the Quebec Conference that he was given command of a much-expanded Chindit force which was to be flown into Burma and dropped behind Japanese lines to support the campaign in the north. Stilwell also raised a guerrilla force of his own, 5307 Composite Unit (Provisional), commanded by his Chief of Staff Brigadier General Frank D. Merrill and manned by US troops that specifically included Sioux Indians and Japanese Americans. The American force trained with the Chindits and became better – although unofficially – known as Merrill's Marauders.

To the south in the Arakan XV Corps, commanded by Lieutenant General Christison, would advance south to capture Akyab, while on the central front IV Corps, commanded by Lieutenant General Scoones, would make probing attacks from Imphal into the provinces of Tiddim and Tamu with units of the 17th and 20th Indian Divisions respectively.

The Japanese also made significant changes to their command structure during 1943. Ground forces were reorganized into the Burma Area Army under Lieutenant General Kawabe Masakazu, with Lieutenant General Mutaguchi Renya replacing Iida in command of the Fifteenth Army. Mutaguchi was a fire-eater with a colourful background. In 1937 the first shots of the China Incident were fired by his troops, in the process fanning the flames of conflict against the wishes and instructions of the Japanese government of the day. While the invasion of India was never avowed Japanese policy it is believed that General Tojo, Mutaguchi's Commanding Officer at the time of the China Incident and now Japan's Prime Minister, clandestinely planned with Mutaguchi to use the Indian National Army (INA),[1] units of which were based with the Fifteenth Army, to precede Japanese forces into India, take advantage of Indian pressure for independence, foment trouble for the British and create an excuse for Japanese troops to enter – much as the previously mentioned China Incident preceded Japanese incursions into China.

To counter anticipated Allied offensive operations two new Japanese armies were created, the Twenty-Eighth, under the command of Lieutenant General Sakurai Shozo, in the Arakan, and the Thirty-Third, under the command of Lieutenant General Honda Masaki, in northern Burma. To accompany the formation of the new armies the Imperial High Command devised two major operations of their own. HA-GO tasked Sakurai's Thirty-Third Army with the envelopment and annihilation of the 5th and 7th Divisions of Christison's XV Corps, in the process preventing the reinforcement of the Allied centre where the much more ambitious operation U-GO was planned. For this attack Mutaguchi's Fifteenth Army was to destroy Scoones's IV Corps around Imphal and Kohima preparatory to an advance into India, initially to cut the Bengal–Assam railway which fed the airfields from which supplies were flown to China, and thereafter seize the airfields themselves. With the successful completion of these operations there remained the very real possibility of an advance farther into India with the assistance of the INA.

Denied amphibious resources Slim's plan for the Arakan was necessarily limited, involving an advance by 5th and 7th Indian Divisions along the spine and both sides of the Mayu Range to capture the small port of Maungdaw, and the road leading from there to Buthidaung in the valley of the Kalapanzin River. This was the only road to traverse the entire length of the Mayu Range, although some 5 miles to the north a narrow footpath crossed through the Ngakyedauk Pass – known to the British contingent among the Allied infantry as the 'Okedoke' Pass. Farther still to the east 81st West African Division would advance down the Kaladan Valley both to act as flank guard and threaten the main

Japanese east–west line of communications. Because of the nature of the terrain to be traversed the West Africans would be the first large army formation – the Chindits were essentially guerrillas – to be supplied completely by air.

Opposing this advance the Japanese Twenty-Eighth Army had in place the 55th Division with units around Akyab and in the Kaladan Valley, plus reinforcements in the shape of the 54th Division.

Air forces available to the Allies for the pivotal months of campaigning to come were 48 RAF and 17 USAAF squadrons in January 1944, rising to 64 and 28 respectively by May.

The Second Arakan campaign began with Christison's XV Corps offensive, which began on 30 November 1943. Meeting stiff resistance the Allied advance made slow progress and it was not until the first week of January 1944 that Maungdaw was captured. The port was immediately put into shape to receive reinforcements and supplies, but with Japanese forces still holding the road to Buthidaung in strength, 7th Division Engineers east of the Mayu Range constructed an unmetalled road of their own across the Ngakyedauk Pass to connect them with the 5th Division on the crest and the coastal plain. This road would suffice for a time but the main road still had to be taken and to do so Razabil fortress, prepared by the Japanese for defence to the last, would have to be taken. To precede the infantry attack air strikes were called in to reduce the defences.

With Spitfires making their appearance in numbers for the RAF, the IAF also reaped the benefits to be had from operating more up-to-date equipment No. 8 Squadron achieved combat-ready status in mid December equipped with Vultee Vengeance dive-bombers, and were assigned to ground support operations on the Arakan front. The Vengeances would usually fly in groups of six, dive at a speed of some 300 mph, release their bombs and pull out of their dive at around 2,000 feet from the ground, achieving a high degree of accuracy in the process. At this time practically all dive-bombing operations on the southern front were carried out by No. 8 Squadron IAF and No. 82 Squadron RAF, also equipped with the Vengeance. On occasion these two squadrons would mount more than fifty sorties per day between them.

On 22 January, No. 8 Squadron moved to Joari Strip, during the course of that month flying 217 sorties totalling 354 hours 26 minutes. It was from here that on 26 January the Vengeances were called upon to attack the Razabil area, but with Japanese entrenchments extending to as much as 30 feet below ground the dive-bombers were unable to carry sufficient weight of bombs to make much impression. Christison therefore called for the assistance of the Strategic Air Force, which attacked with 16 Liberator B24 heavy bombers and 10 Mitchell B25 medium bombers of the USAAF, supported by 24 Vengeances of the RAF and IAF. The total bomb load dropped amounted to 145,250 lb, of which 50 per cent from the Liberators found the target, 70 per cent from the Mitchells and 100 per cent from the Vengeances, but with little appreciable effect. This was put down to the large area under attack – 1,000 × 600 yards – and the depth of the dugouts. An additional problem was the time lapse between completing the air raid and follow-up assaults by the Army, allowing Japanese infantry time to retake their positions and prepare to receive the attack.

While attempts continued to take Razabil, a decision was taken to attack Buthidaung via the Ngakyedauk Pass, and reinforcements duly tramped their way eastwards across the Mayu. Where the eastern end of the improvised roadway reached the Kalapanzin valley a maintenance area was established at Sinzweya containing supply depots, ammunition dumps, vehicle parks and main dressing stations for the wounded. With reinforcing troops moving off toward Buthidaung and those on the western side of the range fully occupied at Razabil, the maintenance area was left isolated, a fact which both played into the hands of, and ultimately became a thorn in the side of, the Japanese. Operation HA-GO, the planned Japanese offensive in the Arakan, now went forward and in true Japanese style aimed to cut off 7th Division in the Kalapanzin Valley by swinging around their left. Slim had anticipated such a move but admits to being caught by surprise when, on the morning of 4 February, Japanese troops appeared in strength 5 or 6 miles in rear of the Division and within 2 or 3 of the Ngakyedauk Pass.[2] With that heady mixture of skill and luck that attends a great many military victories, General Shozo had placed his troops perfectly, debouching as they did into the Kalapanzin Valley to cut off 7th Indian Division and with little more than the clerks and medical units of the maintenance area between them and the Pass. Should Ngakyedauk fall to this attack Christison's XV Corps would be cut in half and open to the grave risk of being comprehensively defeated in detail, opening up the flank of 5th Indian Division in the process.

The maintenance area at Sinzweya, shortly to become better known as the 'Admin Box', was located in a natural depression approximately one mile long by half a mile wide and enclosed on all sides by jungle-clad hills. General Messervy, the commander of 7th Division, had located his Headquarters some 3 miles or so north-east of the maintenance area and had pushed all available troops forward, including the Sikh battalion assigned as HQ guard, consequently with the approach of the Japanese flank attack, defence devolved upon the

HQ staff, in particular the Divisional Signals unit and a company of Indian Engineers, who conducted a fighting retreat to Sinzweya.

The situation in which XV Corps now found itself was perilous in the extreme, but, despite his being surprised by the timing, the attack was not only what General Slim expected but had in fact planned for. During his time campaigning against the Japanese in Burma Slim had observed that they operated to very tight logistical limits and aimed to turn this chink in their armour to his advantage. Japanese attacks almost invariably went forward carrying with them very little in the way of supplies, fully expecting that once outflanked the British and Commonwealth troops would dissolve into retreat and the attackers would press forward using food and other equipment left by their opponents in their rush to escape the trap. Prior to the opening of the campaigning season Slim issued orders to all Allied troops that if outflanked they were NOT to retreat but dig in where they were and be reinforced and provisioned from the air. In this way Slim hoped to deny Allied supplies to the Japanese who, as their own were used up, would be severely hampered by long land-based lines of communication open to the threat of continual disruption from the air. Slim hoped that Japanese ground troops could in this way be 'bled dry' of the means to wage war and be comprehensively defeated in the process. The strategy applied to the whole of the Allied front in Burma/India and was first tested in the heat of battle at Sinzweya, where the clerks and admin staff did not retreat, but dug in as ordered and prepared to fight it out.

General Slim's strategy had the brilliant simplicity of the true masterstroke, but inevitably was not without risk. From the perspective of the air forces the Japanese offensive in the Arakan coincided with advanced preparations for Stilwell's forward movement from China and Wingate's second Chindit expedition, both of which placed high demand upon available transport aircraft, in addition to which existing operations had to be maintained, including the considerable task of maintaining 81st West African Division in the Kaladan Valley. In order to enable Troop Carrier Command to carry out all its commitments without reduction in the scope of any of the ground operations Admiral Mountbatten approached the Combined Chiefs of Staff to request the temporary diversion of transport aircraft from 'The Hump' route while the 7th Division emergency existed. Permission was duly given and twenty-five Curtiss C46 Commandos flew south to commence operations over the Arakan from the third week of February.

Large-scale transport operations could not be carried out, however, without achieving air superiority in the north and maintaining the air superiority gained in the south with the advent of the Spitfire. The JAAF introduction of the Ki-44 Tojo to supplement the Ki-43 Oscar fighters was accompanied by another change in tactics which involved Japanese aircraft adopting a defensive circle and splitting into small groups when the circle was broken. When operating at their optimum performance height, around 10,000 feet, this method put a premium on the manoeuvrability of the JAAF aircraft against the superior performance of the Spitfire Mk VIII in particular, the experience of No. 136 Squadron RAF, the first to be equipped with the Mk VIII, showing that attacks tended to be delivered at too high a speed leading to a falling off in marksmanship.

Still equipped with their Mk Vs, 607 Squadron was one of those at the sharp end of the battle to maintain the RAF's grip on the skies above the Arakan. Wilfred Goold recalls the period:

February opened up with even more aggression by the Japanese Air Force. Scrambles were an almost daily occurrence with anywhere from 50+ to 100+ usually about 7 to 8 in the morning. Nervous pees were the order of the day and this became a problem. When the phone rang in the dispersal there was a mad rush to get to our planes, only to find it was Ops wanting a weather report!! DOC solved it by having the phones in a separate basha, and, if a scramble was on, a Klaxon horn was blown. At the same time, Sigs rigged up a system where the ground crew could listen in to the interception, which was great for morale.

Intense activity continued and I see on February 9, 70+ and I recall that we intercepted with good height, with the Japs everywhere as usual. I, with my No. 2, dived in, attacked this Oscar, saw hits on his tail assembly – then he was gone. I pulled up and repeated the exercise, but this time it was a melee, with planes turning everywhere. Pulling up again, I lost my No. 2 and then dived into the beehive again without success. Pulling up again, this time I formated (sic) with three Jap Oscars, the leader had a bright orange cowl. I don't know who was the more surprised!!

As I was on my own and there were three of them, I decided to get out, so I put everything in the corner, pushed the throttle through the gate and headed for the deck. This time they didn't follow me, so I levelled off at tree top and headed for home. Almost immediately I saw two Oscars ahead and up a bit. I was closing fast. I opened fire on the left plane and saw heavy strikes on his fuselage, and his canopy shattered; he did a violent turn to the left. I switched to the other and as he also turned left, hit him in the tail unit and fuselage. I didn't hang around to see the results as the Japs had been using this tactic to get to unsuspecting planes returning north. I expected that there would be others around!

I had no sooner landed and got out when some Oscars followed our Spits back to base. They made a run down the runway, strafing what they could. My claims for this sortie were one probable, two damaged. The next day the Army confirmed two Jap fighters crashing in the area where I had made my claim, so my claims for those two were confirmed.[3]

Under cover of the fighter squadrons the transports flew resupply missions over the 'Admin Box' as the 7th Division stood its ground. Pressure on both ground troops and aircrew was intense, and as the Japanese pressed forward the DZ available to the transports on which to parachute their cargoes shrank to 200 × 60 yards. Despite the attentions of the JAAF and accurate small-arms fire from the ground, only one Dakota was lost during the battle, the 31 Squadron aircraft of Flight Lieutenant J.A. 'Johnnie' Walker of the RCAF, shot down by an Oscar on 8 February. Nat Gould, the aircraft wireless operator, survived the crash and walked back to base through enemy lines.[4] The lack of casualties among the lumbering transports may seem surprising but appears to stem from a fundamental error by the JAAF, who completely failed to appreciate the significance of resupply from the air, not only in the Arakan but in later battles, preferring to attack Allied fighters and bombers while leaving the transports, without which Allied ground operations could not proceed, relatively untouched. Possibly there was something in the 'warrior code' which made attacking unarmed transports beneath the Japanese fighter pilots of the day. If so, it was a blunder of monumental proportions.

With one eye on the impending Operation U-GO, 5th *Hikoshidan* concentrated most of its strength in the Imphal area. Operations on the Arakan front were carried out by 7th *Hikodan* supported by 4th *Hikodan*, having been instructed to keep the Allied air forces in the south busy by concentrating a high rate of activity into the ten-day period before the main Japanese ground assault at Imphal was due to begin. At times as many as eighty sorties would be launched per day, nearly all with fighters, rarely with bombers.

One of the many dogfights in which the JAAF attempted to wrest air superiority back from the RAF erupted over Maungdaw on 8 February. Colonel Yoshio Hirose, commander of the 64th *Hikosentai*, claimed as his personal tally three Spitfires, while three Ki-43 Oscars were lost from his command.[5]

The period of greatest danger for the 7th Division was the fortnight between 7 and 20 February, during which RAF and USAAF transports flew 639 sorties and their fighter escorts 342. In addition to the necessary weapons and supplies of war, unessential items such as the new SEAC newspaper, cigarettes and mail from home were also parachuted into the 'Box' to instil into the men on the ground the idea that their situation was temporary, not hopeless. At the beginning of the airlift, General Slim, wise in the ways of the 'poor bloody infantryman', helpfully suggested that perhaps a case of rum might be put into every fourth or fifth aircraft to make sure that the troops on the ground *really* searched for the supplies that had been parachuted to them. Major General Alfred

Snelling, Slim's officer in charge of administration, patiently explained that he had already given orders that a case of rum should be put into *every* aircraft for just that purpose![6] One area of air supply where Slim did have an appreciable effect was in the matter of parachutes. As with everything else in South East Asia the silken variety were in very short supply while the demand for dropping as opposed to landing supplies soared. Slim believed that an acceptable alternative capable of being used for dropping supplies (not men) could be made from jute – in plentiful supply in Bengal. Having sent his personal representatives to the – at the time mainly British – leaders of the jute industry in Calcutta, Slim received an enthusiastic response and following a month of trial and error the 'parajute' was born, made entirely of jute, even the ropes, and 85 per cent as efficient as its more elaborate silken cousin. A side benefit that might be thought to have brought a wintry smile to the denizens of the Treasury was the cost – £1 for a parajute set against £20 for a silk parachute. In fact a display of the worst type of narrow civil service mind set saw to it that Slim was the recipient not of congratulations but a rebuke from Whitehall for not obtaining supply through the proper channels![7]

The battle of the 'Admin Box' lasted for seventeen days, and not only did 7th Indian Division not retreat, but, reinforced and supplied by air it became one of the jaws of a pincer movement which, combined with reinforcements approaching from the north, in turn trapped the Japanese. Denied Allied supplies by Slim's strategy and by now chronically short of food and ammunition, the hitherto unbeatable Japanese infantry broke and ran, leaving an estimated 5,000 of the 8,000 or so who initially carried out the attack dead on the battlefield. With the Allied assault at Anzio in the balance and the Russian spring offensive under way little attention was given to the victory in Burma by the world's media, but the effect on the morale of Fourteenth Army was electric. The enemy, until recently believed to be virtually invincible, had been soundly beaten and would never again boast the almost hypnotic advantage gained during the Allied disasters of the early days of the war in South East Asia.

The Allied ground troops fought brilliantly but the victory could not have been won without resupply from the air, and the transports would not have been able to operate without the air superiority gained by the fighters. Ground and air forces had become completely interdependent and would remain so for the great battles still to be fought in India and Burma.

During the course of the Second Arakan offensive RAF and USAAF transports delivered over 10,000 tons of supplies to the 5th, 7th and 81st Divisions in just over 3,000 sorties.[8]

Brewster Buffaloes – 'The Flying Barrel'. Although modern these aircraft were unloved by the RAF and outclassed by Japanese fighters.
Imperial War Museum Photo KI 196.

Curtiss P40 Warhawks (Tomahawks in RAF nomenclature) of the American Volunteer Group being assembled. They have not yet received their distinctive 'shark's teeth' paintwork.
Imperial War Museum Photo KI 161.

Above & below: Two views of the Nakajima Ki-27 Nate fighter showing the distinctive fixed undercarriage and spatted wheels.
National Archive Maryland USA Photo No. 8-G-15376.

An RAF Blenheim bombing Pauktaw, Burma, 20 May 1943. Bomb bursts can clearly be seen below the aircraft. The venerable Blenheims performed good service but were phased out shortly afterwards. *Royal Air Force Museum London Photo AC97/98/13.*

A Vultee Vengence dive-bomber lands at a forward airstrip ready to be prepared for its next raid. *Imperial War Museum Photo IND 3185.*

Squadron Leader Narinjan Prasad of the Indian Air Force, CO of an IAF Vengence squadron. The IAF successfully operated two such squadrons. *Imperial War Museum Photo IND 3114.*

Nakajima Ki-43 Oscar, the principal fighter operated by the Japanese Army Air Force in the China/Burma/India theatre.
National Archive Maryland USA Photo No. 80-G-603454.

Hawker Hurricane MkIIC. Although outperformed by the Japanese Oscar the Hurricane did great service, first as a fighter and later in its 'Hurribomber' fighter-bomber role.
Imperial War Museum Photo CI 191.

A Vickers Wellington MkX waits on an airstrip as Indian infantry prepare to embark for the front in a nearby transport aircraft, and a monsoon storm blots out the mountains in the background. *Imperial War Museum Photo CF 154.*

Fast, high-flying Mitsubishi Ki-46 Dinah reconnaissance aircraft, invulnerable to Allied interception attempts until the arrival of the Spitfire in late 1943. *Imperial War Museum Photo E 1285.*

RAF Consolidated B24 Liberator heavy bombers over Ramree Island. *Imperial War Museum Photo C4939.*

A Douglas C47 Dakota transport of 2nd Troop Carrier Squadron USAAF. Note the permanently open fuselage door for supply dropping operations.

Royal Air Force Museum Photo Group B1125.

Brigadier General William D. Old USAAF, AOC Troop Carrier Command.

Watched by curious Burmese, 152 Squadron motor transport echelon calls a halt on the Magwe/Meiktila road to brew a cup of 'Char'. *Photo: Ronald White, 152 Squadron.*

Mitsubishi Ki-21 Sally heavy bombers.

Left to right: Air Commodore (later Air Vice-Marshal) Vincent, Field Marshal Wavell, the Maharaja of Patiala, Air Chief Marshal Sir Richard Peirse.

Imperial War Museum Photo IND 1901.

Flight Sergeant Alex (Paddy) Calvert shaking hands with Air Vice-Marshal Bouchier, AOC 221 Group. Squadron Leader Pegge, Officer Commanding 607 Squadron, stands behind the Air Vice-Marshal. *Photo: Alex Calvert, 607 Squadron.*

USAAF Curtiss C46 Commando transports on the tarmac awaiting loads for the besieged defenders of Imphal.
Royal Air Force Museum London Photo Group B1126.

Men of the RAF Regiment in the Imphal valley. Top left is Squadron Leader T.F. Ryalls, Officer Commanding all RAF Regimental units in the valley.

Imperial War Museum photo CI692

The Dimapur/Kohima 'road' along which reinforcements had to fight their way while the besieged defenders of the Imphal Plain were supplied from the air.

Photo: Ronald White, 152 Squadron

Aerial view of Rangoon jail clearly showing the messages JAPS GONE and EXTRACT DIGIT.
Royal Air Force Museum London photo AC97/98/18

A subdued group of Japanese envoys arrive at Mingaladon Airfield near Rangoon for the surrender, August 1945. *Photo: Ronald White, 152 Squadron.*

Supermarine Spitfire MkVIII of No.155 Squadron RAF operating from a forward airstrip in Burma. More than any other aircraft it was the Spitfire that enabled the RAF to wrest air superiority from the Japanese Army Air Force.
Imperial War Museum Photo CF 271.

II

As the glow faded from the embers of the battles around Sinzweya Christison's XV Corps once more began its advance, but in March 1944 momentous events were taking place elsewhere along the Burma front.

In October 1943, coinciding with the opening of Christison's advance in the Arakan, the American-trained Chinese troops of General Stilwell's Northern Area Combat Command, combined with units of the Nationalist Chinese Army and the 3,000-strong US infantry force led by Brigadier General Merrill (code-named Galahad), began an advance from the Chinese province of Yunnan, their objective the strategically crucial airfield at Myitkyina. The advance made slow progress, the Japanese content to give ground slowly as they husbanded men and materiel for their main assault, Operation U-GO at Imphal. By the spring of 1944 the supply of both men and materiel for the Japanese armies was reaching its limit, added to which their shipping was under constant attack, making deliveries to the far-flung territories under their occupation increasingly difficult. Faced by the slow but inexorable strangulation of their armies the Imperial High Command needed a military victory, one which would bring results quickly and decisively enough to irrevocably shift the balance of power in their favour. They saw their chance at Imphal. Should Mutaguchi's Fifteenth Army be able to destroy IV Corps and break through into Assam the Japanese calculated that they could halt supplies to China, force Chiang Kai-shek to the negotiating table and a peace treaty, and thereby release vast numbers of battle-hardened Japanese troops for operations in the Pacific and elsewhere. Faced with the prospect of a much longer war than anticipated, might not public opinion force the United States Administration to reconsider and sue for peace? And there was always the tantalizing prospect of replacing the British as masters of India.

In the Imphal area General Scoones' IV Corps, comprising three Indian divisions, had been conducting limited advances, constructing roads and making preparations for a major attack when sufficient forces should become available. By February 1944, 17th Indian Division (The Black Cats) had advanced southward through the Chin Hills some 150 miles from Imphal to the area of Tiddim, but had been stopped in its intention to swing left and reach the Chindwin River at Kalewa by stiff Japanese opposition. Eighty or so miles of wild mountainous jungle farther east the 20th Division made a more limited southward movement as far as Palel/Tamu. The remaining division, the 23rd, remained in and around Imphal together with 254 Indian Tank Brigade.

Through an increase in activity on the part of the Japanese plus numerous intelligence reports from ground patrols and air reconnaissance indicating the arrival of substantial reinforcements, Scoones and Slim were by now well aware that a major offensive was coming their way and decided that of the options available the best way to meet it would be to concentrate IV Corps at Imphal and fight the battle on ground of their own choosing. This would oblige Mutaguchi, as with Shozo in the Arakan, to make a major assault at the end of long land-based lines of communication with his forces lightly provisioned and expecting to capitalize on a rapid Allied retreat.

The Imphal plain is approximately 40 miles long by 20 miles wide and forms the only oasis of flat ground to be found among the mountains that separate the Brahmaputra Valley of India from the plains of Central Burma. Used as an Allied base from the time of the retreat in 1942 Imphal boasted orderly military camps, hutted hospitals, supply dumps, ordnance depots, engineer parks and wide tarmac roads, some far-flung across the 600 square miles of the plain but most around the village of Imphal itself and, 25 miles to the south, Palel, their dispersal being according to need and with offensive not defensive operations in mind. An estimated sixty to seventy thousand Indian non-combatants, mostly labourers, also inhabited the plain. One hundred and thirty miles to the north a sizeable military railhead had been hacked out of the jungle at Dimapur, connected by a single mountain road to Kohima and from there down into the plain at Imphal.[9]

The impending monsoon would have considerable bearing on the campaign to come. If IV Corps could hold until the weather broke the Japanese line of communication would be tenuous indeed, but by the same token Allied resupply and reinforcement would have to be flown in, for which possession of the only two all-weather airstrips on the plain, at Imphal and Palel villages, would be vital.

To achieve the decisive victory that he hoped for Slim planned to draw the Japanese onto the plain, then move the 5th and 7th Divisions in by air from the Arakan, to be replaced in the south by troops from India. Slim was also given the Indian Parachute Brigade and arrangements were put in hand to move the 2nd British Division overland from India should the need arise.

With US forces advancing slowly from the north, the Japanese still putting up stubborn resistance in the Arakan to the south, and a make-or-break struggle about to explode in the centre, a fourth large-scale assault was thrown into the mix. This was Major General Wingate's ambitious second Chindit operation, code-named 'Operation Thursday', comprising 12,000 Indian, British and West African troops. The common denominator for all four operations as far as the Allies were concerned was that they all relied heavily on air transport – and there were not enough transport aircraft available to maintain peak activity on several fronts at once. Timing would be crucial – and not just on the part of the Allies. At Imphal Slim and Scoones came to the conclusion that Mutaguchi would attack in early March, however, should the assault commence at a time when Troop Carrier Command was committed to ferrying the Chindits into northern Burma, the result could quite easily be disaster at Imphal.

At the Quebec conference Wingate made a highly favourable impression, particularly on the Americans, who not only backed a second large-scale operation but agreed to provide it with what amounted to its own air force. A major problem with the first Chindit expedition was the exceptional difficulty experienced in bringing out the wounded. At Quebec Mountbatten suggested the formation of a light air-ambulance service using aircraft such as the small American-built Stinson L.1 and L.5 monoplanes, capable of short take-off and landing in restricted jungle clearings and the rapid transportation to safety of several casualties per flight – British forces used de Havilland Tiger Moth and Fox Moth light aircraft for this purpose in the Arakan. The idea was accepted and by the time Operation Thursday entered the final planning stage it had blossomed into the Air Commando Group, comprising not only the air ambulances but B25 Mitchell bombers, P51 Mustang fighter-bombers, C47 Dakota transports, gliders and helicopters. The force was provided by General 'Hap' Arnold, Commanding General of the USAAF, and led by Colonel Philip Cochran, a 34-year-old USAAF fighter pilot. Formally under Air Marshal Baldwin of the Third Tactical Air Force, in fact Cochran planned the air side of the operation directly with Wingate.

While the Air Commando would carry the spearhead of the assault and initially maintain the group once behind enemy lines, such was the scale of the operation – the transportation by air of 10,000 men of the unit total – that the British and American squadrons of Troop Carrier Command would be required to fly in the majority of the personnel and their equipment and subsequently shoulder much of the supply work.

The purpose of the operation was to disrupt the supply network of the Japanese forces facing Stilwell and generally create as many problems for the Imperial Japanese Army as possible. The 2,000 Chindits who were to enter Burma on foot departed in mid February, maintained from the air by Troop Carrier Command, while D-Day for transportation of the initial glider-borne component was set for 5 March.

Given the scarcity of transport aircraft already referred to the scale of effort required for Operation Thursday was daunting. Forty-four Dakotas from Nos 31, 62, 117 and 194 Squadrons RAF combined with thirty-nine from the 27th and 315th Troop Carrier Squadrons and

111

one squadron of the 5318th Air Unit, USAAF, the RAF operating from Tulihal, the USAAF from Lalaghat.[10]

Three landing grounds were selected for the initial landings, code-named 'Piccadilly', 'Broadway' and 'Chowringhee', although only the first two were designated for use on the first night and of these 'Piccadilly' was the primary site. However, with 'tug' aircraft and gliders lined up ready to go on the departure strip at Lalaghat on the evening of the 5th, a plot twist worthy of Hollywood occurred when an officer ran on to the strip bearing a still wet copy of a low-level air reconnaissance photograph taken that afternoon. The image had been taken by Lieutenant Russhon using a hand-held camera from a Mitchell B25 of the Combat Camera Unit, and was now being rapidly transported to a group of high-ranking officers waiting on the strip for the operation to commence. What they saw instead was a photograph showing all too clearly that teak logs hidden with buffalo grass now obstructed 'Piccadilly' to such an extent that it could not be used. Fortunately the officers present at Lalaghat included Wingate, Air Marshal Baldwin, General Slim, General Stratemeyer, Air Vice-Marshal Williams, General Old and Colonel Cochran (at whose instigation the Mitchell had been despatched on its last-minute reconnaissance). The group immediately went into a huddle amid much discussion around the question of whether the enemy had discovered the operation and whether departure of the troops should be delayed for a few days while further investigation was carried out, or even cancelled altogether. Also under discussion was the fact that the same Mitchell had also photographed 'Broadway', which was clear, opening up the possibility that the Japanese had set up an ambush at that location.

What finally decided the issue was the fact that 'Piccadilly' had been used once during the first Chindit expedition and a photograph of the strip had appeared in the American *Life* magazine. The consensus of opinion, therefore, was that the Japanese had neutralized a known landing site, not discovered the operation. The airlift was back on but those aircraft briefed for 'Piccadilly' would have to be redirected to 'Broadway'. Given the task of notifying the crews and troops involved, Colonel Cochran knew that such a literally last-minute change would cause consternation among the men and chose to make his approach with a classic display of American 'front'. 'Look boys,' he said, 'we've found a better place to go – Broadway!'[11]

At just after 6.00 pm, not much more than one hour after the officer had appeared on the strip with the photograph, the first Dakota lifted off, and almost immediately there arose another problem. Gliders had been rigged to their 'tug' aircraft in pairs owing to the shortage of transports, a system which in practice proved to be unwieldy in the extreme. Buffeted by evening turbulence and the slipstream from the Dakotas, a total of nine gliders, heavy with their loads of troops, bulldozers and other equipment, broke free from their tow ropes during the course of the flight and crashed. Tow rope failure was in part put down to the fact that being made of nylon the ropes had necessarily been laid out along the edge of the airstrip at Lalaghat for around two weeks in order that kinks could be removed, but while there trucks had driven over them weakening the threads. This, added to the high rate of climb necessary to clear the mountains, caused a number of failures.

Arriving over 'Broadway' gliders were set free but on landing found that the strip contained numerous undulations not visible from photographs. Several crashes ensued, each wrecked glider becoming a hazard to those that followed. With darkness falling and disaster beckoning Lieutenant Colonel Allison of the USAAF rapidly improvised a system of airfield control, signalled news of the problems on the airstrip and got the fly-in stopped while the obstructions were cleared. Of the sixty-one gliders despatched on the night of 5/6 March only thirty-five reached 'Broadway', but by the following evening an American airborne engineer unit assisted by British and Gurkha troops had levelled the strip sufficiently for C47 Dakotas to be able to land. As was his habit Brigadier General W.D. Old was in the forefront of the operation, personally piloting the first C47 to land at 'Broadway'. With transports arriving and leaving at a rate of one every three minutes during the night hours the backlog of personnel and equipment was rapidly cleared and by D plus six 9,052 personnel, 175 ponies, 1,183 mules, and 509,083 lb of stores had been transported.[12] Seventy-eight Dakotas landed at 'Chowringhee' on the night of 8/9 March and a further forty on the night of 9/10 March, completing the schedule for this airstrip which was then abandoned.[13]

Aided by diversionary bombing raids around Bhamo and Indaw, such was the success of diversionary measures employed that the Japanese did not discover 'Broadway' until two waves of fifteen JAAF fighters swept the area on 13 March, by which time a detachment of Spitfires from No. 81 Squadron RAF had been stationed there and shot down three of the interlopers, damaging a further six. One Spitfire was lost and one Japanese fighter brought down by anti-aircraft fire. On 23 March the final Chindit brigade was landed at a further improvised airstrip, code-named 'Aberdeen'. Not one transport aircraft had been lost but, ironically, the following day, 24 March, Wingate was killed when his personal aircraft, a Mitchell bomber, crashed in the Naga Hills during a storm. Command devolved upon a seasoned Chindit campaigner, Brigadier Lentaigne.

*

As Operation Thursday commenced the military temperature in the centre around Imphal also began to rise significantly. On 6 March troops of the Japanese 33rd Division attacked 17th Division units around Tiddim and in accordance with their usual practice attempted to work their way around the flanks to cut the road to Imphal. The assault increased in strength over succeeding days until on 13 March Scoones ordered 17th Division to withdraw to the Imphal plain.

Further north, across the Chindwin and facing the 20th Division, Mutaguchi massed his 15th and 31st Divisions and on the night of 15/16 March both moved forward in earnest, crossing the Chindwin in strength. Slim describes these attacks, which developed to the north of Imphal, as resembling the probing fingers of an extended hand, moving to cut off Kohima from both the railhead at Dimapur and Imphal, isolating Imphal itself in the process. When the columns converged and the fingers of the hand closed the Japanese fully expected the British to be annihilated on that front.

By the end of March Japanese forces had cut the road from Tiddim to Imphal, the road from Imphal to Kohima, and swept around to Bishenpur to the west of the plain. The bulk of IV Corps was now surrounded, the garrison at Kohima besieged, both relying on support from the air to avoid destruction. The situation was in some ways similar to that which developed around the 'Admin Box', but on a much larger scale, in addition to which IV Corps had its own air cover in the shape of 221 Group, also based on the Imphal Plain. For Slim's plan to work IV Corps had to be maintained in fighting trim by air while the Japanese, without an air transport system in any way comparable to that of the Allies, used up what supplies they had. Large-scale resupply by capturing Allied reserves would be denied them, as would bringing supplies overland, with Allied fighters and bombers creating havoc along Mutaguchi's extended road and rail communications. The plan had already begun to work in a small way. Japanese troops attacking 17th Division around Tiddim planned to capture and use the extensive divisional motor transport, but the Division retreated in good order and took its transport back to Imphal.

Of crucial importance to the outcome of the battles on the Imphal plain, the Allied air transport system now found itself hard pressed, not only by the extensive demands in the centre, but the requirements of Operation Thursday and Stilwell's advance from the north. As can now be seen, had the Chindit operation been delayed by a few days, as at one point seemed likely, the main Japanese assault at Imphal would have coincided with a significant proportion of Troop Carrier Command ferrying Wingate's troops into northern Burma – with a high degree of probability that disaster would have overtaken either IV Corps or the

Chindits as a result. As it was Troop Carrier Command was stretched to the limit and on 16 March Mountbatten ordered that once again transports should be diverted from 'The Hump' route, this time twenty Curtiss C46 Commandos. The Combined Chiefs of Staff backed the move but stipulated that they must be returned within one month.

5th *Hikoshidan* also found its objectives unexpectedly split and instead of committing its full force to the support of Fifteenth Army's assault at Imphal was required to dilute its offensive capability by attacking both IV Corps and the Chindit operation farther north. As an instance on 15–17 March raids were carried out on the defenders at Imphal, but on the 16th at least part of the available force was required to attack Wingate's raiders as they attempted to establish new airstrips. On the 18th the main air offensive was switched from Imphal to the Chindits in support of a ground attack which in the event did not materialize for some days thereafter. Such had been the requirement for support from the air, first over the Arakan, then the Chindit operation and Imphal, that at a crucial juncture in the latter operation, the four days from 20 March, 5th *Hikoshidan* was withdrawn completely in an attempt to replenish losses in men and materiel. To bolster its efforts 5th *Hikoshidan* received temporary reinforcement in the shape of the 62nd *Hikosentai* (heavy bombers) which arrived in Burma in the middle of March and remained until the middle of August, and 87th *Hikosentai* (fighters) which arrived in Burma on 7 March and remained for two weeks before returning to Sumatra. A significant loss to the *Hikoshidan* during the course of the campaign was the removal to the Pacific theatre of 7th *Hikosentai* (heavy bombers) in the middle of July. A definitive account of the activities of 5th *Hikoshidan* during the Chindit/Imphal campaigns is problematical due to the scarcity of surviving records, however, in so far as is possible a list of operations is given at Appendix II.[14]

The JAAF losses were in part due to the equipping of USAAF fighter units in Assam with long-range P51 North American Mustangs and P38 Lockheed Lightnings, which inflicted heavy casualties on the JAAF both in the air and on the ground. Mustangs and P40 Tomahawks intercepted an incoming enemy raid in the Digboi area on 27 March, claiming 26 destroyed and 4 probables, for the loss of 2 Allied aircraft. Army reconnaissance later discovered twenty-two crashed enemy aircraft in the area of the dogfight. No. 459 Squadron USAAF, equipped with Lightnings, began operations with 224 Group, and in conjunction with the Mustangs was able to supplement Spitfires which were still in comparatively short supply and retained for defensive interceptions. An inevitable but serious contraction of the early warning system around Imphal as the Japanese advanced was offset to some extent by the use of the American long-range fighters to interdict enemy formations as they returned to their bases on the central Irrawaddy plain.

In addition to ordering the C46 Commandos to the Imphal battle area, Mountbatten, in the US General Hospital at Ledo at the time with a serious eye injury, ordered 5th Indian Division to be transported by air in its entirety from Arakan to Imphal, the first time such an operation had been attempted. The task was allotted to 194 Squadron RAF, plus a number of USAAF C46s, and was completed in 758 sorties commencing on 19 March and ending in early April. Combined with the successful withdrawal of 17th Division, this meant that the Japanese now faced four divisions rather than the anticipated two, in addition to which XXXIII Indian Corps plus one brigade of the 5th Division moved to Manipur to begin operations to relieve Kohima from Assam. This, however, would take many weeks of campaigning and in the meantime the demands upon Troop Carrier Command were unrelenting.

Mountbatten despatched General Wedemeyer of his staff to Washington in an effort to arrive at a solution to ease the problems, and on 25 March General Arnold offered to set up four special Combat Cargo Groups for ACSEA, plus four additional Air Commandos along the lines of Cochran's unit operating with the Chindits. This, however, was a long-term solution to the problem which would not produce additional aircraft until July, and in any event the principle of the Air Commando was not universally popular. Air Chief Marshal Peirse for one thought that they gave rise to the danger of committing fighter and bomber aircraft permanently and exclusively to one particular Army formation, with consequential risks arising from a damaging lack of flexibility, plus duplication of effort which the air arm could ill afford either in terms of men or aircraft.[15]

To alleviate the immediate problem Mountbatten was therefore obliged once more to approach the Combined Chiefs of Staff to request the retention of the C46 Commandos borrowed from 'The Hump' route for longer than one month. The Combined Chiefs felt unable to agree but opted to divert 64th Troop Carrier Group USAAF, comprising sixty-four Dakotas, from the Middle East, plus a detachment of fifteen similar aircraft from 216 Squadron RAF, for a period of one month. These transports arrived in early April and went into service immediately. General Stratemeyer, in day-to-day command of Allied air operations, subsequently appealed to Mountbatten through Peirse for retention of the Middle East units until the arrival of the first of the new US Cargo Groups in July. If this could be arranged Stratemeyer felt that the C46s on loan from 'The Hump' could be returned. Mountbatten realized that he could not expect to retain all the aircraft currently on loan and that a quick decision had to be arrived at in order to deal with the knife-edge situation at Imphal. He therefore immediately ordered the twenty C46s back to 'The Hump' route and contacted the Combined Chiefs to apprise them of his decision, while at the same time requesting that the Middle East units be allowed to remain.

The decision now facing the Combined Chiefs of Staff was a highly complex one concerning not just the war in India/Burma but operations worldwide, top of the list being the Normandy invasion scheduled for June, a mere two months away, which would require massive air transport capacity. To further complicate their deliberations a high-level inter-service conference at Comilla on 17 and 18 April established the daily air supply requirement for the defenders of Imphal at 540 tons, although commitments to the other fronts in Burma plus the treacherous flying conditions certain to be encountered during the approaching monsoon season would mean that this figure was unlikely to be achieved. Under heavy attack, Imphal would be unable to survive a shortfall in its supply requirements for an extended period of time.

As it was, despite the unceasing efforts of the air arm, during the course of April the besieged soldiers' and airmen's rations dropped to 65 per cent of regular field standard, and the stockpile of supplies fell to danger levels. The reasons for this critical situation boil down to a severe shortage of transport aircraft, competing demands being many:

- Aircraft being diverted to meet the pressing needs of Special Forces in North Burma.
- 57 Parachute Brigade required transportation from north-west India to Imphal.
- The commitment to the West Africans in the Kaladan Valley proved to be heavier and longer than anticipated.
- Early in May over 300 tons of bituminized hessian ('bithess') required transportation from Calcutta in an attempt to make the airstrip at Tulihal, just south of Imphal village, weatherproof.
- Transportation of an Army Air Support Control unit required from Poona for service in Assam with XXXIII Corps, and the routine (and essential) movement by air of the servicing echelons of tactical squadrons.
- Inclement weather in April and May prevented the flying of supplies to Imphal for hours, sometimes days, and inevitably concentrated supply operations into periods of fair weather. This had the knock-on effect of greatly increasing the strain, congestion and workload on the already highly pressurized facilities at Imphal and base airfields.

Everything that could be tried was tried. General Stratemeyer diverted Mitchell and Wellington bombers to ferry operations carrying bombs to the Imphal squadrons, releasing transports for supply operations. The

117

comments of one Dakota pilot illustrate the varied nature of their tasks at the time:

> All our jobs are mixed up. One day we take in reinforcements to Imphal, the next day go to Comilla and collect flour, ammunition and petrol from the dumps for delivery to Imphal, where we pick up a load of "useless mouths" [administrative personnel whose presence was not essential. During May 30,000 were flown out of Imphal] and return them to the Brahmaputra. Then we take casualties from the Kohima battle and the next day we are back again on the old supply-dropping job in the Kaladan. It means seven hours flying a day, every day, a strain which I don't think we could have kept up except for the nervous tension of the crisis.[16]

The pilot here refers to the transportation of casualties and it is worth noting that in the first five months of 1944 Troop Carrier Command evacuated 23,000 sick and wounded to safety. It is no exaggeration to say that air transport saved the lives of the majority of these men, who otherwise would have faced a journey of many days by sampan, mule and ambulance. Casualties evacuated from the Chindit columns amounted to 2,126 by the end of May, most of whom would have been unlikely to survive without the L.1 and L.5 ambulances transferring them from the depths of the jungle to airstrips where they could be picked up by Dakotas.

Given the number of casualties flown out of battle areas it is surprising to realize that at no time during this critical period could transport aircraft be spared specifically for the removal of wounded, but then rarely did they ever return from forward airstrips empty – there were always sick and injured to be flown out. Medical care at forward airstrips in the Arakan and at Imphal was officially an RAF responsibility, but developed by necessity into a joint RAF/Army task.

On 1 May the activities of Troop Carrier Command were combined with Third Tactical Air Force under the overall command of Air Marshal Baldwin. Although this streamlining of operations resulted in the most efficient use possible of the transport aircraft, it made no practical difference to the shortfall at Imphal, and on 4 June Troop Carrier Command was disbanded. The transport squadrons were to remain with 3rd TAF until a new organization could be formed.

This was just a fraction of the background against which the Combined Chiefs had to make their decision concerning the C46 transports, and it was not until 16 May that they were able to inform Mountbatten that the seventy-nine aircraft on loan from the Middle East could remain until July when the first Combat Cargo Group was scheduled to arrive. Air Chief Marshal Peirse was of the opinion that had these seventy-nine aircraft not been retained by SEAC Stilwell would have been forced to withdraw to Ledo, the Imphal plain would have become untenable, the air route to China threatened, and recently installed all-weather airfields and warning systems in the Brahmaputra and Surma valleys lost.[17] All of which added up to the level of military catastrophe for the Allies that the Japanese were hoping for.

III

On the Imphal plain itself 221 Group had the two principal all-weather airstrips – Imphal Main to the north and Palel to the south – plus four additional strips at Tulihal, Wangjing, Sapam and Kangla. Tulihal, as has been mentioned, was largely covered with bithess to convert it to all-weather capability and was something of an anomaly, being a massive 6,000 yards long by 150 yards wide. The story goes it was built by British engineers to a specification provided by the USAAF and as the Americans worked in feet and the British in yards it ended up three times as large as it needed to be. In addition to bithess to improve the runways and taxiways, PSP, an American Meccano-like invention comprising interlocking metal sections was also used at Tulihal.

The other strips were little more than dirt runways, Kangla in particular being described as 'just plain paddy', and 'the most awful place which I can recall. When it rained we lived with gruesome fish which were endemic during the monsoon. I never ceased to wonder where these fish came from, since they were between a half and a pound in weight'.[18]

221 Group was under the command of Air Vice-Marshal Stanley F. Vincent, a fighter pilot during the First World War and by 1940 in command of a fighter station in England. However, rather like the American Brigadier General W.D. Old, it was, despite his rank and position, difficult to keep Vincent out of the cockpit. During the Battle of Britain he often took to the air and on more than one occasion was caught up in the fighting. As AOC 221 Group he was still known to fly on raids and reconnaissance missions, his radio call sign in the air being the distinctive 'Bullshit One'.

Having surrounded Kohima in the north, Japanese forces also invested the village and airstrip at Palel to the south. Harold Staines joined the RAF in 1940 and was posted to 34 Squadron, arriving in Burma in February 1942. By May 1944 Harold had transferred to the RAF Regiment and found himself occupying one of the many box trenches defending the vital all-weather airstrip just outside the tiny village. The box trenches were self-contained but placed so as to offer covering fire for each other and crossfire to the enemy. Covered with tarpaulins and surrounded with trip wires, everyone, including air crew, was required to perform guard duty in the boxes. Harold recalls the aircraft being pulled close to the boxes at night to await the arrival of Japanese infantry, who would come down to the village and make for the airstrip to try to inflict as much damage as possible on the aircraft. One night they succeeded in bypassing the trenches and damaging or destroying a number of aircraft by placing bombs in them before disappearing silently back into the darkness. Even in those dark days there was apparently still room for humour and Harold remembers that to repay some slight that he has long since forgotten, 34 Squadron 'bombed' nearby 42 Squadron with toilet rolls! He also recalls that a tour of duty comprised a daunting 300 operations before being allowed to return home.[19]

At Kohima relentless Japanese pressure drew the noose tighter and tighter around the defenders, the fighting bloody and hand to hand. By the middle of April the defending British and Indian troops were confined to an area known as Garrison Hill which, as the Japanese had captured nearby wells, necessitated the accurate air-dropping of drinking water as well as medical and other supplies.

The four Squadrons in the Imphal area equipped with 'Hurribombers', Nos 34, 42, 60 (Air Vice-Marshal Vincent's old Squadron) and 113 RAF, flew over 2,200 sorties during April alone, chiefly against the Japanese road block set up at Kangla-tongbi on the Imphal–Kohima road, the similar road block on the Imphal–Tiddim road and Japanese infantry attempting to move westwards on the Tamu road to tighten their grip on Palel.

On 17 April, 607 Squadron, now equipped with Spitfire Mk VIIIs, moved lock, stock and barrel to the airstrip at Wangjing on the Imphal plain. Wilfred Goold, now Officer Commanding 'B' Flight, does not have particularly fond memories of the place:

It was a dirt strip . . . We all lived in slit trenches exactly the same as World War I. This was really hard living. We were on 100% guard dusk to dawn to guard against Japanese patrols. This was not the type of living and work we were brought up to expect. We considered it highly dangerous . . .

One of the hazards of operating from strips like Wangjing was the dust. In a no wind situation, as it nearly always was in early morning, and you had a Squadron scramble, the first two would get off and the dust would hang there. The following sections took off into this, hoping that the aircraft before hadn't aborted or pranged.

On April 27th the Chota Monsoon arrived and it started to rain. We were scrambled and ordered to get all aircraft to Imphal Main, which was an all weather strip . . . I might add that our wardrobe was very meagre, almost what we stood up in, with some underwear and a toothbrush, so there was no packing up.[20]

120

On arrival at Imphal Main the 607 pilots enquired as to their accommodation and were told there was none so they would have to live in airmen's bashas. Despite having just vacated box trenches at Wangjing this did not sit too well with the pilots. Later, in the mess, Air Vice-Marshal Vincent entered and introduced himself, enquiring if they had any problems. On being told of their billeting difficulties Vincent barked orders to the effect that the 607 pilots were to be given suitable accommodation even if it meant moving others out. Turning back to the 607 pilots he mentioned that he was now living in the War Room, and went on to enquire whether perhaps five of them might like to occupy his bungalow. Goold and four others wasted no time taking up the offer. On one memorable day Vincent notified the pilots that he needed his bungalow for a few hours as a VIP was coming for a confidential 'natter', but first wanted to meet them. At this point Goold and his fellow pilots were introduced to General Slim, who asked them how the air war was progressing and stressed how vitally important it was for air superiority to be maintained. It is often the way for those who have to do the fighting to be critical of the 'top brass' but Goold refers to Vincent as 'a great fellow – a died in the wool fighter pilot', and recalls Slim as being 'a most impressive person'.

To reduce the likelihood of JAAF attacks on transport aircraft a corridor system was introduced which was constantly patrolled by fighters of the RAF and IAF, but such was the intense pressure exerted by Japanese ground and air forces that all fighter squadrons except 607 had to be withdrawn at dusk, to reappear the following dawn. Wilfred Goold and 607 Squadron were constantly in action and he vividly remembers his last sortie with them:

> The last interception I led was on May 18th; we intercepted some 40+ Oscars. They were, as usual, milling around. I led the Squadron in as near line abreast as possible, all picking out a victim. I lined up on an Oscar and saw hits on his fuselage; he flipped left and I kept on. Rather than climbing immediately I slipped under some Oscars and caught this one turning slowly to the left. I opened fire and he burst into flames. Seeing some aggressive looking Oscars, I climbed rapidly and with the Spit VIII this was fantastic. My claim this day was one destroyed, two damaged.
>
> This was my last op. as my repatriation notice had arrived; I was on my way home! A.V.M. Vincent offered me a squadron if I were to remain. However, I felt I had had enough. Sometimes, on reflection, I was becoming over confident in air to air combat and was beginning to stay down and mix it. If I had stayed I might have had more success, but then I could have been shot down.
>
> The most frightening aspect of flying in this part of the world was the weather. You would be scrambled and then when you had to return it was

overcast with these dreadful monsoonal clouds. The valley was only 50 odd miles wide and there were a lot of pilots lost trying to let down through this. It was a nightmare![21]

No. 1 Squadron IAF was called up from Kohat to Imphal to operate in conjunction with No. 28 Squadron RAF in a fighter reconnaissance role, both squadrons being employed on offensive, tactical, photographic and sector reconnaissance sorties. Supporting the closely fought land battles during April, No. 1 Squadron carried out 412 sorties totalling 485 hours, during the course of which the pilots obtained crucial information concerning the condition of roads and bridges leading to Japanese forward positions. Long-range operations had to be curtailed, however, as extra fuel tanks fitted to the Squadron Hurricanes slowed them to such an extent that they became easy prey for Japanese fighters.

On reconnaissance over the Imphal area approaching dusk, Squadron Leader Arjan Singh of the IAF observed an enemy infantry battalion break cover and move towards Allied Headquarters in Imphal village, only 8 miles distant. On receipt of his warning every available pilot from four squadrons, Nos 28, 34 and 42 RAF, plus No. 1 IAF, were scrambled. This in itself was no mean task as both ground and aircrew had believed operations to be over for the day and were already at supper, or relaxing in their canvas baths. Nevertheless within fifteen minutes thirty-three Hurricanes were airborne and over the scrubland where the enemy had been detected. Initially making no contact they dropped to low level and switched on landing lights, at which point the Japanese column was detected. The aircraft immediately attacked and drove back the Japanese advance, later capture of Japanese documentation confirming that thirty-seven officers and 213 men were killed.

This particular reconnaissance resulted in a major strike against the enemy; however, the more usual sortie came to be referred to as the 'merry go round'. Dependent upon the weather, one of the usual routes began by strafing the enemy-held suspension bridge at Falam, followed by an attack on infantry in the nearby village, paying particular attention to the low mud walls separating paddy fields as these, rather than the native huts, were the preferred hiding places for the Japanese. The aircraft would then turn to the winding Tiddim Road, paying particular attention to an enemy-held village where a captured British pilot had been tortured. The Tiddim Road itself was frequently used by Japanese armoured units and its bridges were attacked and new landslides created on a daily basis. From there the pilot would return to base and as he landed another sortie on the 'merry go round' would begin.

Based at Uderbund airstrip near Agartala, the Vultee Vengeance dive-bombers of No. 7 Squadron IAF entered the maelstrom swirling around Imphal on 23 March, and in the few days remaining to the end of the month dropped 126,500 lb of bombs in support of the hard-pressed defenders. Operations continued daily against troop concentrations, mechanized transport, ammunition dumps and dugouts. On 13 April in response to a request from the Army, No. 1 Squadron combined with 110 Squadron RAF, also equipped with the Vengeance, to attack a hill overlooking Imphal village from which Japanese artillery could bombard the airstrip and troops below. With Allied infantry close to the hill a high degree of accuracy was called for and achieved by both squadrons, Japanese casualties from this one operation being estimated at 300. Demonstrating the dangerous nature of the work carried out by ground as well as air crew, a 500 lb bomb exploded while being fused killing seven airmen including the No. 7 Squadron Armaments Officer.

Around Kohima the hard-pressed defenders were supported by Vengeances of the IAF and Hurribombers of the RAF dive-bombing Japanese bunkers and slit trenches, the commander of the garrison later reporting that the sight and sound of Allied aircraft overhead put new heart into his men. Further south dive-bombers and ground-attack fighters repeatedly dispersed concentrations of Japanese troops and vehicles. During May Vengeances flew in excess of 1,000 sorties on the IV Corps and XV Corps fronts, while Hurribombers flew 1,693.

The Strategic Air Force also weighed in with its medium and heavy bombers, Wellingtons of Nos 99 and 215 Squadrons RAF flying 125 sorties assisted by Liberators (12 sorties) and Mitchells (106 sorties) of the USAAF. All but one of these attacks were directed at targets on the Imphal–Tiddim road, particularly around milestones 120 and 87, two points of great importance to the Japanese in their attempts to bring reinforcements to the front. Any movement by the Japanese toward deployment on Imphal plain was rapidly broken up by Vengeances and Hurribombers, which would attack at short notice any troop concentrations in the foothills reported by Allied ground troops through Army Air Support Control.

The make or break Japanese assault at Imphal largely nullified Allied plans for the Strategic Air Force, which, for the duration of the emergency, was called upon not only to provide direct support for the ground forces, but crews for transport operations. Essential tools in the plan to isolate attacking Japanese troops from their supplies, the bombers were extensively employed in raids on rail communications, roads and bridges. The combination of Mitchell bombers and the spiked bombs that came into use during March proved particularly effective, destroying many miles of railway track. A good example of the work of the bombers concerned the strategically important bridge across the Sittang at Mokpalin, which had been destroyed by the Allies during the retreat from Burma. Photo reconnaissance sorties meticulously followed the long and arduous efforts of the Japanese to repair it, and as soon as the work was completed a bomber raid destroyed it again. It was not rebuilt.

On 4 June 1944, after bitter fighting, the Japanese siege of Kohima was finally broken. Units of XXXIII Corps then began to fight their way southward along the road to Imphal, and supported by air supply, across mountain tracks to the east and south-east towards Ukhrul, cutting the communications of Japanese units fighting in the west around Bishenpur. At the same time units of IV Corps fought their way northwards from Imphal. With the pendulum beginning at last to swing the way of the Allies, transport aircraft not only supplied the garrison for the present battles but by airlifting as much as 500 tons per day in treacherous monsoon conditions were able to build a stockpile to exploit the anticipated full-scale Japanese retreat. With improvements in weather conditions the airlift increased still further, and finally, on 22 June 1944, units of IV Corps and XXXIII Corps linked up on the Dimapur Road, 29 miles from Imphal and 109 miles from Dimapur. The siege of Imphal was over.

The resupply and reinforcement of the four divisions of the defence, plus the RAF and IAF units also based on the Imphal plain, was by any standards a phenomenal achievement for the Allied air forces, particularly bearing in mind that it was the first time in military history that ground forces of a size in excess of that of an army corps, 120,000 men, had been maintained entirely by air transport and for a period in excess of three months. During the course of the battle RAF and USAAF transport aircraft, the latter being in the majority, flew in a fully equipped division and evacuated 50,000 administrative personnel plus 10,000 sick and wounded. All arms of air power interlocked to provide a protective umbrella over the ground troops – fighters and fighter-bombers maintained the air superiority that allowed the transports relatively unhindered access, photo reconnaissance located troop con-centrations and supply convoys, and bombers and fighters raided the enemy continually, ultimately disrupting them to such an extent that the Japanese Fifteenth Army was forced to withdraw. For each and every squadron there were the ground crew, without whom the great success achieved by the air arm would not have been possible, working as they routinely did all hours of the day and night to keep their aircraft in the air.

As Slim had planned, his strategy turned the tables on the Japanese and it was they, not IV Corps, who ran out of food and ammunition.

Now Mutaguchi's army was in retreat and Fourteenth Army was ready to finish the job.

At Singapore Japan had inflicted on British forces the greatest military defeat in their history. The wheel having perhaps not yet come quite full circle, at Imphal British and Commonwealth forces, with the indispensable aid of Allied air power, inflicted on the Japanese military the greatest defeat in their history.

Notes

1. At the instigation of Prittam Singh of the Indian Independence League and Major Fujiwara Iwaichi, the INA was formed in February 1942 from Indian Army prisoners of war captured by the Japanese. The INA failed militarily during the Second World War but was instrumental in helping to gain India's independence from Britain in 1947.
2. Slim, Field Marshal Viscount, *Defeat Into Victory* (Pan Grand Strategy Series, 1999), p. 235.
3. Flight Lieutenant Wilfred Goold DFC, in correspondence with the author.
4. Franks, Norman L.R., *First in the Indian Skies* (The RAF Collection in conjunction with the 31 Squadron Royal Air Force Association, 1981), p. 105.
5. Hata, Ikuhiko, *Japanese Army Air Force Units and their Aces 1931–1945* (Grub Street, 2002), pp. 200–1.
6. *Op. cit.*, Note 2, p. 236.
7. *Op. cit.*, Note 2, pp. 225–6.
8. TNA Air 41/37, *Air Supply Operations in Burma 1942–1945*, p. 14.
9. *Op. cit.*, Note 2, p. 286.
10. *Op. cit.*, Note 8, p. 16.
11. *Wings of the Phoenix* (HMSO, 1949), p. 59.
12. TNA Air 2/7906, *Air Operations in South East Asia 16 November 1943 to 31 May 1944*, Air Chief Marshal Sir Richard Peirse, p. 1386.
13. *Op. cit.*, Note 8, p. 18.
14. *Japanese Monograph No. 64* (The Library of Congress, Washington DC), p. 67.
15. *Op. cit.*, Note 12, p. 1387.
16. *Op. cit.*, Note 8, quoted on p. 24.
17. *Op. cit.*, Note 12, p. 1387.
18. Sergeant F.H. Thomas, 5866 Mobile Signals Unit, quoted in Franks, Norman, *The Air Battle of Imphal* (Wm. Kimber, 1985), p. 21.
19. Harold Staines in conversation with the author.
20. *Op. cit.*. Note 3.
21. *Op. cit.*, Note 3.

Chapter Six

'Play Ball'

I

As part of the essential build-up of Allied transport capability 2nd Troop Carrier Squadron USAAF completed a tortuous journey that started at Pope Field, Fort Bragg, North Carolina on 23 January 1943 and culminated at Yangkai, China, the best part of two months later. Flying Douglas C47 Dakotas – more popularly known to American crews as 'Gooney Birds' – and Commanded by Captain Frank E. Sears Jr., the Squadron was initially attached to the India-China wing of ATC and commenced operations 'flying the Hump' across the Himalayas to Chabua, India on 17 March 1943. Having successfully completed many hundreds of these operations, on 1 July 1943 the squadron was transferred to the Tenth Air Force and based at Dinjan in Assam, its new role dropping supplies to Allied troops and civilians in Burma.

Up to this point the squadron had been fortunate enough to escape more or less unscathed but in a few short months all that was to change. In October and November 1943 two aircraft crashed killing their entire crews, one on a supply dropping mission into Burma, one on a trans-India flight. During December the squadron mounted a six-aircraft supply mission to the Sumprabum area which was attacked by twelve Japanese fighters. Three Dakotas were lost, but one of the remainder managed to lure an attacking Oscar into a manoeuvre that resulted in the Japanese aircraft crashing into the crest of a ridge. In January 1944 a squadron operation to Ngumla comprising three Dakotas escorted by eight P51 Mustangs was intercepted by an estimated eighteen Japanese fighters in the Fort Hertz area. All three Dakotas were lost. Well and truly initiated into the hazards of flying unarmed transport aircraft the aircrews of 2nd Troop Carrier, like their compatriots in the growing number of Allied transport squadrons, were required to learn their trade fast.

Detached in a wide 'left hook' from Stilwell's advance, in May 1944 Brigadier Merrill's Ranger battalions were closing in on the vitally important airfield at Myitkyina, assisted by Chinese units and native Kachins. Merrill himself had suffered two heart attacks and the 3,000-strong 'Galahad' force was led for the most part by Colonel Charles Hunter and supplied, amongst others, by 2nd Troop Carrier Squadron, now under the command of Captain Allan L. Dickey. For these operations the normal squadron complement of 66 assigned officers and 227 enlisted men was increased to 70 officers plus 4 attached, and 240 men plus 34 attached.

During the course of April, 1st and 2nd Troop Carrier Squadrons flew an entire Chinese division, over 14,000 men, to Maungkwan and in the first two weeks of May, 2nd Troop Carrier alone dropped 1,709.8 tons of food, ammunition, medical supplies and equipment to 'Galahad' force plus Stilwell's 22nd and 38th Chinese divisions. On 2 May the perils of flying during the monsoon were once again brought home when a C47 disappeared into Himalayan thunderheads and was not heard of again until its wreckage was discovered weeks later close to the summit of Digboi Mountain. Captain Evon V. Jones, the sole surviving pilot from the original complement to arrive in China, had two close shaves in succession during the month. Running out of fuel in flight he managed to glide his C47 into a paddy field, and on a later occasion had a tyre blow out on landing. Captain Jones and his crew survived both encounters unhurt, but the aircraft was badly damaged by the second.

With the Allied noose tightening around Myitkyina the 2nd Troop Carrier Operations Room became the nerve centre for planning and coordinating airborne supply and reinforcement of the ground troops. On the night of 15 May the pilots, co-pilots and navigators of the Second and Fourth Troop Carrier Squadrons, plus attached glider pilots, were gathered in the Intelligence Room at Dinjan and briefed by Captain Dickey. Utilizing a map of the campaign area and a large photograph of Myitkyina, Dickey explained that Merrill's troops were on the point of capturing the airfield and that as soon as this had been accomplished the 1st, 2nd, 4th and 18th Troop Carrier Squadrons would fly in supplies and reinforcements to consolidate its capture and facilitate further advances. 'Play Ball' would be the signal for the airlift to begin.

All available aircraft were checked and rechecked regardless of the increased workload on ground crews. Anti-aircraft guns, radar units and ancillary equipment were prepared for immediate shipment to Myitkyina and 'Galahad' rear echelon supply units at Moran and Jorhat were alerted. 2nd Troop Carrier ground station, code-named 'Bike', was designated to handle ground-to-air communications for 2nd and 4th

Troop, while 1st Troop ground station, code-named 'Pipestone', would handle 1st and 18th. To ensure the successful coordination of the supply effort a receiver was installed at 2nd Troop Operations Room to receive 'Pipestone', with any transmissions being handled by 'Bike's' regular channels. Glider pilots designated to fly in reinforcements left for Shingbwiyang on 16 May to pick up gliders and 'tug' aircraft, and with the transport squadrons on 48-hour alert the men were fed 'on the line' and camp beds were shifted into Operations and Engineering offices to allow them to sleep close by their aircraft.

Normal operations continued until 1530 hrs on 17 May when 'Play Ball' was received. Within twenty minutes the first three C47s were airborne and followed a pre-planned route from Dinjan to Moran/Jorhat and then on to Myitkyina, carrying radar equipment and the generators necessary to allow operations to continue at the airstrip around the clock. The first Allied aircraft to land at Myitkyina following its recapture was the 2nd Troop Carrier C47 of Lieutenant Roy Mack, flying in through a hail of ground fire that riddled the aircraft and peppered the hydraulics.

On the ground with the 'Galahad' force and assigned to Colonel Hunter was Captain Hoyt E. Hagar, the 2nd Troop Carrier air control officer. With Allied ground forces fighting for control of the airport Hagar first called in air strikes on Japanese positions, thereafter calling in Lieutenant Mack for his landing, followed by four more C47s. Close behind these transports Brigadier General W.D. Old himself piloted the first tug aircraft of the glider contingent bringing the engineers whose job it was to have the airstrip working at full capacity in the shortest possible time. The engineers of Company A, 879th Airborne must have wondered what they had let themselves in for when they emerged from their glider to be greeted by a brusque 'You're in the way!' They need not have worried for the reception that the Imperial Japanese Army had prepared for them was much warmer, and soon the engineers were busy defending themselves with hand grenades.

Once on the airfield Captain Hagar operated an SCR 284 radio from a revetment dubbed the Fox Hole Tower, along with two enlisted men, one of whom relentlessly churned the handle of a hand grinder generator that powered the ground-to-air radio. The other was a Tennessee mountain boy who acted as Hagar's bodyguard and appears to have been kept very busy. Hagar estimated that his Tennessee guardian angel must have killed around a dozen Japanese who tried to infiltrate the Fox Hole position, and at one point manned a naval deck gun that had been set up nearby and shot down a Japanese fighter.

Hot on the trail of the gliders came thirteen more C47s bringing anti-aircraft guns, including twelve Bofors guns with their British crews,[1] plus Chinese troops and supplies. As usually happens with the best laid plans a hitch occurred and although a 24-hour schedule had been the intention, the weather intervened and operations were halted from 2200 hrs on the 17th to 0430 hrs on the 18th. Immediately the weather lifted the C47s were again in the air and encountering severe ground fire from the many Japanese still surrounding the airstrip, returning bullet ridden to Dinjan to be patched up in record time ready for their next flight.

Existing almost entirely on cigarettes, K-rations, coffee and sandwiches a number of the aircrew became so fatigued by the relentless schedule that they resorted to Benzedrine to stay awake. At last all the effort began to have its effect and reinforced US, Chinese and Kachin ground forces cleared the Japanese from the airstrip and drove them into Myitkyina town.[2]

Myitkyina was the focal point for road, rail and water transport in northern Burma and being possessed of an all-weather airfield had been used extensively by the JAAF to harass traffic across 'The Hump' to China. Now, however, the boot was on the other foot and within two days of the capture of the airstrip, fighter and dive-bomber units of the Tenth Air Force moved in to begin ground support operations against an enemy that was at times not more than 1,000 yards away. Taking advantage of the massive build-up at the vital airfield, transport aircraft reverted to the original more southerly route via Myitkyina to China, avoiding the treacherous Himalayan leg of the journey.

While the all-weather airstrip remained in operation the monsoon still took its toll, virtually continuous heavy rain causing aircraft to sink into the mud at their dispersal points and requiring them to be parked at the southern end of the runway itself, where they proved to be one more hazard to add to the list headed by air turbulence and enemy fire. Despite the difficulties take-offs and landings built up to a truly impressive total of 500 per day, and at periods of peak activity averaged one per minute.

Despite the Allied build-up Japanese ground forces held on to Myitkyina town for eleven weeks following the capture of the airfield. This was in part due to the exhausted state of the American Rangers and in part due to a certain amount of confusion among their allies in the Chinese contingent, who appear to have mistaken each other for Japanese and inflicted severe casualties on their own troops before discovering their error. In the ensuing confusion the Japanese were able to bring in reinforcements, greatly adding to the time required to capture the town.

Between May and October 1944 some 14,000 landings were made at Myitkyina transporting over 40,000 tons of cargo, including personnel.

The Old Soldier in General Stilwell steadfastly refused to accept that an army could be supplied from the air, and as his troops advanced engineers following along behind constructed a roadway from Ledo designed to become a major artery for supplies to the Chinese-American ground forces. In practice the roadway was often closed by rain, particularly during the monsoon, and it was not without a certain amount of irony that during these periods the road builders themselves became totally reliant on air supply. It was to be six months after the capture of Myitkyina airfield that the first ground convoy reached the town, during which time the road made little impact on supply to the forward troops. Even after it was in operation a report by Brigadier General Godfrey USAAF, Chief Engineer of American Air Service Command, calculated that the seventy-five Dakotas on the air lift to Myitkyina handled the equivalent cargo of twelve hundred 2½-ton trucks, in the process utilizing half the manpower required had the roadway been ready. The report further calculated that the building of airstrips in northern Burma as Allied troops advanced required one-fifth of the manpower needed for the building and maintenance of roads, due to the nature of the terrain to be traversed.[3]

In addition to all other requirements to be met, supplies airlifted to China continued unabated, the tonnage moved improving dramatically in the closing months of 1944 and substantially exceeding expectations:

	Proposed deliveries (tons)	Actual deliveries (tons)
August	13,000	23,675
September	14,000	22,314
October	20,500	24,715
November	27,500	34,914
December	31,000	31,935[4]

The average number of transports in commission monthly on the Hump route rose from 108.4 in June to 249.6 in December, the number of trips rising over the same period from 3,702 to 7,612. A bottleneck had long existed at Kunming where aircraft stacked up over the airfield in all weathers awaiting their turn to land, however the opening of all-weather airstrips at Luliang and Chanyi greatly eased the problem.

From June 1944 one hundred B29 Boeing Superfortress long-range heavy bombers of 20th Bomber Command USAAF, under General Curtis le May, were based at newly constructed airfields around Kharagpur, to the west of Calcutta. Their prime mission was to fly to forward bases in China and from there on to targets in Japan proper, however, many of the forty-nine missions carried out by these 'super heavies' before they were transferred to the Pacific were long-range tactical targets provided by SEAC including Rangoon, Saigon and the docks complex at Singapore. The B29 forward bases in China inevitably necessitated an increase in supply tonnage moved by the hard-worked transports.

As had been mentioned previously construction and maintenance of airfields in Assam for the China airlift was the responsibility of the British Army, specifically Allied Land Forces, South East Asia engineer resources. By November 1944 a substantial amount of work had been undertaken as the following table shows:

Description	Completed	Under construction
Runways	13 miles	–
Taxiing tracks	25 miles	7 miles
Aircraft standings	486	20
Aircraft parking aprons	37 acres	23 acres
Roads	80 miles	23 miles
Accommodation	for 33,106 men	–
Covered storage	63 acres	4.25 acres[5]

Supply dropping of the intensity required by several fronts being in closely fought action simultaneously inevitably gave rise to some hair-raising experiences. One dispatcher was hooked out of an aircraft by a parachute, wafting gently to terra firma perched on a box of rations, while a Dakota force-landing with a load of 7,000 pounds of petrol finished up with a wingtip in the open fireplace of a Naga's hut. Fortunately for all concerned the fire did not spread. The weather, as ever, took a hand, the crew of a Hudson transport flying into a storm discovering the perils of the torrential rain, lightning flashes along the wingtips of the aircraft and the stomach-churning sensation of the Hudson dropping like a stone from 16,000 to 12,000 feet in seconds, the pilot managing to regain control with much difficulty.

Perhaps one of the narrowest – but by no means unique – escapes occurred to the crew of a Dakota of 194 Squadron on a supply drop to No. 34 Chindit column in northern Burma. Loaded, and quite probably overloaded, with bags of rice for a free-fall drop the aircraft took off from Agartala with eleven others, soon to find themselves flying above dense cloud completely obscuring the ground. With the aircraft at an altitude of 8,500 feet in order to safely clear mountain peaks which rose to 7,000 feet, a guesstimate was arrived at that the DZ must be below, causing the pilot (Warrant Officer, later Group Captain, Deryck Groocock) to instruct the wireless operator to prepare the aircraft for the drop. This entailed piling bags of rice by the open door in the fuselage, the cargo then usually being ejected by two despatch men, popularly known as 'kickers' by virtue of the fact that they lay on the floor of the aircraft hanging on to straps while literally kicking supplies out of the door.

In this instance, with bags piled up by the door, the Dakota's airspeed, normally around 125 mph, dropped away for no obvious reason. The more power Groocock applied the more the airspeed slowed. With the aircraft approaching a stall and the pilot unable to keep the nose down, the Dakota reared up and flipped over into a right-hand spin, descending at a mind-numbing rate of around 2,000 feet per minute. For those aboard able to make the calculation this gave them around forty-five seconds before hitting the mountains, still hidden beneath the cloud below. Warrant Officer Groocock took normal spin recovery action, full opposite rudder and joystick forward and sat mesmerized watching the altimeter drop to 6,000, 5,500 and 5,000 feet. Finally at 4,500 feet the aircraft plunged out of the cloud and into a valley with great mountain peaks disappearing into the clouds on either side. Regaining control and suffering a bad attack of the shakes, in company with the rest of the crew, Groocock came to the conclusion that the aircraft must have been badly loaded at Agartala and stacking rice sacks by the door had put its centre of gravity outside operable limits. With the Dakota in a spin the sacks fell forward, restoring the balance and enabling the pilot to regain control.

Continuing their flight along the valley while Groocock and his crew regained their composure, a column of smoke was spotted ahead and to their amazement the intended DZ appeared below. With considerable relief and no little care so as not to upset the balance again, the cargo was successfully dropped.

Of the twelve aircraft on that particular operation Groocock's was the only one to penetrate the cloud cover and find the DZ, the remainder returning with their loads. The crew subsequently had the satisfaction of receiving a 'thank you' signal from the Commanding Officer of 34 Column for the successful drop.[6]

With the rapidly increasing reliance upon air transport the Army set up its own units to handle the loading of aircraft from its stores depots, one Rear Airfield Maintenance Organisation (RAMO) being located at each airfield together with one or more Air Despatch Companies. The duties of these units encompassed the packing and loading of supplies and in the case of parachute or free-fall loads the ejection of supplies from the aircraft. Supplies held at each individual RAMO would form the basic requirements of dependent ground forces including petrol, rations and ammunition. Specialist items such as engineering stores, heavy ordnance and medical supplies would be held at depots where transport facilities offered the best access to airfields. The Army felt that while imposing certain limitations the system offered the only practical compromise between splitting stocks and complete air flexibility.

Unloading at forward airfields was also the responsibility of Army units, the Forward Airfield Maintenance Organisations (FAMOs). Landing strips in forward areas were much the preferred option as parachute or free-fall drops generally resulted in around 25 per cent wastage. In the case of a C46 Commando or C47 Dakota the target time for unloading by the FAMO would be fifteen minutes, notwithstanding the fact that many cargoes – Bailey bridging for example – would be both heavy and unwieldy. Once unloaded cargoes would be removed to nearby depots from which bulk issue would be made to the relevant formations. An exception would be made for troops in the vicinity of the airfield who would receive supplies from a Detail Issue Depot.

Both RAMOs and FAMOs necessarily made high demands upon labour, a factor which was to prove a source of friction in the campaigning to come, the RAF maintaining that a shortfall existed in Army manpower allotted to RAMOs and FAMOs which exacerbated the stresses and strains inherent in a system already working close to its limits. Problems also arose in respect of RAMOs in so far as they received their daily tasks from the corps which they were supplying, subsequently applying to the Air Forces for the required number of aircraft. Demands on transport aircraft being what they were a shortfall in aircraft availability would often occur and time-consuming confusion would result. With air supply on this scale being developed 'on the hoof' no workable system for the allocation of priorities had been evolved. The problem was addressed with the formation of the Combined Army-Air Transport Organisation (CAATO) to receive and collate daily requests, assess their urgency, and, being in full possession of current aircraft availability, allot tasks accordingly.

II

In addition to the make or break confrontation at Imphal, attacks on Japanese lines of communication were carried out over a wide area and for a protracted length of time. The persistent efforts over many months of two Beaufighter squadrons, Nos 27 and 177 RAF, in both day and night raids, succeeded in forcing the main weight of enemy transport firstly from road to river, and then from river to rail. By early 1944 most large-scale Japanese movements of supplies were made at night, while for protection during the day a complex system of camouflage was combined with an extensive network of gun emplacements in an attempt to keep Allied aircraft at bay. Daily Beaufighter raids were carried out along the Tuangup pass road, against shipping on the Irrawaddy, and the Ye-u and Myitkyina railway lines. With the arrival of Lightnings and Mustangs the USAAF extended disruption of Japanese lines of communication still farther afield.

Completed in November 1943 the infamous Burma–Siam railway became a prime target. Stretching for over 244 miles, traversing jungle and mountains, the line was built by native slave labour and Allied prisoners of war, 11,000 of whom died, mostly from malaria and brutal treatment at the hands of their captors. A prime source of supply for the Japanese, the line made its way across no less than 688 bridges traversing rivers and ravines from 100 to 1,200 feet wide. Over 2,700 tons of bombs were dropped on the railway to ensure that at no time did it achieve anything like its full potential. Also extensively attacked were the railway junction at Thanbyuzayat, ferry terminals at Moulmein and Martaban, and the all-important railway junction at Pegu.

The Japanese did not accept these attacks on their vital railway lines of communication unchallenged, and being the masters of innovation that they are came up with the ingenious 'loco truck'. This comprised a small diesel engine locomotive with two sets of wheels – one set to run along rails, one set fitted with tyres – and equipped with two jacks, one at the front, one at the rear. On arriving at a break in the railway line a rail would be placed under each jack at right angles to the track enabling the loco truck to be lifted off the railway, lowered onto the wheels equipped with tyres, driven past the break and returned to the track. The loco truck became a prized target for fighter and bomber pilots.

The attrition rate for Allied pilots engaged in this work was high, a fairly typical example being that of a Beaufighter squadron that lost seventy-five aircrew killed or missing over an eighteen-month period. Thirteen were subsequently released from prisoner-of-war camps, but the majority of those lost paid the price exacted by low-level flying, night flying and operations undertaken in blinding Burmese storms.

The Beaufighters of Nos 27 and 177 Squadrons were armed with 20 mm cannon and machine guns, and proved exceptionally successful at attacking enemy transport targets, but in January 1944 a third squadron of Beaufighters, No. 211 RAF, made an appearance operating aircraft armed with rocket projectiles (RPs). As a central part of their attempts to thwart the menace of air attack to their transport system Japanese engineers constructed a network of pens and shelters to protect railway locomotives, these shelters being designed to withstand cannon or machine-gun fire but often proving vulnerable to rocket attack. The opening of the Burma–Siam railway allowed the Japanese to bring replacement locomotives quickly and easily into Burma, consequently the emphasis of air raids tended to shift to stations, water towers and curved sections of track, all of which were difficult and time consuming to replace and ideal targets for RPs. The delay fuse used to arm rockets, however, proved unsuitable for attacking bridges and these targets were increasingly left to the medium and heavy bombers of the Strategic Air Force.

Evidence of the growing versatility of the Allied air forces was provided by the destruction of the strategically important Shweli suspension bridge. Attacked many times by bombers it had remained undamaged, however the arrival of No. 1 Air Commando USAAF, equipped with long-range Lightnings, enabled not only the rapid destruction of the suspension bridge but also that of its emergency replacement two weeks later. Mustangs and Lightnings of the USAAF carried out many raids against the Mandalay–Myitkyina railway, particularly the section between Shwebo and Wuntho which supplied Japanese divisions attacking Imphal during the emergency, and units opposing the Chindits.

In addition to land operations the air forces were also called upon to patrol vast areas of the Indian Ocean, the Mozambique Channel, the Gulf of Aden, the Gulf of Oman and the Bay of Bengal. These operations were designed both to cover Allied convoys and discover those of the enemy, and were broadly controlled by AOC 222 Group in conjunction with the appropriate area naval authority plus, where necessary, the South African military. This naturally placed extended responsibilities on AOC 222 Group, who therefore had not only his own Group to command but also the organization and direction of seaward General Reconnaissance operations in the areas mentioned. To assist him with this latter duty a new command structure was introduced – Indian Ocean General Reconnaissance Operations (IOGROPS) – with a Deputy AOC and supporting staff, the area of responsibility for the new group being broadly similar to that of Coastal Command in the UK. 222 Group remained involved in maritime work, however, particularly in the area of mine laying.

Anti-shipping operations were usually confined to attacks on coastal and river traffic, but one much more tempting target did come the way of Beaufighters of Eastern Air Command operating at extreme range over the Andaman Sea. A convoy of ocean-going Japanese merchant vessels was discovered and despite not being armed with bombs, the Beaufighters swept in using rockets and machine guns. For thirty-three hours the attacks kept on, aircraft returning to base time and again to rearm and refuel before heading back to the fray. Fourteen merchant ships, two sloops and a gunboat were left burning wrecks, making the operation the biggest air-sea strike in the history of EAC.

Towards the end of 1943 a decision was taken that, in order to relieve pressure on the overworked Bengal infrastructure, reinforcements for Fourteenth Army would be transhipped by sea from ports along the east coast of India to Chittagong. Commencing on 6 December round-the-clock air patrols of the shipping lanes to be used were initiated, culminating at midday on the 9th when the ships reached their destination. Only one Japanese submarine, believed to be an 'I' class vessel, was located during these operations and while it could not be sunk neither was it able to launch an attack. Two JAAF aircraft were seen over the Bay of Bengal but kept well away from the convoy area.

With the surrender of the Italian fleet in September 1943, by the end of that year reinforcements for the Royal Navy's Eastern Fleet were at last beginning to arrive, and as a consequence increased patrols became necessary. During December No. 354 Squadron RAF, operating long-range Liberators, took over General Reconnaissance patrols, extending them to cover the north-eastern area of the Bay of Bengal and the Arakan coast. By February there were thought to be ten Japanese submarines in the Indian Ocean, aided by several U-boats of the *Kriegsmarine*, and the number of sinkings rose as a result. These included on the 12th of the month the tragic loss from convoy KR8 of the elderly troopship *Khedive Ishmail*. The vessel carried a crew of 183 plus 1,300 military and naval personnel, of which only 214 survived. The Japanese submarine *I-27* was sunk during the encounter but the destroyer *Paladin*, recently arrived from the Mediterranean, was also badly damaged. Experience in the Atlantic had long since established the value of air escort for convoys, but due to a lack of available aircraft and the presence of two Royal Navy destroyers, air cover for KR8 had not been provided.

Air-sea rescue entailed many long and arduous hours of flying as witnessed by efforts to locate survivors from a tanker torpedoed in the Seychelles area, finally rescued after the crew of at least one Catalina of the several utilized had flown for forty-two hours over a 48-hour period. Gradually the increase in air patrols, including carrier-based aircraft from the growing Eastern Fleet, had its effect, and by April the number of Axis submarines in the Indian Ocean had fallen to an estimated two. During the first quarter of 1944 searches by aircraft resulted in the rescue of 535 survivors from ships torpedoed in the waters around India.

By the beginning of 1944 the only area of Allied air operations to remain under separate command was Photographic Reconnaissance, No. 171 Wing RAF, comprising Nos 681 and 684 Squadrons, being placed under the control of Strategic Air Force while the 9th Photographic

Reconnaissance Squadron remained under the control of 10th USAAF. This often resulted in wasteful duplication of effort and on 1 February the joint Photographic Reconnaissance Force was formed under Group Captain S.G. Wise RAF.

Significant innovations in photographic reconnaissance were developed in the 10th USAAF area, in particular the varied use made of aerial photography for tactical operations – low-level verticals, reconnaissance strips, obliques and pinpoint shots. A simple grid system, common to both ground and air forces, was used for marking photographs. This was of particular relevance in the NCAC area of operations which consisted largely of expanses of jungle-clad hills with few natural features to use as points of reference.

Aerial reconnaissance as far away as Rangoon, Bassein, and Lashio came to be regarded as routine by suitably adapted Lightnings and Spitfires, but the arrival in theatre of the de Havilland DH.98 Mosquito greatly extended the range and scope of PR operations. On 27 March a Mosquito of 684 Squadron photographed a lengthy section of the Bangkok–Singapore railway during a flight of 1,860 miles, the longest to date. During April the number of requests from Fourteenth Army for photographic intelligence of the Imphal battle and reinforcement areas inevitably increased dramatically, and a Mosquito broke the previous record by covering 2,172 miles photographing sections of the Malay Peninsula railway. The record for any theatre of the war, however, was a flight by a Mk XVI Mosquito in March 1945, flying 2,493 miles in eight hours forty-five minutes to reconnoitre the Bangkok–Singapore railway to a point south of the Malay border. Being of largely wooden construction Mosquitoes had particular problems adjusting to the climatic conditions in India/Burma, the plywood webs of the spars either shrinking or swelling in the humid atmosphere. Ultimately, however, they proved their worth.[7]

Manpower shortages continued, the overall shortfall being some 12 per cent, a not exceptional figure but one which for the air forces manifested itself principally in the form of a shortage of skilled tradesmen. A number of solutions were tried, from the recruitment and retraining of Indian labour to the substitution of women, a proposal which culminated in a mission from the Air Ministry led by Air Chief Commandant Dame Trefusis J. Forbes.

The dearth of skilled mechanics and engineers was felt principally in the areas of repair and maintenance, which also suffered from an inability to call upon civilian contractors' working parties for assistance due to the low level of industrialization and consequent skills short-fall in evidence at that time in India. This factor resulted in plans to produce metal long-range jettisonable fuel tanks locally taking so long to implement that a plywood alternative had to be developed. Certain types of industrial production were available in India, however, the monthly output of supply-dropping parachutes – Slim's 'parajutes' – increasing from 35,000 to 144,000, with a target of 250,000 per month by the end of 1943.

With an envisaged operational target of 156 squadrons, quick and efficient aircraft maintenance was, nevertheless, a crucial requirement and some attempts at expansion were put in place. No. 2 Command Maintenance Unit, Trichinopoly, manned principally by civilians, was doubled in size and three new CMUs were formed. No. 322 Maintenance Unit, Cawnpore, became the largest service base repair depot in India, ultimately capable of undertaking major repairs to fifty-five large aircraft and a monthly engine overhaul capacity approaching 500 units.

Emergencies would put still further strain on available manpower, the Imphal siege being a notable illustration. Such was the requirement for transport aircraft that all available repair and maintenance manpower was switched to Dakotas, the monthly output of these aircraft from repair depots rising from two in December to eleven in May, but at the cost of practically no work being carried out on other types.

With aircraft lost or out of commission, availability of replacements became an essential requirement and a number of Aircraft Storage Units (ASUs) and Reserve Aircraft Pools (RAPs) came into being, covering the whole of India by dividing the sub-continent into three zones. ASUs were to hold two months' reserve, while RAPs were to hold two weeks' reserve of aircraft ready for immediate issue. The efficient operation of these units resulted in the regular replacement of aircraft within twenty-four hours.

Problems remained, however, notably – and apparently interminably – with regard to spares, which were now for the most part available but lacked the means by which to store them safely. By late 1943 the lack of construction of new storage space resulted in some 30,000 cases of RAF stores languishing in the open in all weathers. Despite the high degree of cooperation achieved certain areas of inter-service discord remained, ACM Peirse complaining that construction priorities awarded to the RAF in the Fourteenth Army area were subject to delay and alteration by army commanders diverting labour and materials without reference to the AOC concerned. Application of suitable levels of manpower for RAF construction work was to become a source of friction between Army and Air Force.

A cause of much perplexed head scratching was the difficulty encountered in recovering aircraft which crashed or force-landed away from an airfield, an occurrence which all too often led to the writing off of repairable aircraft due to the nature of road and rail transport in India. Even if damaged aircraft were to be delivered to a railway, further damage suffered during trans-shipment to a repair depot more often than not rendered the casualty fit only for scrap on arrival. One useful method of countering this problem was the formation in November 1943 of an Airborne Salvage Section, which flew to crash scenes in a specially adapted transport aircraft capable of carrying spares, tools and engines. On reaching the crash site damaged aircraft would be patched up and flown to the nearest repair depot. The Airborne Salvage Section operated a C47 Dakota – which it had previously salvaged – in which the mainplanes of large aircraft, and even complete Spitfires, were on occasion carried.

Cooperation between the RAF and USAAF remained at a very high level in the maintenance sphere, evidenced during the Imphal siege when Air Service Command USAAF released to the RAF one third of the total stocks of Dakota spares held by them in India.

The joint structuring of Eastern Air Command produced a high degree of cross-fertilization between the RAF and USAAF in the area of radar and signals, two British GCI radar stations being sited to cover US bases in the Brahmaputra valley, and another at Shingbwiyang to provide early warning for Stilwell's troops in the Hukawng valley. An additional set was modified for transportation by air and made available to the US military. New American Light Warning sets were tested by both the RAF and USAAF and the results of British research into radio counter-measures were provided to US forces. To reduce the potential for costly errors all USAAF units in theatre adopted the RAF call sign procedure.

The specific need for mobile signals and communications units was met by the adoption of specialist signals vehicles with the result that Group and Wing headquarters became fully self-contained and mobile in respect of signals requirements. Additional experiments in mobility were carried out with the installation of GCI units into barges, a jeep, an amphibious jeep and an amphibious DUKW. Specialist training for signals and radar personnel under field conditions was addressed by the formation of No. 5 Base Signals Unit. RAF Air Formation Signals units suffered their share of the shortage of qualified manpower, a situation exacerbated by the need to supply the Chindits with 185 wireless operators and mechanics plus eight officers.

Flight Control in India/Burma was of prime importance due to the extremes of weather encountered allied to the lack of land-line communications and the exceptionally wide dispersal of landing grounds. Despite this requirement in November 1943 only 30 trained British

139

Flying Control officers existed, augmented by 30 IAF officers and 30 resting aircrew. This complement left forty main airfields along the reinforcement route and in Ceylon without either trained airmen or flight control equipment. Despite attempts at remedies by May 1944 there still existed a shortfall of 150 officers and 100 airfield controllers.

On a more positive note a joint RAF/USAAF system of Air Traffic Control was under active discussion and an application was made to USAAF Headquarters for a supply of officers trained in the joint system then in operation in the UK.

In a climate such as that to be encountered in India/Burma there were many infections, ailments, and diseases to threaten the health of the Allied servicemen, the most serious cause of sickness being malaria. In an effort to combat the disease a senior medical officer specializing in malariology was appointed to reorganize measures for control and initiate by propaganda and instruction personal awareness of anti-malaria discipline. Additionally a flight from No. 134 Squadron RAF was detailed to spray known mosquito breeding grounds with the newly arrived DDT chemical agent.

In order to ease the shortage of hospital beds for the rapidly growing air arm, work began to convert the buildings of the La Martiniere School, Calcutta, to a 500-bed medical centre, the first in SEAC for the RAF, although there were already four RAF Mobile Field Hospitals in operation. It was hoped that by having the La Martiniere complex as a central administrative as well as medical centre for RAF health requirements that the supply of stores and equipment to the mobile units, which tended to be haphazard, would be greatly improved.[8]

III

Having thoroughly disrupted enemy communications the Chindits drew Operation Thursday to a close, some marching north to join with Stilwell's forces, some airlifted out before the monsoon turned the 'kutcha' airstrips to mud. Those making their way north marched out of range of the light air ambulances, giving rise to one of the more unusual aspects of air support for the columns – the use of two RAF Sunderland flying boats to evacuate sick and wounded from the jungle. The two four-engine flying boats were summoned from Ceylon and moored on the Brahmaputra in Assam until given word that the columns were in position. Taking off in weather that made fighter escort impossible they flew at their 10,000 feet operational ceiling to Indawgyi Lake, a four-hour flight which they made several times, bringing in food and replacements, lifting out over 500 casualties and in the process becoming affectionately know to the Chindits as 'Gert' and 'Daisy'.

Transport aircraft in general were known to the Chindits as 'DCs' and one British private, bearded and exhausted after many months of marching and fighting, on alighting from the aircraft that brought him out of the jungle turned back and patted the fuselage affectionately, commenting to the pilot 'as far as I'm concerned, sir, they can keep their VCs and their MCs. Give me the DCs!'[9]

With the collapse of the assault on Imphal 5th *Hikoshidan* shifted the emphasis of its operations to the north. The principles and importance of air transport were never grasped by the JAAF and although several types of transport aircraft were built they were never available in great numbers and were decidedly thin on the ground in Burma. Despite this the air dropping of supplies became necessary when Japanese ground forces were surrounded by Stilwell's advancing Chinese-American troops, 5th *Hikoshidan* carrying out ten such operations, of which only six were judged successful due to a combination of bad weather and enemy interception.

Having already lost the heavy bombers of 7th *Hikosentai*, the JAAF in Burma became further weakened during the 1944 monsoon by the withdrawal of 98th *Hikosentai* (heavy bombers), returned to Japan for retraining in torpedo operations, and 12th *Hikosentai* (heavy bombers), reassigned to the Pacific together with 7th *Hikodan Shireibu*.

Units available for operations in Burma were:

Hikoshidan Shireibu	Rangoon.
4th *Hikodan Shireibu*	Heho.
50th *Hikosentai* (19 fighters)	Mingaladon.
8th *Hikosentai* (11 light bombers)	Mingaladon.
204th *Hikosentai* (11 fighters)	Main force at Phnomh Penh, detached unit at Pegu.
64th *Hikosentai* (6 fighters)	Whereabouts uncertain.
81st *Hikosentai* (two reconnaissance aircraft)	Saigon.

Although not nearly enough in terms of numbers, some improvement in equipment was possible, 64th and 204th *Hikosentai* upgrading from Type 2 to Type 3 Ki-43 Oscars and 50th *Hikosentai* from Type 2 Oscars to the new Nakajima Ki-84 Frank, although a number of operational defects were experienced with this latter aircraft.

Due to an alarming loss of experienced aircrew an intensive training programme was introduced for the mainly inexperienced replacements arriving for duty with the *chutai*. Because of the serious shortage of bombers, training of fighter pilots included particular reference to strafing and bombing in an effort to fill the gap. For those bombers remaining, daylight operations became extremely hazardous and retraining for night raids was introduced. Due to the high attrition rate suffered by reconnaissance aircraft following the introduction of Spitfires, daylight operations were curtailed and replaced by sorties at dawn, dusk and during night hours, for which retraining was also required.

Replacements for aircraft losses were by now extremely difficult to come by and strenuous efforts were made to reduce losses to a minimum by the maintenance, recovery and rebuilding of as many aircraft as possible. Allied amphibious landings along the Burma coast were anticipated and joint operations in conjunction with the JNAF planned.[10]

Still having no landing or ancillary craft Slim was in fact unable to consider any form of amphibious assault in his campaign to retake Burma, and had decided on an overland advance from the north. With the Japanese now in disorganized retreat Slim believed that if it were possible to drive Mutaguchi's Fifteenth Army back across the Chindwin and be ready to push a substantial force into the central plain of Burma by the end of monsoon, he could force a second decisive battle in front of Mandalay before the Japanese command had recovered from its totally unexpected defeat at Imphal. For this campaign his ground forces would again need supply almost entirely from the air.

The major battles fought along the entire front during the course of spring and summer 1944 taught many lessons as far as air transport was concerned. For one, the disbandment of Troop Carrier Command and subsequent control of transport squadrons passing to Third Tactical Air Force had not proven entirely satisfactory. A decision was therefore taken to organize an integrated US/British formation to be known as Combat Cargo Task Force (CCTF), with responsibility for the control and planning of air transport operations supporting all land forces except Stilwell's command in northern Burma, who would be supplied by the Tenth USAAF. Command of CCTF fell to Brigadier General F.W. Evans USAAF, with Air Commodore J.D.I. Hardman as his deputy and in command of the RAF component of the force.

While the Imphal battles were in progress Admiral Mountbatten took the decision to move his headquarters from Calcutta, which he intensely disliked, to Kandy in Ceylon, taking the principal military headquarters with him, although advanced headquarters in Burma, closer to the scene of action, was still the norm. With the reorganization of the transport squadrons there came a number of other Allied command changes, including Air Chief Marshal Sir Richard Peirse, who left the command in November 1944 following persistent rumours of an affair with Lady Auchinleck, and despite the fact that Mountbatten got on well with him and would have preferred to retain his services. Peirse's replacement was to be Air Chief Marshal Sir Trafford Leigh-Mallory but the aircraft in which he was travelling crashed in the French Alps on 14 November, killing all on board. The appointment finally went to the New Zealander Air Chief Marshal Sir Keith Park, who took up his post on 24 February 1945. For the intervening months Air Marshal Sir Guy Garrod became acting Allied Air C-in-C. General Stilwell left for a new post in the USA, replaced as Deputy Supreme Allied Commander by the American General Wheeler. General Sultan, formerly Stilwell's deputy, became commander of all US and Chinese forces in India and Burma, and General Wedemeyer, formerly Mountbatten's Deputy Chief of Staff, replaced Stilwell as Chief of Staff to Chiang Kai-shek and commander of all US forces in China. A new Headquarters to oversee all Allied land forces in SEAC was established under Lieutenant General Sir Oliver Leese. In the Arakan Air Commodore the Earl of Bandon – popularly known to his men as the Abandoned Earl – took command of 224 Group in support of XV Corps, which had been detached from Slim's Fourteenth Army to come under the direct control of General Leese. Vincent's 221 Group continued its support of Fourteenth Army in the centre.

From June 1944 10th USAAF based in Assam had been released from 3rd Tactical Air Force to become an independent formation under Eastern Air Command. As a consequence, in October 1944 an administrative streamlining took place involving the disbandment of Headquarters 3rd Tactical Air Force, direct operational control of all subordinate formations being assumed by Headquarters Eastern Air Command and an expanded Headquarters 221 Group. Air Marshal Baldwin, formerly AOC 3rd TAF, became Deputy Air Commander, Eastern Air Command, and Air Marshal Commanding, RAF Bengal-Burma.

The principal Fourteenth Army offensive commenced at the end of November 1944, and in one of those incidences in warfare that can all too easily have disastrous results, coincided with a renewed westward assault by Japanese forces in China that threatened to engulf both Chungking and Kunming, the vital terminal at the China end of the airlift. With Chinese resistance crumbling the 1st, 2nd and 4th Combat Cargo Squadrons USAAF were transferred from Burma operations to China to airlift supplies and reinforcements, including the 14th and 22nd Chinese Divisions from the northern Burma front.

To make up the shortfall as far as Fourteenth Army were concerned Nos 117 and 194 Squadrons RAF, previously withdrawn for rest and retraining, were returned to service to augment the four squadrons still in operation, Nos 31 and 62 RAF at Comilla, plus 2nd and 4th Troop Carrier USAAF at Dinjan. As if being shot at by the Japanese was not bad enough, on 19 December a 2nd Troop aircraft returning from a supply drop encountered four bursts of anti-aircraft tracer from an area that should have been firmly under Allied control. Later investigations revealed the culprits to be a US battery being 'playful'. The game reportedly scared the 'daylights' – no doubt the cleaned-up version – out of the crew of the aircraft.

The following day, 20 December, welcome transport reinforcement materialized with the arrival of No. 435 Squadron RCAF at Tulihal, to be joined shortly thereafter by No. 436 Squadron RCAF at nearby Kangla. Also on 20 December, the first airstrip in Burma to be opened in support of Fourteenth Army's advance came into operation at Indainggale.

Further improvements in equipment arriving in SEAC for the air forces necessitated the return to India of nine Hurricane squadrons to re-equip with the Republic P47 Thunderbolt. The Thunderbolt was a fine aircraft, a fighter-bomber, but bore distinct differences to the Hurricane. For one thing it was heavy; at around 20,700 lb (9,390 kg) it was heavier than a loaded Dornier Do17 bomber! For another it was, by the standards of the time, large, RAF pilots commenting that they could dodge enemy fire by running around in the cockpit. But when they got used to it, they liked it. Despite the size and weight of the aircraft the big 18-cylinder 2,535 hp Pratt & Whitney engine had enough 'grunt' to take the Thunderbolt to an impressive 433 mph.

Until its acquisition of the Vultee Vengeance the RAF had not had much time for dive-bombers, but having had success with that aircraft opted to use the Thunderbolt in the dive-bomber role when the occasion demanded. Unfortunately this method of attack brought to light a highly dangerous fault with the fuel 'header' tanks which had a tendency to split – with the aircraft in a dive this caused petrol to pour onto the hot engine and explode. The defect was put down to one of a number of reasons – sloppy craftsmanship, bad storage or bad fitting. Whatever the cause a number of pilots were needlessly killed before the problem was rectified.[11]

Even with the partial switch to Thunderbolts the Hurricane, despite the fact that production had ceased, remained for SEAC a front-line weapon in its 'Hurribomber' role, strafing troops and mechanized transport, attacking defensive positions, gun emplacements and jungle hide-outs.

Further changes resulted in four Vengeance squadrons retraining for Mosquitoes, and the comparatively slow Wellingtons, which had been so successful, being retired in favour of Liberators. The Liberator proved itself to be an adaptable aircraft, Wing Commander J. Blackburn RAF, finding that by experimenting with fuel consumption his squadron could reach Bangkok 1,100 miles away, and more than double the aircraft's normal bomb load on such sorties, from 3,000 to 8,000 lb. His example was not unnaturally followed throughout the Strategic Air Force.

Technological advances had enabled the Italian Regia Aeronautica to develop a radio-controlled flying bomb, and in Burma the radio-controlled Azon bomb came into use for the Allies. The Italian version was a 500 lb monster placed in a drone controlled by radio from an accompanying aircraft. The Azon bomb, while smaller, was similar in so far as the direction of its fall was controlled by radio signal from the bomber. Psychological warfare also took a hand, leaflet drops by the Strategic Air Force warning Burmese and Siamese workers to stay away from railway lines pending raids, whereupon essential trackmen, switchmen and labourers suddenly discovered urgent reasons to be somewhere else, bringing about a crippling shortage of labour over the entire Japanese-controlled railway system.

Fourteenth Army's advance now assumed rapid proportions, an event to be welcomed in itself but bringing in its wake significant supply problems that threatened to slow momentum and give Japanese forces breathing space. In his later report on this period General Leese refers to 'difficulties which, on occasion, are bound to arise when one Service is largely dependent on another for all the essentials of its existence under adverse conditions of climate and terrain'.[12] This is a considered reflection on a situation which, in the heat of the moment, provoked a certain amount of inter-service strife at the highest levels of Army and Air Forces. In January 1945 Admiral Mountbatten visited the forward areas and General Leese, dissatisfied with the amount of air supply that CCTF was providing to Fourteenth Army and fearful of the consequences, took the opportunity to circulate a memorandum stating that unless more transport aircraft became available not only might the Fourteenth Army advance come to a halt, the Army might also be forced to withdraw back beyond the Chindwin for the 1945 monsoon. This was without doubt a nightmare scenario and arose from a number of difficulties chafing both Army and Air Forces, which, instead of being rationally addressed and corrected, were overblown by the pressure cooker atmosphere of the time. Nevertheless it does need to be fully appreciated that this was the first time in military history that a modern mechanized army had succeeded in conducting a campaign hundreds of miles from its supply bases, with no lines of communication other than those of the sky, so there were bound to be difficulties.

In Northern Combat Area Command a high degree of cooperation existed between ground and air forces, but a similar ability for each arm to trust the other without being tempted to stray onto each other's turf cannot be said to have existed between CCTF and CAATO. CCTF, for instance, complained that the Army attempted to quote and work on flying hours per aircraft without any knowledge of aircraft availability. CCTF also became exercised at what was perceived to be unnecessary delays emanating from RAMOs without appreciating that the British and Indian Army officers and other ranks there were strained to breaking point, often being required to work 72-hour shifts to complete their tasks.[13] Comparisons between US packing and loading agencies at Dinjan and the Air Supply Companies at Hathezari reflected badly on the British units who, the air arm considered, were not given by the Army the personnel, facilities and organizing skills necessary for the scale of the job.[14] For his part General Leese, in an attempt to smooth out problem areas, appointed a senior officer, Brigadier J.A. Dawson, to the command of CAATO.

As a direct result of General Leese's representations Mountbatten put forward an urgent request to the Chiefs of Staff for additional transport squadrons, answered in March by the arrival in SEAC of Nos 238 and 267 RAF. Significantly, CCTF itself foresaw problems in maintaining a suitable level of supply to keep the Army moving at its rapid pace, but in contrast to General Leese considered that the root of the problem lay not with the provision of more aircraft but with the growing need for bases suitable for transports closer to the forward areas. In this respect the operations of XV Corps in the Arakan assumed prime importance as Akyab and Ramree islands, both of which already contained airfields, appeared ideally situated for development as main transport bases.

Joint Air/Army planning sessions concluded that, even with the limited amphibious resources available, with Japanese forces in any event slowly but steadily withdrawing, a series of assaults could be launched along the Arakan coast to secure these objectives in conjunction with 81st West African Division in the Kaladan Valley. These plans came to fruition when a series of small but effective amphibious attacks by elements of XV Corps succeeded in capturing Akyab, Myebon, Ramree, Kangaw, Ru-ywa and Letpan, while elements of the Royal Navy's reinvigorated East Indies Fleet under Vice Admiral Sir Arthur Power, including the battleship *Queen Elizabeth*, captured Cheduba.

The original intention for these forward bases was for Akyab to have an all-weather airstrip by 30 April, and Kyaukpyu on Ramree Island by 15 May. Such was the rate of advance of the ground troops, however, that this was not nearly early enough and fair-weather strips were developed alongside the all-weather versions. As a result two squadrons of Dakotas began supply operations from Akyab on 20 March in conjunction with No. 1 RAMO which had been transferred from Imphal. An additional two squadrons were in operation by the end of March, plus half a squadron operating from Kyaukpyu for the supply of troops in the Arakan. With the securing of adequate facilities along the coast March also saw quantities of supplies arriving by sea for onward transmission by air.

Air support for the Arakan operations was provided by 224 Group and highlighted two significant developments: the first the use of Spitfires in a fighter-bomber role (including No. 8 Squadron IAF); the second the utilization of two teams of light aircraft as airborne Visual Control Posts, flying at low level to seek out targets well camouflaged by coastal jungle. On discovering enemy positions their location would be passed to attack aircraft waiting above. The Visual Control Post system was subsequently enlarged to encompass ground-based units placed with forward infantry groups, ten such units being in operation by the end of 1944, rising to thirty-four by May 1945.

Resistance on the islands of Akyab and Ramree had been light, Akyab in fact being undefended, the Japanese 55th Division having been withdrawn to meet pressure from the West Africans in the Kaladan Valley. Amphibious landings on the mainland, however, attracted greater opposition the farther inland they progressed, developing into close-quarter fighting among the chaungs (streams) and mangrove swamps. To cut off the Japanese defenders from their lines of communication, fighters and fighter-bombers continually pounded the roadway southward to Toungup, the mountain road from Toungup to the railhead at Prome and the roadway eastward from An to Minbu. Such was the importance accorded by the Army to the interdiction of supplies along the mountain road to Prome that heavy bombers of the Strategic Air Force were also called into play, despite the fact that damage to the road would hinder the supply of Fourteenth Army itself once the area had been retaken. Targets along the Prome–Rangoon railway were also attacked, the Lightnings of 459 Squadron USAAF being particularly effective at the destruction of bridges along the line.

For the JAAF there were now few places left in Burma where they could count on being safe from attack. A prime example of this was the raid by forty P51 Mustangs of the USAAF led by Lieutenant Colonel Levi Chase. Taking off from Cox's Bazaar in the Arakan they embarked on the longest single-engine fighter raid of the war, flying 780 miles to Don Muang airfield 12 miles north of Bangkok, where they destroyed thirty-one aircraft and returned to base having lost only one Mustang.

The Japanese aircraft attacked were, among others, the fighters of 204th *Hikosentai* which had been moved to Don Muang while a proposed move to the Philippines was under discussion.

With 1945 only a few weeks old Admiral Mountbatten received a directive from the Combined Chiefs of Staff to the effect that Burma was to be liberated by the earliest possible date, an event which was to lead as quickly as possible to the liberation of Malaya and the opening of the Straits of Malacca. At a conference held in Calcutta to discuss strategy, Mountbatten asked Air Chief Marshal Park whether Eastern Air Command could take on the job of supporting Fourteenth Army on an overland campaign to capture Rangoon. It would be an immense task responded Park, but it could be done. Immediately the decision was taken to head overland to Rangoon a deadline imposed itself on ground and air forces alike. The principal port and capital of Burma had to be taken by May and the onset of the monsoon. If the operation was successful the gigantic task of feeding more than 300,000 men could be taken up by shipping supplies into the port – if not the job would have to be continued through a further five months of appalling weather by CCTF.

A plan for the reconquest of Burma as far as Mandalay, code-named 'Capital', had been under discussion since September. Developed and fine-tuned by General Slim it envisaged the encirclement of the Japanese Army, considered to have lost its finest troops at Imphal, in and around the city. 36th British Division was to march south from Myitkyina supported by Tenth USAAF; XXXIII Corps would advance on Mandalay from the north and west supported by 221 Group. All of which would hopefully take Japanese eyes off General Slim's tactical masterpiece, the clandestine movement of IV Corps from its positions around Kalewa on the left flank of Fourteenth Army, on a wide 'right hook' to Meiktila, 80 miles south of Mandalay and directly astride the main Japanese artery of supply from Rangoon. As soon as this vital Japanese strongpoint was taken, transports would fly in a fresh British brigade while bombers completed the encirclement of Mandalay.

In addition to XXXIII Corps, 221 Group would also support IV Corps on its march south. To effect close cooperation the headquarters of both Fourteenth Army and 221 Group had been established at Imphal, but now moved forward jointly to Monywa in anticipation of the opening of the campaign. As IV Corps moved south the area of operations covered by 221 Group grew to a front 200 miles long by approximately the same in depth, and was destined to grow much larger as the months progressed. As the battle front moved outwards so the squadrons became scattered over a wide area, fighters in particular

148

keeping pace with the front line and moving onto forward airstrips days after an area was taken. While the aircraft were able to fly in, ground crew, kept to a minimum to aid mobility, plus spares and ancillary equipment had to be brought in by transports.

All aircraft engaged in close, as distinct from tactical, support of Fourteenth Army were controlled by HQ 221 Group. For a crucial period in the campaign to take Meiktila, two exceptions were made to this command arrangement with regard to two US Air Commando Groups, which were operated directly from HQ Eastern Air Command, and the Mustangs of Second Air Commando USAAF, which were operated from the advanced HQ of CCTF as it moved forward together with HQ IV Corps.

An exception was also made in the case of the four Thunderbolt squadrons of 905 Wing RAF, which, being based in the Arakan but assigned to the support of Fourteenth Army remained under 224 Group.

Faced with attacks along the whole front from China in the north to the Arakan in the south, the new Japanese C-in-C, Lieutenant General Kimura Hyotaro, realized that the battle for Burma hinged on the central sector around Mandalay and developed a plan of his own. Anticipating an attempt by Fourteenth Army to cross the Irrawaddy, he would concentrate much of his available force around Mandalay at the expense of the Arakan and the northern front, so as to attack Fourteenth Army while it was split by the river, with its divisions on the west bank isolated. Getting wind of Japanese reinforcement Slim urged increased pressure from XV Corps in the south and the Chinese-American forces to the north, also requesting that the 36th Division be moved to the centre as reinforcement. Mountbatten and Leese both recognized the need but the division was some distance to the north, and without transport aircraft to spare time would be needed to bring it south by road.

The only reinforcement available for the centre was 5th Indian Division, which Slim ordered up.

Notes

1. Chindits who had just been flown out of Burma but were immediately flown back due to the pressing need for anti-aircraft batteries – one more example of the flexibility that air power gave to the Allied commanders.
2. Smith, W.E. (ed.), *2nd Troop Carrier Squadron USAAF – CBI – WWII* (The Gregath Company, 1987), pp. 100–5.
3. TNA Air 41/37, *Air Supply Operations in Burma 1942–1943*, p. 27.
4. Craven, W.F. and Cate J.L. (eds), *The Army Air Forces in World War II*, Vol. VII (University of Chicago Press, 1958), p. 138.

5. TNA Air 2/9883, *Operations in Burma from 12 November 1944 to 15 August 1945*, Lieutenant General Sir Oliver Leese, Bart., p. 1946.
6. Williams, Flight Lieutenant Douglas, *194 Squadron Royal Air Force – 'The Friendly Firm' (Burma Campaign)*, (Merlin Books, 1987), pp. 43–6.
7. TNA Air 2/7906, *Air Operations in South East Asia, 16 November 1943 to 31 May 1944*, Air Chief Marshal Sir Richard E. Peirse, and TNA Air 2/7908, p. 19.
8. *Op. cit.*, Note 3, p. 1405.
9. *Wings of the Phoenix* (HMSO, 1949), p. 68.
10. *Japanese Monograph No. 64* (The Library of Congress, Washington DC), pp. 75–81.
11. Probert, Air Commodore Henry, *The Forgotten Air Force* (Brassey's, 1995), p. 233.
12. *Op. cit.*, Note 5.
13. *Op. cit.*, Note 3, p. 50.
14. TNA Air 2/7908, *Air Operations in South East Asia, 1 June 1944 to 2 May 1945*, Air Chief Marshal Sir Keith Park, p. 9.

Chapter Seven

End Game

I

The long southward trek by General Messervy's IV Corps met its first serious obstacle at Gangaw in the Kabaw Valley, which was held by well entrenched Japanese infantry. Messervy's problem was that he could not attack in full strength without giving away the presence of his corps, and being only able to use light spearhead forces he called on EAC to achieve the rapid removal of the obstruction. EAC had developed two plans to meet situations such as this, code-named 'Earthquake Major' and 'Earthquake Minor'. For the former, Liberator heavy bombers would bomb the target followed up by fighter-bombers strafing as ground forces advanced. Fighters would then make low-level dummy attacks to keep the enemy's heads down as Allied infantry closed in. Earthquake Minor followed the same principle with the exception that Mitchell medium bombers would be used for the initial assault. In the event, 'Earthquake Minor' was ordered for Gangaw and carried out by four Mitchell squadrons of the USAAF plus Thunderbolts and Hurricanes of the RAF, fighter cover being provided by RAF Spitfires. RAF air control officers, experienced from operations with the Chindits and located with forward infantry companies, then called down strikes by Hurricanes onto any positions still intact after Earthquake. Ninety minutes after the air assault ceased five of the six main enemy positions were in IV Corps hands for the loss of two infantry wounded. The subsequent ease with which the Japanese were cleared from the area was attributed to a significant lowering of morale caused by the bombing.

Transport pilots watching the advance of IV Corps from the air said that a line of red dust thrown up by Corps vehicles, including everything from Sherman tanks to bullock carts, could be seen for miles as the column passed through Gangaw. Fortunately JAAF air reconnaissance was negligible and any aircraft that might have made the attempt was kept at a respectable distance by fighter cover. As IV Corps advanced, transport aircraft operating from the newly secured airstrips at Akyab and elsewhere in the Arakan parachuted supplies into designated Corps drop zones in dry river beds or landed at freshly bulldozed landing strips.

As the leading elements of IV Corps approached the Irrawaddy, 221 Group was called upon to instigate a game of subterfuge to confuse the enemy. Operation Cloak was designed to simulate flare-ups at numerous points along the river and draw enemy forces away from the village of Pagan, the location of the actual crossing. In similar fashion to operations carried out during the run-up to the Normandy landings, dummy parachutists were dropped as well as devices known as 'canned battle' which, on hitting the ground, precisely imitated the sound of rifle-fire punctuated by the explosion of hand grenades. Similarly 'Aquakit', when dropped onto water, sent up Very lights. These operations were carried out for several days from 6 February onwards and had the desired effect, 7th Division making their way over the river to establish a bridgehead through which IV Corps could pass. Air support during the river crossing included the use of both explosive and liquid-fire napalm bombs, which had now arrived in theatre. Napalm has since acquired a thoroughly unpleasant reputation and its effects on those unfortunate enough to be so attacked are truly horrific. Nevertheless, rightly or wrongly, its use was sanctioned against Japanese troops in part as a response to their barbarous treatment of Allied prisoners of war.

With a bridgehead secured, between 18 and 21 February the lead units of IV Corps, 17th Division plus 255 Tank Brigade, were brought across the Irrawaddy. On the 21st, with rear echelons still making the crossing, the Division struck out eastwards for Meiktila.

For 5th *Hikoshidan* the situation from the end of the 1944 monsoon onwards became increasingly critical, with too few aircraft to cover the exceptionally large combat area. Its main priority was fixed at support for the Burma Area Army as it withdrew from Imphal to positions around Mandalay, but should the seaborne attack so feared and expected materialize operations against amphibious assaults would take precedence.

Cover for the ground forces retreat was principally the responsibility of 4th *Hikodan*, comprising the 50th and 8th *Hikosentai* (fighters and light bombers respectively). Reconnaissance patrols over the Bay of Bengal as far as Chittagong were to be maintained to give ample warning of the anticipated seaborne attack.

Demonstrating the extreme shortage of aircraft available to Japanese forces in general at this time, a proposal was put forward that 5th *Hikoshidan* should be withdrawn to the Philippines in its entirety to assist with the campaign to drive back MacArthur's invasion, which had begun on 20 October. This would of course leave Burma Area Army without air cover at all and following representations to the High Command it was agreed that a skeleton force of two fighter *sentai*, a single light bomber *sentai*, and one air reconnaissance company should remain. Air strength available to the Japanese in Burma now fell well below minimum effective operational levels for the tasks at hand and comprised the following:

Hikoshidan Shireibu	Rangoon.
50th *Hikosentai* re-equipping with Ki-84 Frank fighters	Bangkok.
64th *Hikosentai* twenty Type 3 Ki-43 Oscar fighters	Central Burma.
8th *Hikosentai* twenty-five Ki-48 Lily light bombers	Indo China.
81st *Hikosentai* thirteen Type 2 & 3 Ki-46 Dinah reconnaissance aircraft	Dispersed.[1]

During the latter part of October fighter units were concentrated on the airfields around Rangoon, while 8th *Hikosentai* carried out a series of small-scale night raids, all that it was now capable of, across Burma and into China:

27 October	Attack by four light bombers on Myitkyina.
28 October	Three light bombers attack Chakaria and Cox's Bazaar.
29 October	Three light bombers raid Feni & surrounding airstrips.
24 November	Raid on Kunming.
25 November	Raid on Myitkyina.
28 November	Raid on Yunnan.
29 November	Raid on Kunming.

All of the November raids were carried out by three or four light bombers.[2]

On 7 December, 8th *Hikosentai* attempted a raid on the B29 Superfortresses of 20th Bomber Command at Midonapur, near Calcutta. Blackout in the area had been discontinued, perhaps a little prematurely, even if it was close to a year since the JAAF had paid Calcutta any attention, but still the raid met with little success. Another attempt was made on 25 December but was intercepted by the fighter defence.

While 8th *Hikosentai* did what it could the fighters were not idle, carrying out a number of strafing raids on airfields and ground support targets. On 14 December a raid carried out by eleven Oscars of the 64th *Hikosentai* failed to find its target, but on their way back to base the

153

raiders happened across a number of transport aircraft with covering fighters, claiming six transports and two Thunderbolts for the loss of two Oscars in the ensuing engagement.

As the Burma Area Army concentrated around Mandalay a decision was taken to move all railway rolling stock to the south of the city for future operations. The movement was consistently hampered by Allied aircraft bombing the Minbu bridge, and to effect the transfer the entire strength of 64th *Hikosentai* was sent to patrol the area of the bridge towards the end of December, as a result of which the trains were successfully moved south between the 29th and 31st of the month.

50th *Hikosentai* completed re-equipping during December, its final complement fourteen Ki-84 Frank fighters and four Ki-43 Oscars. The unit immediately carried out a ground support attack on an Allied mechanized column threatening to cut off the Japanese 15th Division in the Shwebo area, claiming 150 trucks destroyed, the 20 mm cannon of the Frank proving particularly effective in this role.

As the fighting along the Irrawaddy intensified the entire 50th *Hikosentai* and a portion of 8th *Hikosentai* were transferred to Indo China to counter air strikes from a US Navy carrier task force, further crippling Japanese air cover for the impending battles around Meiktila.

II

From the Irrawaddy crossing to Meiktila, 17th Division had to cover 85 miles. On meeting light opposition forward units captured Mahlang, 20 miles from Meiktila, on 25 February. The vital Thabutkon airfield now lay just 10 miles from Mahlang and 255 Tank Brigade forged on to effect its capture on the 26th. Working overnight to repair damage inflicted by retreating Japanese, by the following day the Brigade had Thabutkon in good enough repair for the fly-in of supplies and reinforcements to begin.

The 4,000 men of 17th Division's 99 Airborne Brigade were the first to arrive and over the next four and a half days transports made a staggering 655 trips to the airfield, the majority by squadrons of the USAAF, although Nos 31, 62, 117, 194, 267 and 435 RAF also played an important part. In addition to infantry reinforcements these first few days saw significant stores of petrol, ammunition and rations landed, many aircrew averaging more than twelve hours' flying time per day.

Recovering from the setback the local Japanese commander, Major General Kasuya, launched heavy attacks on all sides of the airfield, transports landing and discharging their loads under fire. One aircraft taking on wounded for its return journey had a shell explode inside the

154

fuselage, causing additional injuries. Two Dakotas were destroyed by a 75 mm gun firing from a position at the end of the runway, and such was the determined nature of Japanese attempts to retake the airfield that at times they would recapture the strip at night and have to be driven off the following morning, two field squadrons of the RAF Regiment playing a significant part in these operations. So precarious did the situation become that landings were stopped and supplies dropped instead by parachute, with all the attendant risk of loss or damage and the knock-on effect of increased demands on the transports.

The allocation of a single FAMO to Thabutkon during the initial landings also caused its share of problems, the officer in charge being obliged to guide aircraft to unloading points when he should have been free to organize their rapid turnaround under fire.

Major General Kasuya had under command some 12,000 men but they were scattered over a wide area protecting dumps, airfields and communications. In Meiktila itself he had around 1,500 miscellaneous base troops, but recognizing the importance of the village he showed considerable energy and determination to hold out, organizing improvised infantry companies from administrative units and whatever came to hand, arranging his perimeter into sectors with reserves, and constructing defensive positions. Every available soldier was pressed into line, including wounded from the local hospital. Ordnance depots were opened and automatic weapons and ammunition issued to every man capable of using a gun. Drawing in airfield defence battalions he sited anti-aircraft guns as anti-tank weapons and at the last moment had the extreme good fortune to receive substantial reinforcements. In response to Kimura's orders drawing units to the Mandalay area, most of the Japanese 49th Infantry Regiment arrived in Meiktila, and Kasuya kept them there. Captured records later showed that 3,200 men, well armed and equipped, defended the town.[3]

The overall tactical situation was now delicately balanced. Around Mandalay Kimura was beginning operations designed to overwhelm the advance by XXXIII Corps, which he believed to be the bulk of Fourteenth Army. Both to relieve the pressure on XXXIII Corps and spring the trap, Slim had to capture Meiktila quickly, forcing Kimura to react to a large force astride his principal line of communications. When he did XXXIII Corps would launch an all-out offensive of its own – the hammer to IV Corps' anvil, with Kimura's Burma Area Army in between.

All-out conflict now raged along a vast concave battle line stretching from northern Burma through Mandalay to Meiktila. Allied transport squadrons were in constant operation and in grave danger of being swamped by the demands made upon them. Recalling the period General Slim commented:

> We were never without acute anxiety on the supply and transport side. Almost daily there was a crisis of some kind. The reserves of some basic ration would fall frighteningly low, guns would be silent for want of ammunition, river craft out of action for want of spares, wounded collecting in some hard-pressed spot with no means of evacuating them. Petrol was always desperately short.[4]

Into this exceedingly close-run situation burst a metaphorical bombshell that threatened to unravel Allied plans entirely. Having halted the Japanese attack in China previously referred to, Chiang Kai-shek now decided on an offensive of his own and on 23 February Slim was notified that all US and Chinese forces then in northern Burma were to be withdrawn, and that pending their withdrawal they were to advance no further than a line stretching from Lashio through Hsipaw to Kyaukme – 80 miles north-east of Mandalay. Kimura would, therefore, be free to transfer practically his entire force in the north to the Fourteenth Army front, while Slim would be responsible for maintaining an extended line that included the newly recaptured Burma–China road. As if that problem was not enough, Slim was also notified that the USAAF transport squadrons then supplying the Chinese would be required to fly them out, while the squadrons allocated to Fourteenth Army would now additionally be required to supply both 36th Division and the Chinese awaiting transfer.

With the assault on Meiktila under way both Slim and General Leese protested in the strongest terms and Mountbatten flew to Chungking to try to redress the situation with the Generalissimo in person, but to no avail. The loss of the US and Chinese troops was a hammer blow to Slim's plans, but his greatest anxiety was reserved for the reduction in available transport aircraft.

Rising to the challenge Mountbatten, backed by the British Chiefs of Staff, was able to persuade the US Chiefs of Staff to leave the great majority of their transport squadrons in Burma until either the capture of Rangoon or 1 June, whichever proved to be the sooner. The latter would see the 1945 monsoon in full fury, and as things now stood the prospects for a rapid capture of Rangoon did not look as rosy as they had. Slim, however, was much relieved by the decision and decided to let June look after itself for the time being while he pressed on with the assaults on Mandalay and Meiktila.

Responding to Kasuya's orders to concentrate there, Japanese units closed on Meiktila, the village and the surrounding area becoming a boiling cauldron of combat. 17th Division began its attack on

28 February and in four days of intense fighting, during which the fanatical defenders were practically wiped out to a man, finally captured the vital strongpoint.

As anticipated Kimura reacted swiftly by changing his point of concentration to Meiktila and enabling the XXXIII Corps attack on Mandalay to gain momentum, with frequent calls for air support to remove obstacles to its progress. To the north of the ancient town the Japanese brought up heavy artillery to blast a corps bridgehead at Singu. Over a 48-hour period Mitchells and Thunderbolts kept up a continual assault on the Japanese position until the guns were silenced. Ahead of the troops, by day and night, Mosquitoes, Hurricanes and Beaufighters attacked again and again, clearing Japanese entrenchments and strong-points from the path of the advancing infantry. XXXIII Corps invested Mandalay from the north, west and south, the Japanese assuming that the main thrust would come from the west at Myinmu. Highlighting their lack of intention to fight in open country the Japanese had but one tank regiment in Burma, which they now committed at Myinmu. The presence of tanks was suspected by Fourteenth Army but not confirmed, and aerial reconnaissance flights were asked to keep a particular eye out for them.

Circling the Mandalay battle area two Hurricanes, one piloted by Flight Lieutenant James Farquharson, the other by Flight Lieutenant R.J. Ballard, awaited a target call from a Visual Control Post, but received instead a message over the R/T that while there was nothing presently in view they should keep a sharp lookout for Japanese armour. Farquharson in particular had a reputation for successful reconnaissance and spotted tracks that might have belonged to a tank disappearing into scrub. Radioing his find to the VCP and Ballard, the second Hurricane joined him and they circled the area until they spotted what appeared to be a small native hut in a nullah. The hut was camouflaged with tree branches but there were no trees anywhere nearby. Farquharson loosed off a couple of cannon shells which blew away the branches to reveal a tank. Armed with 40 mm cannon the two Hurricanes quickly disposed of the tank then extended their search to the south, calling up reinforcements as they did so. During the course of the day thirteen tanks were discovered and all were destroyed with cannon or rocket fire in what proved to be the heaviest concentration of Japanese armour during the campaign for Burma. Curiously, the Japanese relied entirely on camouflage to protect the tanks, having no anti-aircraft guns in place – until the following day when it was too late. An exultant message to the Hurricane squadron from the division facing the tanks read: 'Nippon Hardware Corporation has gone bust. Nice work. Tanks a million!'[5]

With so large a battle area in a continuous state of flux, air reconnaissance was an essential component of the Allied campaign. Closely involved in these operations was No. 1 Squadron IAF, despite the fact that on the night of 4 March a single Japanese bomber – almost certainly despatched by 8th *Hikosentai* – bombed the Squadron base damaging nine Hurricanes and causing a number of injuries. Despite their reduced numbers squadron aircraft covered the length and breadth of Burma, paying particular attention to strategic road and rail junctions such as Meiktila and carrying out a number of sorties per day in order to provide the most up-to-date intelligence possible of both Japanese movements and the location of the widely dispersed Allied forces. At the end of March the Squadron was withdrawn, bringing to a close a fourteen-month tour of duty during which 4,813 operational sorties were undertaken totalling 7,219 hours 45 minutes, and garnering in the process much praise from ground forces for the high standard of their reconnaissance work. Their place was taken by No. 7 Squadron IAF.[6]

The battle for Mandalay culminated with the Japanese defenders inside the formidable 45-foot-thick earth backed walls of Fort Dufferin, entirely surrounded by a moat. Unable to spare sufficient troops to take the defences by storm, Slim asked for help from the air forces, who had studied the problem of reducing Dufferin with bombs and rockets, and put their plan into action. Assisted by Hurricanes and American Mitchells, Thunderbolts in a bomber role were the principal weapon. Commanding the Thunderbolts was Group Captain B.A. Chacksfield RAF, who adopted a 'Master-bomber' technique, circling above the target directing his Wing by radio. Watching the first aircraft swoop in he observed the bombs hit the earthen slopes on the inside of the walls and bounce outside before exploding. Switching the attack around he had succeeding aircraft bomb from the outside in, advising on the correct approach, height and precise spot at which to keep aiming. Finally twenty-six gaps were blown through the great walls and when attacking infantry entered they found that the defenders had fled through a secret sewer. On 20 March 1945 Fourteenth Army hoisted its flag over historic Mandalay, a day of triumph in the north where it seemed that the Japanese defence of Burma was collapsing like a leaky balloon. The issue, however, did not appear so clear cut around Meiktila.

III

CCTF mustered seventeen squadrons with which to supply and maintain Fourteenth Army in the field, plus the bulk of XV Corps in the Arakan. Every transport aircraft was desperately required but Meiktila took a heavy toll. Now receiving the brunt of Kimura's attacks as his Burma Area Army flooded south from Mandalay, IV Corps was desperately in need of supply and reinforcement, but the airfield at Thabutkon remained a fiercely contested strip of tarmac. Japanese artillery and sniper fire continued to sweep the area and on 20 March, the day the flag was hoisted over Mandalay, twelve artillery shells dropped with pinpoint accuracy into a Dakota parking bay. Seven aircraft were severely damaged and many casualties suffered. Showing considerable coolness under fire an Army captain from the FAMO guided those aircraft still undamaged out of the dispersal area and onto the strip for take-off.

Allied fighters and fighter-bombers constantly patrolled the skies above the battle area, swooping to attack targets as soon as they were pinpointed by Visual Control Posts, often bombing and strafing only a hundred yards or so in front of IV Corps infantry.

Despite its reduced resources 5th *Hikoshidan* was also committed to the battle for Meiktila, the Ki-48 Lily light bombers of 8th *Hikosentai* raiding the airfield in twos and threes on 8, 12, 14 and 20 March. With priorities now fixed elsewhere 5th *Hikoshidan* was under orders to move to the Siam/Indo China area, leaving skeleton forces only in Burma. However, before leaving it put together one final series of raids using the forces available:

50th and 64th *Hikosentai*, 17 fighters in total.
8th *Hikosentai*, 9 light bombers.
58th *Hikosentai*, 4 heavy bombers.
81st *Hikosentai*, 3 reconnaissance aircraft.

Operating from airfields around Rangoon these units carried out a series of raids on Allied airfields at Shwebo, Thmadaw, Kalemyo, Cox's Bazaar, Akyab and Kyaukpyu, and ground support operations, principally fighter sorties, in the Toungoo area.

At Meiktila it became the unenviable task of the men of the RAF Regiment to comb the airstrip before dawn to winkle out any Japanese infiltrators before the Dakotas arrived. Strung out in a line the 400 men of the Regiment would investigate every shell crater, gully and fox-hole for snipers. The patrols would take two hours to complete but were in the main successful. One morning the Japanese sent in two companies of infantry to make a determined attack and while the Tank Regiment got into position to drive the intruders off, it fell to the two field squadrons of the RAF Regiment to hold the attackers back, which they did, inflicting forty-eight killed for the loss of seven of their own number.

So fluid was the situation that should an aircraft be sufficiently damaged as to require leaving on the airstrip overnight it would almost certainly be blown up by enemy patrols before morning. With the attrition rate for transports escalating dangerously, for some days at the end of March landings were stopped and supplies parachuted in. Despite the embargo L.5 Sentinels of the air ambulance service were still required to land, flying 550 sick and wounded to Casualty Air Evacuation Units in the hospital zones.

One of the many shortages in the campaigns for Burma concerned air ambulance nursing orderlies. Of the 150 required only twenty-seven were ever supplied, one of whom was Leading Aircraftsman Ian Fiddes. On Dakota flights it was the job of the nursing orderlies to accompany patients, administer oxygen or morphine should they be required and generally attend to the well-being of their charges. Stretchers would be arranged on brackets inside the fuselage of the aircraft which, in the turbulence of monsoon storms, were apt to break and it would be the responsibility of the orderly to bring order to the resulting confusion, usually in the dark.

For nine days in every ten, over a continuous period of five months, Leading Aircraftsman Fiddes averaged ten hours per day on such flights, at times being required to put in as many as thirteen hours. At the end of March he was sent to Meiktila. Such was the build-up of casualties that the embargo on Dakotas was lifted temporarily and the aircraft in which Fiddes travelled swept low over the heads of Japanese infantry on the perimeter of the airfield and landed amid a fierce firefight. With the aircraft under fire stores were unloaded and, assisted by RAF servicing commandos, Fiddes carried casualties aboard, including a brigade major seriously wounded by a shell, and a badly burned Sikh swathed in bandages. With explosions from enemy mortar bombs creeping ever closer, an anti-tank gun fired over open sights from a position only 200 yards away. A mortar bomb destroyed the port undercarriage, splinters ripping through the fuselage; a second destroyed the tail section. With the aircraft now in no condition to take off Fiddes, the RAF crew and the commandos began to carry the stretcher-cases, including the brigade major, now with another serious head wound, to blast pens intended for aircraft. Returning for the Sikh, his last case, Fiddes found that his patient had managed, despite his burns, to crawl to a crater. With the aircraft still under fire Fiddes once more climbed aboard to retrieve his medical kit and oxygen and then made his way to the craters along the perimeter to offer what help he could to the wounded.

With the area still under heavy mortar fire Fiddes commandeered a jeep and driver, placed the major aboard and sent him off to the Casualty Clearing Station. Locating an ambulance he filled the vehicle with stretcher cases until the ambulance itself became a target. Unloading the vehicle again Fiddes carried the wounded back to a shelter until, during a lull in the firing, he was able to carry them one by one to an assembly point a quarter of a mile away where they were collected by ambulances.

Already exhausted, Fiddes returned to the RAF defensive box at the airstrip and continued his first aid work. The box remained under sustained attack for another forty-eight hours, Fiddes spending his time for the most part in the open rescuing wounded.

A short airstrip on the other side of Meiktila had been opened and RAF and USAAF Sentinels were landing to take off wounded. Hearing that air ambulances were operating, the defenders of the box decided to evacuate their casualties by means of a three-ton truck, and thirty wounded were loaded aboard. Fiddes opted to accompany them. En route the lorry became caught in crossfire and the Leading Aircraftsman either led or carried his charges to craters along the roadside. They were finally rescued by Gurkha infantry, who dispatched the Japanese and helped reload the lorry. At the airstrip Leading Aircraftsman Fiddes saw all his wounded safely away then went out himself on the last Sentinel. It had been his first time under fire. His next assignment was in a Dakota back to Meiktila.[7]

Gradually IV Corps tightened its grip on the vital road and rail junction until finally, in the early part of April, Japanese pressure lessened as their forces began to drain away southward towards Rangoon. The gruesome task of body counts indicated that the Japanese lost around 250 dead per day during their furious assaults on Meiktila, the daily count sometimes reaching as high as 400. As some indication of their growing desperation, the blackest day for Japanese losses came at the end of their attempts to take the town. On 10 April, 1,100 bodies were counted.

By this time air supply to Fourteenth Army had reached an astonishing 74,000 tons per month – the transports lifting 95,000 tons if all Allied formations in Burma are included – a system virtually ignored by the JAAF both in terms of the interdiction of Allied transport aircraft and the supply of their own troops.

Kimura now faced attack from three directions across the huge Mandalay/Meiktila front. Denied air supply – although what remained of 5th *Hikoshidan* did attempt to drop medical supplies – and with the few ground-based lines of communication remaining open constantly bombed and strafed by Eastern Air Command, by the middle of April 1945 the once mighty Japanese Burma Area Army, unable to re-equip with any of the essentials of war, began to fall apart.

Despite their straitened circumstances ad hoc resistance by Japanese units continued and a deadline was growing in importance to General Slim – the six to eight weeks remaining before the onset of the monsoon. Should the weather break before the capture of Rangoon, Fourteenth Army might still be forced into a withdrawal by the weather, allowing the Japanese time to re-equip and reorganize, with all the protracted campaigning and losses in men and materiel that would entail.

The drawing up of plans for a combined air/land/sea reconquest of Burma went back almost as far as 1942, but combined operations had always been thwarted by lack of equipment, particularly amphibious craft and naval escorts. However, with the necessary resources now becoming available one such plan, code-named 'Dracula', had been approved by the Joint Chiefs of Staff in September 1944. With its objectives modified to the capture of Rangoon it was now proposed to put Dracula into operation combined with a landward thrust from Fourteenth Army.

By this time Akyab was fully operational as a base for transport aircraft, Nos 62, 194, 267 and 436 Squadrons RAF being based there, Nos 194 and 436 commencing operations on 20 March, and Nos 62 and 267 on 1 April. Also during the course of April, Ramree Island opened as a transport base, detachments from Nos 31, 62 and 436 Squadrons operating there from the 16th of the month. CCTF also benefited from the arrival of two additional squadrons, Nos 96 and 215 RAF.

With his manpower limited Slim organized the dash for Rangoon by advancing Fourteenth Army in two armoured columns: XXXIII Corps south-westwards along the Irrawaddy Valley; and IV Corps southwards down the Mandalay–Rangoon railway. One notable date for the RAF in the advance of XXXIII Corps was 18 April when Magwe, the scene of the RAF's greatest disaster in Burma, was retaken.

Being farther to the south and with the more direct route the main thrust for Rangoon would be that of IV Corps, and to facilitate the advance two airborne operations, 'Gumption' and 'Freeborn', were put into place. These involved the use of glider-borne engineer battalions of the US Army, forward landed to repair transport airstrips and facilitate the rapid receipt and dispersal of the supplies necessary to keep IV Corps on the move. By the middle of April materiel for Gumption – fifty-five gliders and 86,000 gallons of aviation fuel – had been stock-piled at Meiktila. Bypassing Pyinmana, forward elements of IV Corps made rapid progress to the airfield at Lewe, which was captured on 20 April and prepared by British and American engineers sufficiently for gliders from the pool at Meiktila to fly in the following day. The gliders carried with them quantities of essential equipment including bulldozers, jeeps, tractors, food and water. Skirmishing continued all day as the engineers went about their essential tasks, and on the 22nd the JAAF managed one of its fighter raids, eight Oscars strafing the gliders, five of which were destroyed. Ten minutes after the Oscars departed the first supply-dropping transports arrived overhead.

As the engineers completed their work at Lewe leading elements of 5th Indian Division pushed forward into Toungoo, capturing the town against light opposition. While 5th Division continued their advance, six of the Meiktila gliders were flown in to Tennant airfield at Toungoo, disgorging US engineers – for which the RAF had no equivalent organization – and loads similar to those at Lewe. Craters were filled, essential repairs carried out and a 6,000-foot-long airstrip made serviceable. On 24 April Tennant witnessed the landing of fifty-six heavily laden CCTF transports.[8]

With IV Corps closing in on Rangoon and Operation Dracula scheduled to commence within a few days, on 29 April Operation Freeborn was launched. With the first storms of the monsoon beginning to blow, Freeborn entailed the airlifting of a battalion group of 9 Brigade to Pyuntaza airfield north of Pegu, itself some 40 miles north of Rangoon, to cut off any Japanese escape route eastwards from the capital. Twenty-eight transports duly ferried in infantry, ammunition, small arms, jeeps, trailers and a fully equipped mobile radio station. Immediately upon landing the troops set off for Pegu, clearing half the town of the enemy that same day, discovering as they did so some 400 British and American prisoners of war in the process of being marched by their captors from Rangoon jail, intending to take them across the Sittang River and into Siam.

The American glider-borne engineers had one more service to perform for IV Corps, flying in to Zayatkwin airfield on 8 May to prepare the airstrip there. Elsewhere, however, momentous events had taken place.

Operation Dracula, as it now stood, entailed a force of paratroops landing to neutralize seaward-facing heavy guns followed by a seaborne invasion, units of XV Corps entering the city from the Rangoon River estuary. Both operations were to be covered by extensive air support from 224 Group, with 221 Group maintaining pressure on any outlying Japanese formations. D-Day was fixed for 2 May, Air Commodore the Earl of Bandon was appointed to command the substantial tactical air operations, while Brigadier General Evans controlled the air transports. Strategic Air Force prepared the way by saturation bombing of supply dumps containing reserves sufficient for an estimated six months, these attacks including the Superfortresses of 20 Bomber Command.

Extensive photographic reconnaissance had located some 1,700 widely dispersed storage units of which approximately half were destroyed. Roads, railway yards, rolling stock, radar and gun emplacements, bridges, airfields and enemy troops all received the undivided attention of the air forces. RAF Liberators mined the river, forcing those Japanese attempting to escape to make their way either overland towards Pegu and the waiting IV Corps, or eastwards through swamps and across the Bay of Martaban.

Allied fighters and fighter bombers enjoyed something of a field day from the middle of April to early May, the rapid advance of Fourteenth Army having flushed from cover an unusual number of enemy MT units. On 19 April a Hurricane squadron attacked a heavily loaded and camouflaged convoy forty strong at a standstill just south of Pyinmana, leaving seventeen vehicles in flames and many more damaged. The same squadron located a larger column approaching the bridge over the Sittang at Mokpalin on the 30th, leaving forty-three lorries in flames. The approaches west of the Sittang Bridge in fact became a happy hunting ground for the fighters as the bridge was one of the main escape routes for the thousands of Japanese now attempting to make their way to Siam. The Mustangs of Second Air Commando Group and the Beaufighters of 224 Group made significant strikes in the area during the latter part of April.

On 1 May the initial phase of Dracula got under way when two pathfinder aircraft and thirty-eight transports of the 317th and 319th Troop Carrier Squadrons USAAF lifted off from Akyab carrying Gurkha paratroops, which they successfully dropped without opposition over their intended landing ground at Elephant Point, south of Rangoon. The following day Dakotas of Nos 194 and 267 Squadrons RAF dropped rations and ammunition at Elephant Point.

That same day, 2 May, another airborne operation took place. Wing Commander Saunders, Officer Commanding 110 Squadron RAF, took his Mosquito on a low-level reconnaissance over Rangoon. Detecting a surprising absence of Japanese he flew over Rangoon jail and saw two notices painted in large letters on the roofs of the prison blocks; the first read: JAPS GONE BRITISH HERE, the second, rather more to the point, stating simply: EXTRACT DIGIT.

Landing at Mingaladon, Saunders hitch-hiked into Rangoon and released a number of prisoners of war. Then, having achieved the single-handed 'liberation' of Rangoon, he borrowed a native boat and rowed downriver to inform the commander of the invasion force that the Japanese had gone, which came as something of a surprise to the Army as they were convinced that the enemy had substantial forces in the city and would defend it to the death.[9]

IV

Japanese resistance did continue as pockets of troops, some of them large, attempted to escape from Burma, but for the moment the principal problem facing the Allies following the recapture of Rangoon was once again supply. Seaborne traffic suffered delays as more work than anticipated was required to bring the docks to something approaching full capacity. On 1 June the joint British/US Eastern Air Command was dissolved, American squadrons, as agreed, being withdrawn to China following the capture of Rangoon. The part played by all US forces in Burma, but the USAAF in particular, was a highly significant one, the number of American squadrons finally involved totalling forty-seven to the fifty-one squadrons of the British and Commonwealth air forces.

The RAF transport units hitherto belonging to CCTF now became 232 Group under Air Commodore J.D.I. Hardman, and operations continued unabated. Also during May, 221 Group found itself with a new AOC, Air Vice-Marshal C.A. Bouchier. On 21 May the outgoing AOC, Air Vice-Marshal Vincent, had been surprised and pleased to receive a captured Japanese 105 mm gun, presented by General Slim in recognition of the unfailing support and invaluable contribution that Vincent and 221 Group had delivered in support of Fourteenth Army. Both Slim and Fourteenth Army were also to leave Burma for Malaya, their place being taken by the newly formed Twelfth Army under Lieutenant General M.G.N. Stopford.

It being too late to cancel, Operation Dracula went ahead and in the event turned into little more than a victory parade, however it did mean that ground forces in the Rangoon area now totalled upwards of 350,000 men and they all had to be fed.

On 10 May, Nos 31, 117 and 436 Squadrons RAF moved from Hathazari to join their detachments already at Ramree, the squadrons being operable from the 15th. Nos 62, 194 and 267 Squadrons RAF continued operations from Akyab, while No. 435 Squadron RCAF operated from Tulihal to supply the civilian population of northern Burma. Nos 96 and 215 RAF, newly arrived, were withdrawn again pending future operations in Malaya, while No. 238 RAF left the theatre completely.

During May, the last full month in which British and Commonwealth transport squadrons operated in conjunction with those of the USAAF, supply to IV, XV and XXXIII Corps, plus the supply drops to civilians in the north, totalled 67,293 tons.

The months of May and June 1945 were remembered by the transport squadrons as being among the most difficult flying conditions that they had to encounter. The southward dash to Rangoon had been accompanied by fine weather, but as soon as the city was captured the monsoon broke with particular ferocity. The airstrip at Ramree Island, despite being reconstructed for an all-weather role, frequently flooded, becoming so waterlogged that aircraft were unable to take off. At the Pyuntaza strip north of Pegu aircraft sank in mud up to their wheel hubs and were obliged to take off along deeply rutted runways.

For the RAF a further complication arose from what they perceived to be inflexible Army planning, which they felt seemed unable to come to grips with the fact that a margin of surplus had been built into supply drops during May. Mechanical difficulties also made their presence felt when, no doubt as a result of the long hours they had been obliged to fly, a rash of main engine bearing failures affected Dakota aircraft, causing an appreciable drop in transport availability.

What does perhaps come as a surprise, given the problems, is that during July, when 232 Group operated without the tremendous assistance of the USAAF, hours flown and tonnages delivered were proportionately greater than had previously been achieved.[10]

The nature of Fourteenth Army's rapid advance south inevitably meant that sizeable concentrations of Japanese troops had been bypassed. Largely disorganized, many of these units congregated in the monsoon-swept hills and ravines of the Pegu Yomas awaiting their chance to escape eastward across the Sittang River and into Siam. Judging the time to be right, around 20 July a mass of Japanese infantry moved eastwards along a 'front' stretching from Toungoo 70 miles south to Nyaunglebin. Being as determined to escape as Fourteenth Army was determined to ensure that they did not, fierce and bloody fighting erupted in what was to become known as the Battle of the Sittang Bend.

While the total number of Japanese troops numbered many thousands, for the most part they were made up of groups of approximately 500, a factor which caused the fighting to lack cohesion, a confused situation in which not just Japanese units but also British and Commonwealth troops were likely to find themselves surrounded. On one such occasion 600 Gurkhas were trapped and hard pressed by fierce Japanese assaults, carried forward with the desperation of men trying to escape the net closing in on them. Flight Lieutenant J.T. Taylor, the RAF Visual Control Post with the Gurkhas, called down air strikes from as many as seventeen aircraft at a time on targets no more than 250 yards in front of him. Despite the air assault the Gurkhas remained in the trap for days, during the course of which Taylor's radio set was put out of action. The only man capable of repairing it was Corporal S.R. Jackson, but as he did so a shell exploded some ten yards from the jeep in which he worked, a splinter opening up his chest over his heart. Despite the severe wound Jackson declined medical treatment until the radio was repaired. With the aid of air support the Gurkhas, with Taylor leading a company, were eventually able to break out.[11]

With monsoon in full flow the cloud ceiling would at times be as low as one hundred feet. Once more ground and air crew endured operations hampered by the extremes of the weather, from heat so fierce that touching aircraft inflicted burns, to being able to sail to work in a dinghy. Transport aircraft of 232 Group supported ground operations throughout these bitter battles, often having to parachute supplies onto DZs less than one hundred yards from enemy forces, despite which on only one occasion did a few containers overshoot and fall into Japanese hands.

Attacked by Allied ground troops and hammered by fighters and bombers of 221 Group, few Japanese managed to escape from the Pegu Yomas, and those who did were relentlessly strafed by fighters as they attempted to flee across open country. By the end of July the battle was over, Japanese resistance in Burma was broken at last.

Japanese casualties in the Battle of the Sittang Bend are difficult to assess accurately, but they were devastating. Over 6,000 bodies were recovered by Allied troops, with hundreds more claimed by Burmese irregulars. Many, possibly hundreds, must just have disappeared in the swamps and long grass. The Japanese themselves stated that between seventeen and eighteen thousand men made the breakout, of whom less than 6,000 starved, exhausted and diseased survivors reached the east bank of the Sittang. Two thousand more, too sick and weak to march, were abandoned to die in the Pegu Yoma.[12]

V

Understandably, since it was an entirely new concept, the realization on the part of the Allies that it was possible to maintain formations of Army-sized proportions entirely from the air took time to develop. Nevertheless, necessity being the mother of invention, in the final year of the war in India/Burma, resources devoted to air supply more than doubled, from 4 British and 7 American squadrons in June 1944, to 9 British and Commonwealth and 16 American squadrons in May 1945. While there never seemed to be enough aircraft available for the task at hand, in truth the source of many of the problems in all probability lay with poor organization on the ground. As an instance, a basic difference of opinion between Army and Air Force that was never entirely overcome concerned what should be stored where. To simplify storage, economize on personnel and facilitate the adjustment of priorities, Army administrators preferred where possible to stock one type of store at one particular airfield. The practicalities of air supply dictated, however, that aircraft rarely carried just one commodity. On the contrary they would carry mixed loads of food, ammunition, water, petrol, and so on, the Army system requiring them to fly from airfield to airfield to collect the ingredients of a varied freight, resulting in significant wastage of flying hours. The preferred Air Forces solution – the mixing of an extensive range of supplies at the RAMOs on each base – was never fully implemented.

Problems encountered were not always of a substantial nature and in his report Air Chief Marshal Sir Keith Park illustrates a few of the minor difficulties that also conspired to increase unnecessarily the workload on air supply. In calm retrospect these problems appear obvious and comparatively easily rectified, but in the heat of battle the obvious can become obscured by the fog of war:

- Adequate distributing facilities must be made available by the land forces at landing grounds to ensure that perishable goods are quickly distributed when unloaded from aircraft (e.g. in March 1945, with air supply requirements at their peak, 10,000 tons of potatoes and onions were flown into Shwebo where, through the lack of an efficient distribution organization, they remained to rot).

- Aircraft should not be detailed to convey food to areas in which the same commodities can be easily obtained by local purchase (e.g. an aircraft detailed to fly pineapples to a location in Burma might arrive to find that the cargo was rotten, but the flight being unnecessary in any event as pineapples could be purchased at a nearby village for eight annas each; extrapolated across the campaign area these wasted flights had the potential to exact a significant toll on aircraft availability).

- Packing of goods must be strong enough to ensure that containers do not burst in transit.

- Adequate facilities must be provided for feeding and resting aircrews engaged on this arduous flying as they are often absent from their bases for as long as ten hours at a time.

- An efficient supply of refuellers and facilities for night maintenance must be arranged, otherwise aircraft which could otherwise be making an effective contribution to the battle will be grounded.[13]

Park was also highly critical of the allocation of resources to air supply, believing for instance the Ledo Road – built to connect Assam with the Burma Road to China – to be 'the longest white elephant in the world'.[14] Bearing in mind that it took 17,000 Allied engineers and US $148 million to build, one can see his point, particularly in view of the fact that although it was started in December 1942 it was not completed until January 1945, and was never of much value in either strategic or supply terms. With presumably unconscious irony, on completion Chiang Kai-shek changed the name to the Stilwell Road, that general never having been much of a believer in large-scale air supply.

This represents a flavouring of the administrative problems that beset air supply; there were in addition a number of practical difficulties to contend with. While ground forces were rarely in a position to be able to locate ideal DZs there was on occasion a tendency to select narrow valleys, the negotiation of which would be a major hazard for the aircraft. Both forward airfield commanders and RAF flight control personnel were slow in appreciating the significance of air supply, keeping transport aircraft circling while tactical aircraft took off on routine missions that would not be affected by a thirty-minute delay.

The ground–air relationship between 10th USAAF and Northern Combat Area Command appears in general to have been much better organized, with much less propensity on the part of ground and air forces to encroach on each other's territory, each being prepared to trust the other to do their job effectively.

Despite all the difficulties, the specific military problem presented to the Allied Command – the reconquest of Burma overland from the north, a feat of arms believed to be impossible, not least by the Japanese – could only be solved by air transport. That it was solved was due to the unstinting efforts of both air and ground forces, both of whom had frequently to make difficult and ground-breaking decisions. To reduce supply requirements the Army was obliged to pare its divisions down to a minimum, cutting motor transport to 50 per cent of normal establishment, drastically reducing the administrative 'tail', and even reducing the number of guns. That this was possible was due to the type of warfare experienced in Burma with its accent on raiding, pursuit and infiltration, as opposed to European-style battle tactics. The Burma divisions were, nevertheless, for extended periods totally dependent on another Service, the air forces, so if army commanders were a little jumpy from time to time it is probably understandable.

Air supply of the scale achieved would not have been possible without the air superiority which the fighter squadrons finally gained over the JAAF with the arrival of the tools to do the job, principally the Spitfire in its various guises, for which the Japanese never really came up with an answer. Having gained the upper hand the Allied air forces were thereafter greatly assisted by a Japanese shortage of both pilots and aircraft, forcing the Imperial Japanese High Command into a sustained policy of withdrawing units from Burma in an attempt to shore up the Pacific front.

Targets for the heavy bombers of Strategic Air Force were limited in number but of great importance, railway communications being of particular significance, the railways of Burma and Siam forming an inter-connected transportation system totalling some 5,000 miles. From Phnom Penh, north-west of Saigon, the railway snakes west and north-west through Bangkok, Pegu and Mandalay, forking into two lines terminating at Lashio and Myitkyina, with branch lines to Rangoon, Bassein, Kyaukpadaung, Myingyan and Ye-u. They were put to use, not just for the transportation of materiel from Japan, but also for the internal movement of the natural resources of the occupied territories upon which the Japanese heavily relied – rice, tungsten, oil, tin and rubber. Up to 50 per cent of the requirements of the Japanese Army in Burma are said to have been produced locally.

The continued interdiction of enemy shipping also remained a high priority and to this end Liberators of No. 160 Squadron RAF carried 833 mines to enemy waters between 21 January and 3 May 1945, a particularly high proportion, 86.9 per cent, being successfully laid. Perhaps the most daunting raid of this type was carried out by Liberators enduring a 21-hour flight of 3,350 miles duration through tropical storms to Singapore to mine the harbour. Long-time mine-laying specialists 159 Squadron were selected to carry out the mission and Squadron veteran Basil Wood remembers that to reduce aircraft weight and achieve the distance carrying two 4,600 lb sea mines, ground crew were required to remove all unnecessary equipment including much of the armament, armour plating and even the chemical toilets. Even so the aircraft returned from their marathon flight with only enough fuel left to keep two or three of the four engines in operation.[15]

No. 354 Squadron RAF (Liberators) retrained for a low-level anti-shipping role, and an additional Liberator Squadron, No. 203 RAF, was also assigned to anti-shipping operations.

Operations against Japanese shipping were greatly assisted by a reconnaissance squadron of Sunderland flying boats operated by 346 Wing RAF based on the depot ship *Manela*. Initially based at Colombo, the vessel sailed to Rangoon via Akyab and provided a significant addition to offensive general reconnaissance in the area.

With the exception of the two Chindit raids, 'Special Operations' behind enemy lines were for the most part low key during the course of the war, but did undergo a rapid increase in the final phase of the campaign to re-capture Rangoon. The first half of 1944 saw some 35 liaison officers and 34 tons of stores parachuted behind enemy lines, rising to 2,100 tons of stores and 1,000 officers, occupying 1,350 air sorties, between November 1944 and May 1945. The air effort detailed to these operations also mushroomed, from two squadrons totalling fifteen aircraft in June 1944 to three squadrons and one flight totalling sixty-one aircraft by the end of April 1945.

The task of the liaison officers was to link up with Burmese guerrilla groups and coordinate as much harassment of the enemy as possible. In this respect guerrillas are credited with playing a significant role in preventing the Japanese Fifteenth Army from participating in the defence of Toungoo during the IV Corps dash for the capital.

During the final fortnight of April 1945, Force 136, the Special Operations group controlling agents operating behind enemy lines, supplied targets sufficient to employ practically the entire long-range fighter and bomber resources of 224 Group and included troop trains, ammunition and petrol dumps, and so on.[16]

The role of the RAF Regiment changed fundamentally in the final year of the war. Initially upwards of two-thirds of personnel were deployed in machine-gun anti-aircraft units, the remainder as field squadrons designed to protect airfields in an infantry role. In 1944–5 a combination of rapid forward movement combined with a shortage of available army personnel meant that advanced airfields, radar and other air force installations would not necessarily be guarded by the Army unless their locations happened to fall into line with tactical operations undertaken by local army formations. This necessitated either the withdrawal of forward air installations to a safe distance, or the defence of these installations by the RAF themselves. Since the former was scarcely an option, the latter had to be undertaken by an expanded RAF Regiment comprising, by the end of 1944, 10 wing headquarters, 20 field squadrons, 3 armoured (holding) squadrons and 10 anti-aircraft squadrons. In the process the balance between ground defence and anti-aircraft operations was completely reversed.

This reorganization proved its worth time and again during the Meiktila operation and the campaign to recapture Rangoon. The transport aircraft, fighters and fighter-bombers essential for the support of IV Corps were necessarily required to operate to and from airstrips close behind the front lines. With garrison troops for the airstrips unavailable from army units, the task fell to the field squadrons of the RAF Regiment.

Despite reservations initially held by a few high-ranking US officers, cooperation between British and Commonwealth and US forces were of the highest order, the actions of Major General Stratemeyer illustrating the point. Initially unconvinced of the military wisdom of a joint command structure, once the system was in place Stratemeyer gave it one hundred per cent effort and support, Admiral Mountbatten later commenting that the General provided 'an outstanding example of how an Allied Air Commander should conduct himself'.

This then was the Burma Air Campaign, a campaign which, due to the topography of the territory over which it was fought, broke all the recognized rules of the time for the supply of large ground formations in combat situations over extended periods of time.

The campaign for Burma cost the Allies 71,244 casualties and the Japanese 106,144, in addition to which 656,000 Japanese troops still in theatre surrendered at the end of hostilities. In the face of the untold suffering inflicted by the megalomania of the Japanese military regime upon civilians and military alike, on the wings of the air forces the Fourteenth Army ultimately achieved its goal – the crushing defeat of its one-time seemingly invincible foe.

Notes

1. *Japanese Monograph No.64* (The Library of Congress, Washington DC), pp. 86–7.
2. *Ibid.*, p. 88.
3. Slim, Field Marshal Viscount, *Defeat Into Victory* (Pan Books, 1999), p. 442.
4. *Ibid.*, pp. 438–9.
5. *Wings of the Phoenix* (HMSO, 1949), p. 126.
6. Gupta, S.C., *History of the Indian Air Force 1933–45* (Combined Inter-Services Historical Section India & Pakistan, 1961), p. 146.
7. *Ibid.*, pp. 129–30.
8. TNA Air 41/37, *Air Supply Operations in Burma 1942–1945*, pp. 34–5.
9. *Ibid.*, p. 36.
10. *Op. cit.*, Note 8.
11. *Op. cit.*, Note 5, p. 140.
12. *Op. cit.*, Note 3, p. 528.
13. TNA Air 2/7908, *Air Operations in South east Asia 1 June 1944 to 2 May 1945*, Air Chief Marshal Sir Keith Park, p. 10.
14. *Ibid.*, p. 11.
15. Basil Wood, in correspondence with the author.
16. *Op. cit.*, Note 13, p. 18.

Principal Allied Air Forces as at June 1943

Air Headquarters

AOC-in-C: Air Chief Marshal Sir Richard Peirse.
Deputy AOC-in-C: Air Marshal Sir Guy Garrod.
Air Officer on Special Duty: Air Marshal Sir J.E.A. Baldwin.
Senior Air Staff Officer: Air Vice-Marshal J.W. Baker.
Air Officer Administration: Air Vice-Marshal A.C. Collier.
Chief Maintenance Officer: Air Commodore O.E. Caster.
Principal Medical Officer: Air Commodore D'Arcy Power.

The following is a listing of the formations of India Command together with their functions and commanding officers.

Formation	Function	AOC
Air HQ Bengal, Barrackpore.	Control of Nos 221 & 224 Groups.	Air Vice-Marshal T.M. Williams.
221 Group, Calcutta.	Heavy & medium bombers & the defence of Calcutta.	Air Commodore H.V. Rowley.
224 Group, Chittagong.	Fighters & night bombers.	Air Commodore A. Gray.
222 Group, Ceylon.	General reconnaissance & defence of Ceylon.	Air Vice-Marshal A. Lees.
225 Group, Bangalore.	General reconnaissance & defence of southern India.	Air Commodore P.H. Mackworth
223 Group, Peshawar.	Operations on the North West Frontier.	Air Commodore H.J.F. Hunter.

173

| 226 Group, Palam, Delhi. | Control of repair & maintenance units. | Air Commodore L.M. Iles. |
| 227 Group, Bombay. | Technical, non-technical & flying training. | Air Commodore F.J. Vincent. |

Average aircraft strength according to role and percentage serviceability.

Fighters & fighter bombers	Average strength 183.3 Serviceability 73%.
Bombers	Average strength 80.1 Serviceability 58.6%.
GR, Transport & PR squadrons	66.8[1] Serviceability 58.5%.

Total aircraft in India Command

Type	With squadrons	Repair/ Storage etc.	Total
Hurricanes	344	323	667
Spitfires	8	5	13
Mohawks	15	53	68
Beaufighters	27	63	90
Beauforts	33	30	63
Blenheims	91	119	210
Mosquitoes	–	2	2
Mitchell B25s	2	–	2
Lysanders	10	34	44
Vultee Vengeance	121	316	437
Liberators	15	5	20
Wellingtons	31	73	104
Dakotas	26	3	29
Hudsons	70	53	123
Douglas DC2/3s	3	13	16
Catalinas	60	–	60
Harvard	73	82	155
Anson	14	11	25
Miscellaneous	172	153	325
Totals	1115	1338	2453

Squadron dispositions and aircraft types, Tenth US Air Force

Pandaveswar
9th Bomber Squadron, Consolidated B24 Liberators.
493rd Bomber Squadron, Consolidated B24 Liberators.
9th Photographic Reconnaissance Squadron.

Dinjan
25th Fighter Squadron, Curtiss P40 Kittyhawks (Tomahawks).
26th Fighter Squadron, Curtiss P40 Kittyhawks.

Chakulia
21st Bomber Squadron, North American B25 Mitchells.
491st Bomber Squadron, North American B25 Mitchells.

Bisnalpur
436th Bomber Squadron, Consolidated B24 Liberators.

Ondal
490th Bomber Squadron, North American B25 Mitchells.

Panagarh
492nd Bomber Squadron, Consolidated B24 Liberators.

Kurmitola
Detachment of 11th Bomber Squadron, North American B25 Mitchells.

China
Kwalien
16th Fighter Squadron, Curtiss P40 Kittyhawks.

Kunming
11th Bomber Squadron, North American B25 Mitchells.

Yangkai
2nd Troop Carrier Squadron, Douglas C47 Dakotas.[2]

Indian Air Force
Nos 1, 2, 4, 6, 7 & 8 Squadrons, Hurricanes.
No. 3 Squadron, converting to Hurricane IIC fighter-bombers, the first
   IAF unit to do so.[3]

Notes

1. Included in this figure are Nos 99 and 215 Squadrons which, although bomber squadrons, operated in a General Reconnaissance role for June and July.
2. TNA Air 2/7907, Appendix 1.
3. Gupta, S.C., *History of the Indian Air Force 1933-45* (Combined Inter-Services Historical Section India & Pakistan, 1961), pp. 9–23.

Approximate list of operations carried out by 5th *Hikoshidan* during the 2nd Chindit/Imphal/ Myitkyina campaigns[1]

Date	Unit/Aircraft type and strength	Objectives	Results claimed
10 March	50th *Hikosentai*, 8th *Hikosentai* 20 fighters, 2 light bombers.	Raid on Chindits.	
11 March	50th, 64th, 204th *Hikosentai* 60 fighters.	Raid on Chindit air control at Chindwin river crossing.	
12 March	8th, 50th, 64th, 204th *Hikosentai* 60 fighters, 6 light bombers.	Raid on Silchar airfield.	8 aircraft destroyed on the ground, 14 shot down.
	64th, 204th *Hikosentai* 35 fighters.	Raid on river crossing.	
13 March	50th, 64th, 204th, 8th *Hikosentai* 55 fighters, 3 light bombers.	Raid on Chindits.	
15 March	8th *Hikosentai* 6 light bombers.	Raid on Silchar airfield, Imphal.	
16 March	50th, 64th, 204th *Hikosentai* 36 fighters.	Dawn attack on Imphal airfield.	
	50th, 8th *Hikosentai* 20 fighters, 6 light bombers.	Attack on Chindits.	
17 March	50th, 204th, 64th *Hikosentai* 18 fighters.	Dawn attack on Imphal airfield.	
	204th *Hikosentai* 15 fighters.	Attack on Chindits.	
18 March	8th, 50th, 64th, 204th, 12th, 62nd *Hikosentai* 54 fighters, 12 heavy & 6 light bombers.	Raid on Chindits.	
19/24 March	*Hikoshidan* withdrawn for maintenance etc.		

25 March	Attack on airfields at Chittagong & Cox's Bazaar.	
26 March	50th, 204th, 8th *Hikosentai* 14 fighters, 6 light bombers.	Raid on Allied units opposing Japanese 33rd Division south of Imphal.
27 March	Attack on Ledo oilfields.	
28 March	Attack on airfields in northern Burma.	
30/31 March	8th *Hikosentai* 2 light bombers.	Parachuting ammunition to units opposing the Chindits.
3 April	50th, 64th, 204th *Hikosentai* 36 fighters.	Night attack on transport aircraft supplying the Chindits.
6 April	12th *Hikosentai* 6 heavy bombers.	Night raid on Imphal.
7/9 April	64th *Hikosentai*.	Attacks on Chindit transports.
12 April	50th *Hikosentai* 9 fighters.	Intended raid on Dimapur.	Called off because of bad weather.
13 April	8th, 50th, 64th *Hikosentai* 47 fighters, 12 light bombers.	Attack on Chindit transports airfield.
14 April	8th, 64th *Hikosentai* 27 fighters, 9 light bombers.	Attack on Chindit transports airfield.
15 April	8th, 50th, 64th *Hikosentai* 50 fighters, 9 light bombers.	Attack on Imphal airfield.
17 April	50th *Hikosentai* 20 fighters.	Ground support operation south of Imphal.
	64th, 12th, 204th *Hikosentai* 50 fighters, 6 heavy bombers.	Raid on Palel airfield.
18 April	204th *Hikosentai* 20 fighters.	Raid on Imphal.
21 April	50th, 204th *Hikosentai* 28 fighters.	Attack on Imphal airfield & reconnoitre strength of reinforcements transported.
22 April	204th *Hikosentai* 20 fighters.	As above.
24 April	50th, 64th, 204th, 8th *Hikosentai* 50 fighters, 6 light bombers.	Ground support, Imphal.
25 April	50th, 64th, 204th, 8th *Hikosentai* 54 fighters, 9 light bombers.	Raids on Imphal airfields.
26 April	50th, 64th, 204th, 8th *Hikosentai*.	Raids on Imphal	9 enemy aircraft shot down, 2 JAAF aircraft lost.
28 April	50th, 64th, 204th *Hikosentai* 40 fighters.	Attack on armoured column.	200 vehicles claimed destroyed.
April 29/ May 3	*Hikoshidan* withdrawn for maintenance.	
4 May	50th, 64th *Hikosentai* 25 fighters.	Raids in support of Japanese 15th Division, Kohima & on Imphal airfields.

5 May	64th, 204th *Hikosentai* 30 fighters.	Raids in support of 15th Division, Kohima.	Partial success due to bad weather.
6 May	64th, 204th *Hikosentai* 25 fighters.	Raids on Imphal	Shot down 2 enemy aircraft & lost 2.
10 May	50th, 204th *Hikosentai* 25 fighters.	Attacks on enemy artillery positions.	
14 May	50th, 64th *Hikosentai* 25 fighters.	Attacks on enemy artillery & armoured units, Kohima.	Inflicted heavy damage.
15 May	8th, 50th, 64th, 87th *Hikosentai* 35 fighters, 6 light bombers.	Raid on airfields in the Hukawng valley.	
18 May	8th, 50th, 64th, 87th *Hikosentai* 35 fighters, 6 light bombers.	As above.	Shot down 12 enemy aircraft.
19 May	8th, 50th, 64th, 87th(?) *Hikosentai* 25 fighters, 8 light bombers.	Attack on airborne troops Myitkyina.	Shot down 17 enemy aircraft.
20 May	50th, 64th, 87th *Hikosentai* 22 fighters.	Raid on flight control positions, Imphal.	Operation hampered by bad weather.
21 May	50th, 64th *Hikosentai* 20 fighters.	Raids in support of 33rd Division, south of Imphal.	
	12th *Hikosentai* 4 heavy bombers.	Night raid on Myitkyina.	
23 May	50th, 64th, 204th *Hikosentai* 35 fighters.	Raids in support of Japanese 15th Division north of Imphal.	4 enemy aircraft shot down.
24 May	50th, 64th, 204th *Hikosentai* 15 fighters.	Attack on Imphal airfields.	
25 May	50th, 64th, 204th *Hikosentai* 15 fighters.	As above.	Shot down 7, lost 1.
29 May	50th, 64th, 204th *Hikosentai* 34 fighters.	Two raids on Imphal airfields.	
30 May	50th, 64th, 204th *Hikosentai* 33 fighters.	Raid on Imphal.	
31 May	As above	As above.	Raid aborted due to bad weather.
1/4 June	No operations due to maintenance and bad weather.		
5/6 June	50th, 64th, 204th *Hikosentai*	Raid on Imphal.	Aborted due to bad weather.
7 June	8 fighters/50th & 204th *Hikosentai* 5 light bombers/ 8th *Hikosentai* HQ reconnaissance aircraft.	At Meiktila.	Remainder of *Hikosentai* aircraft withdrawn to Rangoon.
8 June	50th, 204th, 8th *Hikosentai* 15 fighters, 2 light bombers.	Raid on Imphal followed by night raid on Imphal.	Shot down 6 enemy aircraft.
17 June	50th, 204th *Hikosentai* 14 fighters.	Raid on Imphal.	Shot down 2, lost 4.
22 June	204th *Hikosentai* 9 fighters.	Attacks on Mogaung & Myitkyina.	Shot down 2.

25 June	204th *Hikosentai* 10 fighters.	Parachuted rations to 18th Division.	
28 June	204th *Hikosentai* 6 fighters.	Parachuted ammunition to 56th Division.	
29 June	50th, 204th *Hikosentai* 12 fighters.	Parachuted food & clothing to 18th Division.	Shot down 1 enemy returning to base.
30 June	50th *Hikosentai* 12 fighters.		
2/4 July	50th *Hikosentai* 10 fighters.	Attempted ammunition drops, Myitkyina.	Aborted due to bad weather.
5 July	50th *Hikosentai* 10 fighters.	Successful ammunition drop, Myitkyina.	
7 July	50th, 204th *Hikosentai* 15 fighters.	Raid on enemy-held airfield Myitkyina.	
9 July	50th, 204th *Hikosentai* 24 fighters.	Raid on enemy ground forces Myitkyina.	Shot down 12, lost 3.
14 July	204th *Hikosentai* 8 fighters.	Ammunition drop to Japanese troops, Lameng, China.	
15 July	204th *Hikosentai* 8 fighters.	As above.	
20 July	50th, 204th *Hikosentai* 2 reconnaissance aircraft.	As above.	Operation aborted, bad weather.
21 July	50th, 204th *Hikosentai* 2 reconnaissance aircraft.	Successful ammunition drop to Lameng positions.	
23 July	50th, 204th *Hikosentai* 2 reconnaissance aircraft.	As above.	Aborted due to bad weather.
25 July	50th *Hikosentai* 8 fighters.	Ammunition drop, Lameng.	Aborted.
26 July	As above	Successful ammunition drop, Lameng.	
29 July	50th, 204th *Hikosentai* 22 fighters.	Raid on Myitkyina.	Shot down 6 enemy.
30 July	50th, 204th *Hikosentai* 20 fighters.	Raid on airborne troops Indoshi (Indawgyi?) Lake area.	

Note

1. *Japanese Monograph No. 64* (The Library of Congress, Washington DC).

Outline particulars of principal Allied and Japanese aircraft used in the Burma Air Campaign

Allied Aircraft Types

Fighters

Supermarine Spitfire Mk VB

Powerplant:	Rolls Royce Merlin 45/1,515 hp (1,130 kw) @ 11,000 feet (3,353 m).
Performance:	Max. 374 mph (602 km/h) @ 13,000 ft. Service ceiling 37,000 ft (11,280 m). Range 470 miles (756 km) on internal fuel.
Armament:	2 × 20 mm cannon + 4 × 0.303 in (7.7 mm) machine guns, wing mounted.

Curtiss P40B Warhawk (Tomahawk)

Powerplant:	Allison V-1710-33 1040 hp (776 kw).
Performance:	Max. 345 mph (555 km/h). Service ceiling 30,000 feet (9,145 m). Range 730 miles (1,175 km) on internal fuel.
Armament:	6 × 0.303in machine guns, 4 in wings.

Hawker Hurricane Mk IIC

Powerplant:	Merlin XX 1280 hp (955 kw).

| Performance: | Max. 336 mph (541 km/h). Service ceiling 35,600 feet (10,850 m). Range on internal fuel 460 miles (740 km). |
| Armament: | 4 × 20 mm wing cannon. 2 × 500 lb (227 kg) bombs, or 8 × 60 lb (27.2 kg) rocket projectiles, or 2 × 90 Imperial gallon (409-litre) drop tanks under wings. |

North American P51D Mustang

Powerplant:	Packard V-1650-7 Merlin (Licence-built Rolls Royce), 1,590 hp (1186 kw).
Performance:	Max. 448 mph (721 km/h). Service ceiling 30,000 feet (9,145 m). Range 2,080 miles (3,347 km).
Armament:	6 × 0.5 in (12.7 mm) wing-mounted machine guns. Provision for 2 × 500 lb (227 kg) bombs, or eight rocket projectiles, or other under-wing ordnance in place of drop tanks.

Bristol Type 156 Beaufighter Mk VIF

(Twin-engine night fighter & ground-attack aircraft)

Powerplant:	2 × Bristol Hercules VI or XVI, 2 × 1,670 hp (1,246 kw).
Performance:	Max. 333 mph (536 km/h) @ 15,600 feet (4,755 m). Service ceiling 26,500 feet (8,075 m). Range 1,480 miles (2,382 m).
Armament:	4 × 20 mm cannon in nose. 2 × 0.303 in (7.7 mm) machine guns in port wing. 2 × 0.303 in (7.7 mm) machine guns in starboard wing.

Fitted with AI Mk VIII radar for night interceptions.

Bombers

Consolidated B24 Liberator heavy bomber Mk III (RAF) – B24D (USAAF)

Powerplant:	4 × 1,200 hp (895 kw) Pratt & Whitney.
Performance:	Max. 303 mph (488 km/h). Service ceiling 28,000 feet (8,540 m). Operating radius with 5,000 lb (2,268 kg) bomb load 1,080 miles (1,730 km).
Armament:	Up to three 0.5 in (12.7 mm) nose guns, 2 × 0.5 in dorsal turret, two in tail turret, two in retractable ball turret, in waist positions. Maximum internal bomb load 8,000 lb (3,629 kg).

Vickers 271 Wellington Mk X medium bomber

Powerplant: 2 × Bristol Hercules 2 × 1,675 hp (1,249 kw).

Performance: 250 mph (410 km/h). Service ceiling 22,000 feet (6,710 m). Operating radius 1,540 miles (2,478 km) with 4,500 lb (2,041 kg) bomb load, 2,200 miles (3,540 km) with 1,500 lb (680 kg) bomb load.

Armament: 8 × 0.303in (7.7 mm) machine guns, two in nose, two in tail, two in waist positions. Maximum bomb load 4,500 lb (2,041 kg).

Vultee Vengeance Mk II dive-bomber

Powerplant: 1,600 hp (1,193 kw) Wright Cyclone.

Performance: Max. 275 mph (443 km/h) @ 11,000 feet. Service ceiling 22,500 feet (6,858 m).

Armament: 4 × 0.3 in (7.62 mm) wing-mounted machine guns, 2 × 0.303 in (7.7 mm) machine guns in rear cockpit. Maximum bomb load 2,000 lb (907 kg).

Reconnaissance

de Havilland DH.98 Mosquito PR Type XVI

(Long-range, multi-purpose fighter/bomber/photographic reconnaissance aircraft, from 1944 onwards used extensively in Burma in the latter role.)

Powerplant: 2 high blown Merlin 2 × 1,710 hp (1276 kw).

Performance: 410 mph (660 km/h). Service ceiling 40,000 feet (12,190 m). Pressurized cabin. Range – a Burma-based Type XVI made a round trip of 2,493 miles, a record for any theatre of the war.

Transports

Douglas C47 Dakota (or 'Gooney Bird' to US crews)

Powerplant: 2 × 1,200 hp (895 kw) Pratt & Whitney.

Performance: Max. 230 mph (370 km/h) @ 8,500 feet (2,591 m). Cruising speed 185 mph (298 km/h). Service ceiling 23,200 feet (7,071 m). Range 2,125 miles (3,420 km).

Cargo hold: Equipped with pulley blocks for cargo handling, max. load 6,000 lb (2,722 kg). Alternative usage – 28 fully armed paratroopers in folding bucket-type seats, or 18 stretchers and a medical team of three. Racks & release gear for up to six parachute pack containers could be mounted under fuselage. Also used as glider-tugs.

182

Curtiss C46 Commando

Powerplant: 2 × 2,100 hp (1,566 kw) Pratt & Whitney.

Performance: Max. 270 mph (436 km/h). Cruising speed 235 mph
                     (378 km/h). Service ceiling 22,000 feet (6,706 m).
                     Range 1,800 miles (2,897 km).

Cargo hold: Approximately 7,500 lb (3,402 kg), or 40 fully
                     equipped troops, or up to 33 stretchers.

Japanese Aircraft Types

Fighters

Nakajima Ki-27

Allied code name: Nate

Powerplant: Nakajima Ha-1b 780 hp @ 9,500 feet (2,900 m).

Performance: Max. 292 mph (470 km/h) @ 11,500 feet (3,500 m).
                     Standard range 390 miles (627 km), max. with drop
                     tanks 1,060 miles (1,719 km).

Armament: 2 × 7.7 mm fuselage-mounted machine guns. 4 × 25 kg
                     bombs in place of drop tanks.

Distinctive fixed undercarriage with spatted wheels.

Nakajima Ki-43-II

Allied code name: Oscar

Powerplant: Nakajima Ha-115 1,230 hp.

Performance: Max. 308 mph (495 km/h) @ 13,000 feet (4,000 m).
                     Service ceiling 36,750 feet (11,200 m). Standard range
                     1,095 miles (1,760 km). Maximum 1,990 miles
                     (3,200 km).

Armament: 2 × 12.7 mm wing-mounted machine guns. Max bomb
                     load 2 × 250 kg.

Nakajima Ki-44-II

Allied code name: Tojo

Powerplant: Nakajima Ha-109 1,450 hp.

Performance: Max. 376 mph (605 km/h) @ 17,000 feet (5,200 m).
                     Service ceiling 36,750 feet (11,200 m). Standard range
                     1,060 miles (1,700 km).

Armament: 2 × 12.7 mm wing-mounted machine guns,
                     2 × 7.7 mm fuselage-mounted machine guns.

Bombers

Mitsubishi Ki-21-II heavy bomber

Allied code name: Sally

Powerplant: 2 × Mitsubishi Ha-101 2 × 1,450 hp.

Performance: Max. 302 mph (468 km/h) @ 15,500 feet (4,720 m). Service ceiling 33,000 feet (10,000 m). Range up to 1,680 miles (2,700 m) dependant upon load.

Armament: 6 × 7.7 mm machine guns in forward, dorsal, ventral, tail & beam positions. Max. bomb load 1,000 kg. Normal bomb load 750 kg.

Kawasaki Ki-48-II light bomber

Allied code name: Lily

Powerplant: 2 × Nakajima Ha-115 2 × 1,150 hp

Performance: Max. 314 mph (505 km/h) @ 18,000 feet (5,600 m). Service ceiling 33,000 feet (10,000 m). Standard range 1,275 miles (2,050 km), max range 1,490 miles (2,400 km).

Armament: 3 × 7.7 mm machine guns in forward, dorsal & ventral positions. Normal bomb load 400 kg. Max bomb load 800 kg.

Reconnaissance

Mitsubishi Ki-46-II

Allied code name: Dinah

Powerplant: 2 × Mitsubishi Ha-102 2 × 1,050 hp.

Performance: Max. 375 mph (604 km/h) @ 19,000 feet (5,800 m). Service ceiling 34,000 feet (10,500 m). Range 1,540 miles (2,474 km).

Index

186

187